THE PACIFIC WAR
Day by Day

THE PACIFIC WAR
Day by Day

John Davison

ZENITH PRESS

This edition published in 2004 by
Zenith Press,
an imprint of MBI Publishing Company,
Galtier Plaza,
Suite 200,
380 Jackson Street,
St. Paul, MN 55101-3885 USA

Zenith Press titles are also available at discounts in bulk quantity for industrial or sales-promotional use. For details write to Special Sales Manager at Motorbooks International Wholesalers & Distributors, Galtier Plaza, Suite 200, 380 Jackson Street, St. Paul, MN 55101-3885 USA.

ISBN 0-7603-2067-5

Editorial and design:
The Brown Reference Group plc
8 Chapel Place
Rivington Street
London
EC2A 3DQ
UK
www.brownreference.com

Senior Editor: Peter Darman
Editor: Alan Marshall
Proofreader: Robin Smith
Picture Researcher: Andrew Webb
Designer: Jerry Udall
Production Director: Alastair Gourlay

Printed in China

Page 1: Warships under Japanese attack at Pearl Harbor, December 1941.
Pages 2-3: US troops on Wakde Island, May 1944.
Pages 4-5: US Marines wade ashore on Tinian, July 1944.

CONTENTS

INTRODUCTION

I n the immediate aftermath of World War I, a future conflict between Japan and the United States and European colonial nations seemed an unlikely prospect. Japan had fought on the side of the Allies against Germany's Pacific colonies during the war, and after 1918 was rewarded with territorial acquisitions throughout the Pacific. During the early decades of the twentieth century, Japan had transformed itself into a truly modern industrial society, imitating and improving on Western standards of production and consumption.

The "Second Class" Nation

Despite its contribution to World War I, however, Japan felt – with some justification – that its status in the world was not confirmed. Although Japan had gained some Pacific colonies in the Allied territorial share out, she was also forced to relinquish Chinese regions conquered during the Russo-Japanese War of 1904–5. In Japanese eyes, insult was added to injury in 1922 when the Washington Naval Treaty limited the size of the Japanese Navy to below that of the US and British fleets, despite the fact that the quality and quantity of Japanese shipping could match and even exceed Allied fleets in the Pacific.

To a people with an extremely high concept of respect, the "loss of face" was stinging, particularly amongst the leaders of the Japanese Army whose philosophy retained strong elements of anti-Westernism. Critically, however, the Japanese were aware that their entire

▶ *The Japanese battleship* **Kongo** *in dry dock at Yokosuka in 1930. On the eve of World War II, the Japanese Imperial Navy had 11 battleships in its inventory.*

industrial revolution was dependent upon US and colonial imports. Almost every vital domestic and industrial product, including food, rubber and most metals, had to be imported, and the United States supplied around 60 percent of Japanese oil. The dependence on the outside world rubbed salt into the Japanese wound, and many felt that Japan had been relegated to a second-class nation within a geographical area in which it should have been dominant.

The Japanese were particularly aggrieved by the fact that what they felt was their natural sphere of influence from which they could obtain the raw materials to run a modern economy was largely occupied by colonial powers: the British in Malaya, the French in Indochina, the US in the Philippines, and above all the Dutch in the oil-rich region of the Dutch East Indies – what is now Indonesia.

▼ *Japanese troops on their way to China in the 1930s. Japan had invaded Manchuria on September 30, 1931.*

The one big area where there was no colonial power was on the Asian mainland: China. In 1931 Japan invaded and occupied Manchuria, a northern province semi-independent of China, and rich in mineral resources, and in 1937 Japan invaded China itself. The war between China and Japan turned into a hugely violent and costly eight-year conflict, in which the Japanese Army in particular demonstrated its utter ruthlessness. At Nanking, for example, between December 1937 and March 1938, the occupying Japanese Army murdered around 400,000 civilians and raped an estimated 80,000 women and girls. Yet the military campaign was as professional as it was cruel, and by the end of 1938 almost all of central and southern China was in Japanese hands.

The Japanese expansion and tales of its atrocities infuriated many in the West. The United States was particularly aggrieved. It had long-standing missionary and trade connections with China, and close associations with the Nationalist leader Chiang Kai-shek. China was also militarily important to the US and

European powers, as "extraterritoriality" agreements permitted the Western nations to establish sovereign commercial settlements on Chinese territory with the accompanying ability to station military units. Relations between the West and Japan plunged further during the late 1930s after US and European warships and troops in the region were attacked in localized incidents.

In 1940 Prince Konoye became the Japanese prime minister, introducing a hardline leadership and rejecting political moderation. His minister of war was Hideki Tojo, and his foreign minister was Yosuke Matsuoka. Both of these ministers were strong advocates of expansion by force. On September 27, 1940, with war already raging across Europe, Matsuoka signed the Tripartite Pact with Germany and Italy. The Tripartite Pact committed the signatories to defend the other countries if they were attacked by any nation other than China, or countries already involved in the European conflict. This commitment essentially aligned Japan with the European Axis powers.

INTRODUCTION

▶ *A meeting of Japan's Greater East Asia Co-Prosperity Sphere. Formally announced in August 1940, it was an attempt by Japan to create a bloc of Asian nations free of influence from Western countries.*

In September 1940 Japanese forces entered northern French Indochina. After defeat by Germany earlier that year, the French were in no position to resist. The Indochina acquisition gave Japan tremendous logistical strength for its war against China and numerous coastal bases to prosecute a naval campaign throughout East Asia. By this time, Japan had already formulated a clear imperialist outlook, looking to establish what it called the "Greater East Asia Co-Prosperity Sphere". This envisaged an East Asia free of colonial influence and united under Japanese hegemony. Japan hoped that the Co-Prosperity Sphere would lead many colonial Asian countries to work, violently or otherwise, towards their independence from British, Dutch and US influence.

In July 1941, the Japanese sent their forces into the south of Indochina. This move, however, drove the United States to retaliate. Japanese assets in the US

were seized, and the US placed a ferocious trade embargo on Japan which reduced its oil supplies by 90 percent. The British and the Dutch also imposed their own economic sanctions, and in total Japan's foreign trade was cut by 75 percent.

Minister for War Tojo and the military hawks in the Japanese Government now had a straightforward argument for war. Debate in the Japanese cabinet swung from appeasement through to outright military action, but steadily the latter

won out, mainly through Tojo's persuasive representations that Japan would become a "third class nation" if it did not assert itself – the oil embargo, for example, meant that the Japanese fleet would be confined to port by the spring of 1942. Also in 1941, the US had commit-

▼ *From the start of their occupation of China the Japanese used airpower to enforce their rule. This is Chungking under aerial attack. Between 1939 and 1941, 12,000 died in bombing raids on the city.*

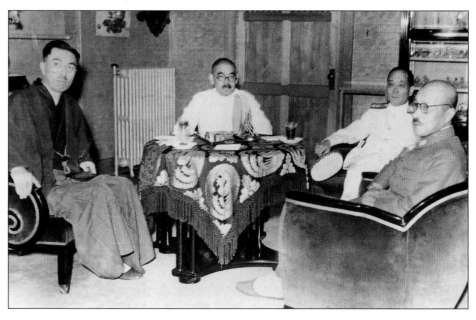

▶ *Prince Konoye (left) became Japanese prime minister in 1940. He resigned in October 1941 after clashing with Tojo.*

ted itself to the Two Ocean Naval Expansion Act, a massive naval building programme which would set a ratio of Japanese to US ships of 3:10 by 1944. If the long-term outlook was bleak, in the short term Tojo also argued that the time was militarily right to launch an attack. In mid-1941 Japan was undeniably the strongest force in the Pacific. The British and Dutch had weak naval forces in the area, and the Japanese Navy had around double the numbers of vessels of all types when compared to the US Pacific Fleet. The Japanese Army had a total manpower of 1,800,000, and was one of the most well-trained and professional forces in the world, specializing in amphibious warfare. Japan's air force numbered well over 2000 aircraft, dwarfing any other air force in the entire East Asian region. Tojo and others argued that although Japan could not compete with US industrial might, a rapid campaign could secure a large expanse of Pacific and Asian territory, which could then be defended at a price too high for the US and Allies to countenance, forcing the Allies to accept Japanese superiority in the East.

In addition, the general world situation in late summer 1941 pushed the Japanese to take a positive view of their prospects if they attacked later that year.

Germany had conquered Western Europe and was engaged in a very successful assault on the Soviet Union. Britain was beleaguered, and the United States was reluctant to commit itself to war. If war was bound to come, as many Japanese believed it would because the Western powers would not give up their colonies in the Far East without a fight, then late 1941 was the time to start it.

On November 5, Emperor Hirohito and the Japanese Government agreed on the course of war should the US not soften its position on the oil embargo by the end of the month. Further debates with

the US during November were fraught, especially as US intelligence had already revealed that Japan's army, navy and air force were making preparations for war. On November 26 the US Secretary of State, Cordell Hull, restated US demands for Japanese withdrawal from Manchuria, China and Indochina and its effective renunciation of the Tripartite Pact. On November 26, 1941, the Japanese Combined Fleet set sail from the Kurile Islands. Its combat destination was Pearl Harbor, Hawaii.

▲ *Mitsubishi A6M Zero fighters outside their assembly plant in Japan. Over 400 had been built by December 1941.*

▶ *US Secretary of State Cordell Hull (1871–1955) became convinced that Japan would attack US bases in the Pacific region.*

1941

The Japanese, achieving total surprise at Pearl Harbor, went on to complete a series of spectacular victories in the western Pacific at the end of 1941. The British, lacking military resources due to their commitments in the European theatre (and defeats at the hands of the Germans), suffered a series of shattering catastrophes that resulted in the loss of Singapore, Hong Kong and most of Malaysia.

NOVEMBER 26

SEA WAR, *PACIFIC OCEAN*

The Japanese First Air Fleet sets sail from the Kurile Islands on a 5440km (3400-mile) journey. Its mission: to destroy the US Pacific Fleet at Pearl Harbor. The Japanese force comprises more than 30 vessels – including six aircraft carriers: the *Akagi, Kagi, Hiryu, Soryu, Zuizaku* and *Shokaku* – and is commanded by Vice-Admiral Chuichi Nagumo.

DECEMBER 6

ATOMIC BOMB, *USA*

President Roosevelt authorizes a secret project known as the Manhattan Engineering District, beginning the development of atomic weaponry under the control of the US Office of Scientific Research and Development. This will eventually be renamed the Manhattan Project.

DECEMBER 7

AIR WAR, *PEARL HARBOR*

The Japanese First Air Fleet launches a massive air assault on the US Pacific Fleet stationed at Pearl Harbor, flying from six carriers positioned 443km (275 miles) north of Hawaii. The first wave begins at 07:55 hours, and US defences are completely unprepared. More than 180 Japanese aircraft attack US warships, sinking six battleships, three cruisers and four other vessels. They damage two other battleships. A total of 188 US mili-

▼ *The busy flight deck of the Japanese carrier* Akagi *prior to the attack on Pearl Harbor. In the foreground are Zero fighters, while towards the rear are massed Aichi D3A Val two-seat dive-bombers.*

▲ The attack on Pearl Harbor as seen from a Japanese aircraft. Here, US ships at anchor around Ford Island are under assault. Just visible is a Japanese aircraft pulling up after bombing the USS Oklahoma.

tary aircraft are destroyed on the ground, and 2403 US military personnel and civilians are killed. More than 1000 US sailors are killed aboard the USS *Arizona* alone, after its magazine explodes. Japanese losses total only 29 aircraft. Most of these are incurred in the second (and final) wave of attack at 08:54 hours, by which time US defences are more prepared. One Japanese I-class submarine and five midget submarines are also sunk. The final Japanese assaults are completed by 10:00 hours. Importantly, the strike at Pearl Harbor fails to destroy any US aircraft carriers, which are out at sea. Many of the damaged ships are repaired quickly. Furthermore, Nagumo calls off a third strike aimed at destroying Pearl Harbor's oil and shore facilities. Such a raid could have rendered Pearl Harbor inoperable. Instead, it continues to function. Although a stunning short-term tactical success, the attack on Pearl Harbor and the onset of the Pacific War effectively consigns Japan to future destruction.

DECEMBER 8

PACIFIC, *JAPANESE OFFENSIVE*
Japanese forces across the Pacific begin campaigns to secure Allied territories in a Blitzkrieg-style offensive.

◀ Vice-Admiral Chuichi Nagumo, the commander of the Japanese carrier strike force at Pearl Harbor. A cautious man, he decided against ordering a third air wave.

KEY MOMENTS

PEARL HARBOR – HOW MUCH DID THE AMERICANS KNOW?

The question of how much the United States knew about the Japanese attack on Pearl Harbor has excited conspiracy theorists and historians alike ever since that fateful day. The more fanciful theories suggest that the US knew an attack was imminent, but allowed it to happen so that the US could enter the war on the Allies' side. They point to the fact that US carriers were not in the harbour when the attack took place, and that the wealth of intelligence pointing to a Japanese attack leading up to December 1941 was impossible to miss. Whilst it was certainly unfortunate that the intelligence collected did not raise the alarm earlier, and the coincidence that the carriers were absent is almost unbelievable, simple intelligence failure seems to be the most likely cause of the surprise.

There were crucial pieces of evidence in the months prior to the attack. US intelligence officials noted that the Japanese carriers had disappeared from their usual moorings. Similarly, in November 1940, low-frequency signals, the kind used by Japan's carriers, were detected northwest of Hawaii but not investigated. Dutch intelligence intercepted an encrypted message sent to the Japanese ambassador in Bangkok suggesting an attack on the Philippines and Hawaii, and the Dutch informed the US, but the warning was dismissed (the US was also aware that the Japanese were telling their diplomatic officials to destroy code books and to prepare for war). Sadly for servicemen who lost their lives at Pearl Harbor, these warnings were missed or mis-read.

► *Smoke billows from the torpedo-damaged cruiser USS* Helena *(left) during the Pearl Harbor assault. Her anti-aircraft guns shot down six enemy aircraft.*

LAND WAR, *MALAYA*

Two Japanese divisions (5th and 18th) invade the northern coastlines of Thailand and Malaya, striking south into the Malayan Peninsula. Their objective is the concentration of British troops around Singapore, and the port itself. Singapore is a vital goal for the Japanese offensive, being the Allies' main port for control of the Malacca Strait between Malaya and the Dutch East Indies.

LAND WAR, *HONG KONG*

British forces opposite Hong Kong on the coast of mainland China are put into retreat after an assault by three Japanese regiments.

LAND WAR, *PHILIPPINES*

Japanese infantry units occupy Bataan Island and land several detachments around Vigan and Aparri on the northern coast.

PACIFIC, *WAKE ISLAND*

The Japanese attempt to take the US outpost of Wake Island (an atoll located between Manila and Pearl Harbor), beginning with a large-scale naval and aerial bombardment.

LAND WAR, *BURMA*

The Japanese Fifteenth Army, commanded by Lieutenant-General Shojiro Iida, occupies the Kra isthmus between Prachuab and Nakhon, beginning Japan's Burma offensive. Occupying Burma will protect the Japanese offensive into Malaya on its northerly flank. It will also sever cross-Burma supply routes to Chinese forces in the north, and secure Burmese oil production.

LAND WAR, *THAILAND*

Japanese forces take Bangkok, the Thai capital. The Japanese campaign into Thailand begins on December 8 with Japanese amphibious landings at Singora and Patani. Today, the Thai prime minister, Field Marshal Pibul Songgram, orders the end of resistance against the Japanese. He will ultimately embrace pro-Japanese tendencies.

LAND WAR, *GILBERT ISLANDS*

Japanese troops land on Tarawa and

▼ *One of the five Japanese Type A midget submarines used in the Pearl Harbor attack (this one beached at Oahu).*

KEY MOMENTS

PEARL HARBOR – ACHIEVING COMPLETE SURPRISE

The Japanese assault on Pearl Harbor was planned by Admiral Isoroku Yamamoto (Commander-in-Chief, Imperial Japanese Navy) and commanded by Vice-Admiral Chuichi Nagumo. It was delivered by a strike force of six aircraft carriers, together containing around 450 aircraft, with a defensive/logistical accompaniment of two battleships, two cruisers, several destroyers and eight support vessels. This large body of shipping managed to sail completely undetected from the Kurile Islands north of Japan to attack positions only 443km (275 miles) north of Hawaii. The reasons for the Japanese achieving such complete secrecy have been hotly debated. Total Japanese radio and communications silence clearly assisted free passage, although British Far East Combined Bureau (FECB) intelligence officers informed Washington of a suspicious halt in fleet communications in mid-November. A front of poor weather protected the strike force from aerial observation, and the US strategic focus on the southern and western Pacific meant that the northern Pacific received little monitoring. A war warning had been issued to US commanders on December 7. However, the belief was that, barring sabotage, Pearl Harbour was safe. Consequently, no anti-torpedo nets were installed (it was believed at the time that Pearl Harbor was too shallow for torpedo runs); most anti-aircraft ammunition was locked away and accessible only to a duty officer; and US aircraft were assembled in the open in large, closely packed groups. US and British intelligence should have heightened security, but inter-service rivalries and inefficiencies negated its value. Crucially, US agents had deciphered messages to the Japanese Consul General in Honolulu instructing spies to map Pearl Harbour in a grid and plot the ships within the grid. This information was not passed on to Rear-Admiral Kimmel (C-in-C, US Pacific Fleet) – it would probably have energized defensive preparations. The final act of Japanese fortune occurred when the attacking air units themselves were detected 212km (132 miles) off the coast by the Opana Mobile Radar Unit. The signals were interpreted as being those of a friendly flight of Boeing B-17 bombers. There can be no doubt that the US left itself open to a surprise attack.

Makin in the Gilbert Islands, extending their field of conquest to the South Central Pacific.

DECEMBER 10–13

LAND WAR, *MALAYA*
The Japanese 5th and 18th Divisions make important advances down through Malaya. British positions at Betong fall on the 10th, and on the 13th the Japanese take Alor Setar on the northwest coast of Malaya, thereby securing important operational airfields in the north of the country.

LAND WAR, *PHILIPPINES*
The Japanese 16th Division goes ashore in the southeast at Lamon Bay, cutting across the island to Tiaong then

▼ *US battleships under attack at Pearl Harbor. From left to right: USS* West Virginia *(badly damaged), USS* Tennessee *(damaged) and USS* Arizona *(sunk with the loss of over 1100 crew).*

KEY MOMENTS

"DAY OF INFAMY"
The shock of the Japanese attack on Pearl Harbor on December 7, 1941, sent reverberations around the world, and caused a virtual earthquake in the United States. The reaction of the American people went from stunned disbelief to fury. In the confusion of the initial reports, fears of an invasion swept across Los Angeles, thousands of men flooded into the streets armed with pistols and rifles, and the National Guard was ordered out. The next day, shortly before 13:00 hours on December 8, 1941, US President Franklin Delano Roosevelt, in an address to Congress and the Supreme Court, asked Congress to declare war on Imperial Japan.

The famous speech began, "Yesterday, December 7, 1941 – a date that will live in infamy – the United States of America was suddenly and deliberately attacked by naval and air forces of the Empire of Japan." It was received to thunderous applause by Congress, and heartfelt cheers across the nation. Aside from becoming one of the most famous pieces of oratory in American, indeed world, history, the Roosevelt address had the effect of uniting a disunited nation. Prior to Pearl Harbor, the United States had been riven by division over whether American should enter the war. Strikes had been called, and the general feeling across the country was by and large anti-war. The Japanese attack and Roosevelt's speech changed all that, and from that point on the American people, assured by the president that they would achieve "absolute victory", threw their weight behind the national cause with verve, vigour and great patriotism.

heading northwards for Manila. US and Filipino forces in the Luzon interior are threatened with encirclement around the capital.

DECEMBER 10

SEA WAR, *SOUTH CHINA SEA*
The British battleships HMS *Prince of Wales* and HMS *Repulse* are sunk by 88 Japanese aircraft in a two-hour attack in the South China Sea, with the death of 840 seamen. The destruction of the two vessels allows the Japanese to make unhindered amphibious landings along the Malayan coastline. A force of 5000 Japanese troops invades Guam,

▼ *Japanese troops invade Burma in December. The British relied on airpower to defend the country, though they had no bombers in Burma!*

▲ *Sailors of the British battleship HMS Prince of Wales abandon ship following an attack by Japanese aircraft.*

easily overcoming a US garrison of fewer than 400 men.

AIR WAR, *MANILA*
Japanese carrier aircraft destroy around half of the US Far East Air Force in the Philippines, striking the aircraft as they sit on the ground at Clark, Ibu and Nicholls airfields. The Japanese now exercise almost total air superiority over the Philippines.

DECEMBER 11

PACIFIC, *WAKE ISLAND*
The Japanese attempt a landing on Wake Island, but a tenacious defence repulses it. Despite having suffered three days of constant bombardment, US shore gunners manage to sink two Japanese destroyers and damage a Japanese cruiser.

DECEMBER 16

LAND WAR, *DUTCH EAST INDIES*
The Japanese 19th Division (part of the Japanese Western Force assaulting Burma, Malaya and the western Dutch East Indies) lands on the northern coastline of Borneo, at Miri and Seria on the coast of Sarawak, sending British and Dutch forces into retreat. In advance of the landings, the Allies set fire to oil installations to deprive the Japanese forces of fuel stocks. Conquest of the Dutch East Indies will bring the Japanese vital natural resources, including oil and rubber, consolidate their control of

▼ *Japanese troops in Malaya in early December. The main landings took place on the 8th at Singora and Patani on the northeast coast.*

DECISIVE WEAPONS

Examples of the Zero version that was built in quantities far greater than any other Japanese aircraft: the A6M5.

MITSUBISHI A6M ZERO

For the first six months of the Pacific War, the Mitsubishi A6M Zeke – otherwise known as the "Zero" – was the best combat aircraft of the theatre. The A6M was designed in 1938, and A6M2 machines were in service aboard carriers by the time of Japan's entry into the war. It combined a highly manoeuvrable airframe with a powerful 708kW (950hp) Nakajima Sakae 12-cylinder radial engine. Its armament of two 20mm cannon and two 7.7mm machine guns gave it a lethal knock-down capability. The most numerous version, the A6M5, had an upgraded Sakae 21 engine which gave it a top speed of 565kmh (351mph). The A6M5 was introduced to counter the new range of US fighters that entered the Pacific War in 1942–43, and ultimately overturned the Zero's superiority. Such aircraft included the Lockheed P-38 Lightning and Grumman F6F

Hellcat. US pilots found the Zero's fatal flaw to be its lack of survivability because of its lightweight frame. Yet the Zero remained a respected aeroplane until the end of the war. Over 10,000 were built in total, many being used for kamikaze attacks.

SPECIFICATIONS:

CREW: one
POWERPLANT: one 820kW (1100hp) Nakajima NK2F Sakae 21 radial piston engine
DIMENSIONS: wing span 11m (36ft); length 9.12m (29.9ft); height 3.51m (11.5ft)
PERFORMANCE: max speed 565kmh (351mph); range 1143km (710 miles); service ceiling 11,740m (38,517ft)
ARMAMENT: two wing-mounted 20mm Type 99 cannon; two 7.7mm Type 97 machine guns (or one 7.7mm and one 13.2mm), both nose-mounted; underwing provision for two 60kg bombs or one 250kg bombs

southwest Pacific seas, and enable them to dominate or invade Australia.
AIR WAR, *BURMA*
The important Allied air base at Victoria Point falls to the Japanese, cutting off aerial resupply of local British forces. Capturing such air bases enables Japanese fighter aircraft to escort bombers on raids into southern Burma, particularly against the Burmese capital Rangoon.

DECEMBER 17

POLITICS, *PACIFIC*
Admiral Husband Kimmel is replaced as commander of the US Pacific Fleet by Rear-Admiral

▶ *Wrecked US aircraft on Wake Island in early December 1941. The Japanese captured the island on the 24th, at a cost of 700 dead. US casualties were 109 killed.*

Chester Nimitz, who is in turn promoted to the rank of Admiral.

DECEMBER 18

POLITICS, *HONG KONG*
The governor of Hong Kong, Sir Mark Young, rejects the third offer from the Japanese for the surrender of the British garrison on the island, despite the fact that the ratio of Japanese to British troops is almost four to one.

DECEMBER 19

LAND WAR, *HONG KONG*
The Japanese 38th Infantry Division crosses from Kowloon Bay to Hong Kong, the 40,000 Japanese soldiers outnumbering the 12,000-strong British garrison.
LAND WAR, *PHILIPPINES*
A Japanese regiment from Palau takes Davao, a major port on Mindanao in the southern Philippines. Davao will be used as a staging post for subsequent Japanese invasions of the Dutch East Indies, and the landing opens another front in the Japanese offensive against the Philippines, which until this point has been concentrated in the north against Luzon.
LAND WAR, *MALAYA*
British forces on Penang, off the northwest coast of Malaya, are forced to abandon the island.

DECEMBER 20

AIR WAR, *CHINA*
Ten Japanese bombers are shot down by the US pilots of the so-called Flying Tiger volunteer force in the Tigers' first engagement.

DECEMBER 21-30

LAND WAR, *MALAYA*
Following further Japanese landings along the western coast of Malaya, and

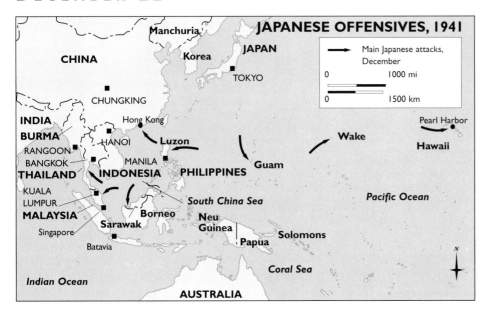

JAPANESE OFFENSIVES, 1941

Main Japanese attacks, December

0 — 1000 mi
0 — 1500 km

CHINA

Manchuria

JAPAN

Korea

TOKYO

CHUNGKING

INDIA
BURMA
RANGOON
BANGKOK
THAILAND
KUALA LUMPUR
MALAYSIA
Singapore
Batavia

Hong Kong

HANOI

Luzon

MANILA

INDONESIA

Sarawak

Borneo

South China Sea

Neu Guinea

Papua

Solomons

Coral Sea

PHILIPPINES

Guam

Wake

Pearl Harbor

Hawaii

Pacific Ocean

Indian Ocean

AUSTRALIA

N

▲ *Japanese Mitsubishi G3M Nell bombers release their bombs over Rangoon on December 24.*

▲ *Japan's offensives during late 1941 were designed to weaken US strength in the Pacific, giving Tokyo time to seize strategic bases and economic resources.*

motivated by the fact that the Japanese have secured four operational airfields, British forces are ordered to withdraw behind the Perak River, a main defensive line in central Malaya, while the 11th Indian Division fights delaying actions. By December 30, the Indian Division itself is in retreat into southern Malaya, and Japanese troops on the east coast of the country have advanced nearly 322km (200 miles) to Kuantan, pushing back the Australian 8th Division.

DECEMBER 22

ALLIES, *POLITICS*
During discussions between US President Franklin D. Roosevelt and British Prime Minister Winston Churchill, the two nations agree on a "Germany First" strategic orientation. The Allied leaders also discuss the establishment of Com-

bined Chiefs of Staff to oversee the Pacific Theatre.

LAND WAR, *PHILIPPINES*
The main Japanese landing in the Philippines takes place at Lingayen Gulf on the western edge of Luzon, as the Japanese 48th Division is landed and begins a southerly advance. With other Japanese forces advancing from the north of the island, the Lingayen Gulf operation threatens to cut off retreating US and Filipino forces around Manila.

DECEMBER 23

LAND WAR, *PHILIPPINES*
Lieutenant-General Douglas MacArthur orders 130,000 US and Filipino troops on Luzon to begin withdrawing into the Bataan Peninsula in an effort to avoid Japanese encirclement of Manila, which MacArthur declares an open city.

▼ *Some of the 43,000 troops of General Homma's Fourteenth Army which landed in Lingayen Gulf, Luzon, 240km (150 miles) north of Manila, on December 22.*

DECEMBER 24

LAND WAR, *WAKE ISLAND*
Two weeks of bombardment against Wake Island finally pays dividends for Japan as a Japanese regiment lands successfully and forces the surrender of remaining US forces.

AIR WAR, *RANGOON*
A major Japanese air offensive is launched against the Burmese capital, Rangoon, which is an important British naval and air base.

LAND WAR, *PHILIPPINES*
A Japanese landing force of around 7000 men goes ashore in Lamon Bay on the east coast of Luzon. The landing prevents US and Filipino forces from retreating through the narrow land passage into the far south of Luzon, and traps them around Manila and on the Bataan Peninsula.

DECEMBER 24-31

LAND WAR, *BORNEO*
The Japanese make an amphibious landing along Borneo's coast, moving 644km (400 miles) along to Kuching. By December 31, the British are in general retreat throughout the Dutch East Indies.

DECEMBER 25

LAND WAR, *HONG KONG*
Resistance by the British garrison on Hong Kong proves futile, and on December 25 the governor, Sir Mark Young, formally surrenders the island.

▲ A bomb explodes on Hong Kong's Kai Tak aerodrome during the Japanese assault on the British crown colony. Hong Kong surrendered on December 25.

DECEMBER 26

POLITICS, *AUSTRALIA*

Fearing the imminent invasion of his country by the Japanese, Australian Prime Minister John Curtin tells the Allies not to give priority to the European war at the expense of the Pacific theatre.

DECEMBER 28

LAND WAR, *SUMATRA*

Japanese paratroopers are dropped on Sumatra. Japan has been training in air-

borne warfare, with German assistance, since 1940; and paratroopers are subsequently used to capture forward air bases throughout the Dutch East Indies.

DECEMBER 31

POLITICS, *PACIFIC*

Admiral Chester Nimitz arrives in the Pacific and assumes command of the US Pacific Fleet.

▼ Victorious Japanese troops enter Hong Kong led by General Sakai.

1942

The year began with Japan continuing its series of victories in the southwest Pacific. The Philippines, Malaya and most of New Guinea fell to the Imperial Army, while Japanese air and naval assets tightened their grip on the Solomons. However, US forces dislodged the Japanese on Guadalcanal, Australian troops pushed back an offensive on New Guinea, and at sea the US won the Battle of Midway.

JANUARY 2

LAND WAR, *PHILIPPINES*

Elements of the Japanese Fourteenth Army enter and occupy Manila while others push up against the Porac Line, the US defensive positions located across the entrance to the Bataan Peninsula. Cavite naval base also falls to the Japanese. An initial attempt to take the Porac Line ends with heavy Japanese casualties, but it forces US and Filipino troops deeper into Bataan.

◀ *Sir Archibald Wavell (third from left), who in January was appointed to head the American-British-Dutch-Australian Command.*

One of the 60,000 Allied soldiers who surrendered to the Japanese Twenty-Fifth Army, commanded by General Yamashita, during its conquest of Malaya.

DUTCH EAST INDIES, *BORNEO*
A Japanese landing force occupies Brunei Bay.

JANUARY 3

POLITICS, *WASHINGTON*
The scattered Allied forces in South-East Asia are brought under a unified command named ABDACOM (American-British-Dutch-Australian Command), with the British General Sir Archibald Wavell as Supreme Commander. This attempt at a joint command structure will prove to be difficult in practice, with international and inter-service rivalries reducing efficiency.

POLITICS, *CHINA*
The Chinese Nationalist leader Chiang Kai-shek is made C-in-C of Allied forces in China.

▼ *Japanese soldiers in landing barges approach a burning Manila in early January. On the advice of President Quezon, General MacArthur had declared it an open city on December 25, 1941.*

JANUARY 4–9

LAND WAR, *MALAYA*
The Indian 11th Division is driven back across the Slim River, only 322km (200 miles) from Singapore. The defence of the Malayan capital, Kuala Lumpur, appears futile, so British forces receive orders to fall back to Johor in the far south of the country.

JANUARY 7–23

LAND WAR, *PHILIPPINES*
Some 80,000 US and Filipino troops fall

▲ *Japanese troops enter Kuala Lumpur. During their conquest of Malaya the Japanese never gave British forces time to regroup.*

back to main defensive positions running down either side of Mount Santa Rosa and Mount Nahib, two high-altitude features occupying central-northern Bataan. The positions are held against numerous Japanese assaults until January 23, when I Corps occupying the western defences and II Corps

in the eastern half are forced to pull back to reserve positions some 48km (30 miles) to the south.

JANUARY 8

LAND WAR, *DUTCH EAST INDIES*
The Japanese occupy the capital of British North Borneo, Jesselton.

JANUARY 10–17

LAND WAR, *DUTCH EAST INDIES*
Two massive Japanese task forces, known as Central Force and Eastern Force, make major landings throughout the Dutch East Indies. On January 11, Central Force goes ashore at Tarakan in northeastern Borneo, while Eastern Force lands on the northernmost tip of Celebes. On January 17, Japanese units land and take the coastal town of Sandakan in British North Borneo.

JANUARY 11

LAND WAR, *MALAYA*
The Japanese advance through Malaya continues, with British and Commonwealth forces establishing defensive lines that are subsequently outflanked by Japanese amphibious "jumps" down the western Malayan coastline.

▼ *The aftermath of a Japanese air raid on Singapore. As the Japanese advanced, the stream of people into Singapore turned into a flood. Soon, medical services were on the verge of collapse.*

STRATEGY AND TACTICS

JAPANESE STRATEGY FOR 1942

The Japanese surprise attack on the American fleet at Pearl Harbor was designed to cripple the American Pacific Fleet to such an extent that the Greater East Asia Co-Prosperity Sphere, Japan's innocent-sounding name for her territorial acquisitions, would be beyond the range of US forces after the American carriers had been destroyed. Though the carriers were never found and destroyed, Japanese strategy for 1942 was built upon this same precept: protection. The Japanese high command in Tokyo decided that the Greater East Asia Co-Prosperity Sphere had to be protected by a defensive line extending south and north of the Marshall Islands. This meant that certain islands that lay within this perimeter had to be taken and fortified. This included the Philippines, where the US had 130,000 men stationed, the key strategic island of Corregidor, New Guinea, the Solomon Islands and the Gilbert Islands.

It was also hoped that by achieving six months of steady and overwhelming military defeats in the Pacific, the US would be forced to negotiate a surrender, or at the very least accept Japan's territorial gains. In the face of an aggressive US counter-strategy (the complete opposite of what the Japanese had actually planned and hoped for), the Imperial Japanese Navy sought to devise a plan whereby the US Pacific Fleet could be engaged in battle and sunk, achieving the same aim as was intended at Pearl Harbor. Away from the ocean, Japanese goals included the capture of Singapore (and the whole of the Malaysian Peninsula), and the conquest of Burma.

SEA WAR, *CENTRAL PACIFIC*
The aircraft carrier USS *Saratoga* is hit by a torpedo fired from a Japanese submarine 805km (500 miles) southwest of Oahu.

JANUARY 12

LAND WAR, *MALAYA*
The Japanese Twenty-Fifth Army occupies the Malayan capital. The capture of the city enables Japanese forces to resupply its units for the subsequent drive into southern Malaya against Johor and Singapore.

JANUARY 15–20

LAND WAR, *BURMA*
The Japanese Fifteenth Army advances northwards from the Kra isthmus and mainland Thailand into Burma. On January 20, it launches its main attack, demolishing the 17th Indian Division and a single Burmese division (both commanded by Lieutenant-General T.J. Hutton) attempting to defend the town of Moulmein.

JANUARY 16

AIR WAR, *SINGAPORE*
In the face of overwhelming Japanese air superiority, almost all British aircraft on Singapore are flown to Sumatra. Although nearly 500 aircraft were committed to the defence of Malaya, most were obsolete types and were useless against Japanese air units, which enjoyed an aircraft numerical superiority of roughly three to one.

JANUARY 18

POLITICS, *BURMA*
The Burmese prime

▶ *A column of Japanese Type 95 light tanks in Malaya. Highly mobile, the Type 95 stayed in production until 1943.*

▲ US troops take cover in a slit trench on Bataan during a Japanese air raid. Note the British-style helmets they are wearing.

▲ Troops of the Japanese Fifteenth Army at the frontier bridge near Moulmein, Burma, at the start of their invasion.

minister, U Saw, is arrested by the British as he attempts to discuss Burmese independence plans with British officials in Palestine.

JANUARY 19

LAND WAR, *MALAYA*
Allied defensive positions around Muar, only 160km (100 miles) from Singapore, are crushed by the Japanese 5th and 8th Divisions. The Allies lose

around 3700 men killed, wounded or captured in the action.

JANUARY 20

AIR WAR, *NEW BRITAIN*
Aircraft from four Japanese carriers begin the bombardment of the port of Rabaul, New Britain.

SEA WAR, *AUSTRALIA*
A Japanese submarine is sunk off the coast of Australia near Darwin by US and Australian warships, heightening

Australian fears that they will soon become victims of a Japanese invasion. Two days later, the Japanese prime minister, General Hideki Tojo, delivers a warning to Australia that, "if you continue your resistance, we Japanese will show you no mercy".

LAND WAR, *SINGAPORE*

Having been driven from mainland Malaya, British and Commonwealth forces under Lieutenant-General Percival cross the Johor Strait bound for

▼ *Two dead Japanese soldiers on Bataan. The Imperial Army suffered heavy losses capturing the peninsula.*

Singapore, the final troops moving to Singapore on the 31st. The Johor causeway across the Strait is badly damaged by British demolition teams to prevent the Japanese making an easy crossing. The island braces itself for the inevitable Japanese onslaught. An air raid against Singapore City on the 20th kills 50 and injures another 150. Southern Singapore is heavily protected from

naval assault by large-calibre coastal guns, but the Japanese will be coming from the opposite direction. An appeal is made for reinforcements of RAF aircraft, as most of the island's remaining RAF planes were evacuated to Sumatra on January 16.

JANUARY 22

LAND WAR, *PHILIPPINES*

The Japanese strengthen their operations in the Philippines by landing reinforcements at Subic Bay in the top western corner of the Bataan Peninsula. In the night, a Japanese battalion makes an amphibious assault down the Bataan coastline and attempts to establish a beachhead on the southern coast of the peninsula

JANUARY 23

LAND WAR, *SOUTHERN PACIFIC*

More than 5000 Japanese troops make amphibious landings on New Britain, New Ireland and Bougainville in the Solomon Islands. Rabaul on the northern tip of New Britain is occupied, and will become one of Japan's most important Pacific naval and aviation bases.

POLITICS, *MANILA*

A puppet government is established in Manila. The Japanese tended to establish such regimes in most of the coun-

▶ *The Burma invasion was intended to secure the flank for the conquest of Malaya, and cut Allied links to China.*

JAPANESE INVASION OF BURMA

tries they conquered, hoping to create the appearance of encouraging independence from European colonial powers for Southeast Asian states.

LAND WAR, *BORNEO*
A major Japanese landing force is put ashore at Balikpapan on the eastern coast of Borneo.

JANUARY 24

LAND WAR, *SAMOA*
A protective force of US Marines occupies Samoa.

SEA WAR, *BORNEO*
Off the coast of Borneo, a Japanese convoy is mauled by US destroyers and Dutch bombers, with four transport vessels sunk. The convoy was heading to reinforce troop landings at Balikpapan.

JANUARY 24–31

LAND WAR, *DUTCH EAST INDIES*
Japanese units in the Dutch East Indies consolidate their coastal gains with more amphibious advances. On January 24, Western Force moves down to Kuching in southern Sarawak, before making two subsequent leaps down to Pemangkat and Pontianak in Borneo on January 27 and 29 respectively. Meanwhile, Central Force and Eastern Force makes several advances through their respective territories, effectively accomplishing a coastal encirclement of Allied forces in the Dutch East Indies.

▲ *The carrier USS* Enterprise, *which was damaged during a suicide aircraft attack in early February 1942.*

▼ *Lieutenant-General Joseph Stilwell (fourth from left) was appointed to lead US forces in China, India and Burma.*

▲ *Manuel Quezon, the president of the Philippines Commonwealth, formed a government-in-exile in the US when Japan occupied the Philippines in 1942.*

JANUARY 25

POLITICS, *THAILAND*
The government of Thailand, basing its outlook on undeniable Japanese successes, declares war on Britain and the US.

JANUARY 26

LAND WAR, *PHILIPPINES*
US forces retreat deeper into the Bataan Peninsula and take up a defensive line stretching from Bagac on the west coast to Orion on the east coast. These posi-

tions become the main battle lines for the next two months, as the Japanese are unable to prosecute their advance through a combination of combat fatigue, heavy casualties and various tropical diseases.

SEA WAR, *MALAYA*
British and Australian naval and aviation units suffer heavy casualties when attacking a Japanese convoy off the Malayan coast. Thirteen of sixty-eight aircraft are shot down and the Aus-

▲ *US internment: people of Japanese ancestry are interned at the Santa Anita Assembly Center, San Pedro, California.*

tralian destroyer *Vampire* and the British destroyer HMS *Thanet* are sunk during the engagements.

JANUARY 30

LAND WAR, *BURMA*
Moulmein is occupied as the Japanese drive towards Rangoon and forge three

▼ *Japanese armour rolls down Orchard Street in Singapore as British resistance collapses.*

other lines of advance. During the course of the advance to Moulmein, several major Allied air bases at Tenasserim, Tavoy and Martaban fall into Japanese hands, severing the British India–Burma air lifeline. A mere 35 operational Allied aircraft in Burma face more than 150 Japanese air opponents.

FEBRUARY 1

SEA WAR, *MARSHALL AND GILBERT ISLANDS*

The US carriers USS *Enterprise* and USS *Yorktown* and the cruisers USS *Northampton* and USS *Salt Lake City*

make an aerial and naval bombardment of Japanese positions at Kwajalein, Wotje, Maloelap, Jaluit and Mili in the Marshall Islands, and Makin in the Gilbert Islands, committing a total force of 92 aircraft. During the raid, the carrier USS *Enterprise* is damaged by a suicide aircraft attack, the earliest example of kamikaze air raids in the war. The attack is more likely to have been opportunistic rather than planned, though.

FEBRUARY 2

APPOINTMENTS, *WASHINGTON*

Lieutenant-General Joseph Stilwell becomes commander-in-chief of the US

▲ *Rangoon under threat. Members of a Japanese artillery battalion train their field gun on Rangoon from high ground outside the city.*

forces in the China-Burma-India theatre, and chief of staff to Chiang Kaishek. Stilwell, who is fluent in Chinese, becomes one of the most successful commanders in the Southeast Asian region.

SEA WAR, *PHILIPPINES*

A Japanese force attempting to land on southwest Bataan behind US lines is defeated at sea by US Navy patrol boats and US aircraft. Several Japanese landings aiming for south Bataan have been defeated over the last week, resulting in the loss of two Japanese battalions.

FEBRUARY 3

AIR WAR, *DUTCH EAST INDIES*

The Dutch naval base at Surabya on Java is damaged severely by a Japanese air attack.

FEBRUARY 4

AIR WAR, *MADURA STRAIT*

An Allied naval force under the command of Rear-Admiral Doorman, Royal Netherlands Navy, suffers a massive air attack as it attempts to intercept a Japanese invasion fleet heading for Borneo. Three cruisers are damaged: one Dutch and two US.

POLITICS, *SOUTH PACIFIC*

The Australia-New Zealand Naval Command is established and led by US Navy Admiral H.F. Leary.

KEY MOMENTS

BATTLE OF THE JAVA SEA

On the night of February 27, 1942, a large naval element of the Japanese Eastern Force comprising 4 cruisers, 14 destroyers and 41 transport vessels sailing for Java was intercepted by a mixed unit of US, Dutch, British and Australian warships. The Allied force consisted of five cruisers and nine destroyers under the command of Dutch Rear-Admiral Karel Doorman. The subsequent action was inauspicious for the Allies, as they suffered from inferior firepower, no reconnaissance aircraft (Doorman had left seaborne aircraft ashore, mistakenly believing they wouldn't be needed in a night action), no air cover and the inexperience of Doorman himself. Two Allied cruisers and three destroyers were sunk, the British cruiser HMS *Exeter* withdrew owing to battle damage, and Doorman was killed. The Japanese force under the command of Vice-

Admiral Takagi Takeo suffered only one damaged destroyer.

The following night, the remaining two Allied cruisers (the USS *Houston* and Australia's HMAS *Perth*) engaged other Japanese shipping west of Batavia, sinking two vessels and damaging four others, though they were subsequently destroyed themselves by a massive retaliation force of 12 Japanese warships. HMS *Exeter* and two other destroyers were also sunk as they attempted to make an escape from Surabaya to Ceylon on March 1. Four US destroyers were the only Allied survivors of the Battle of Java Sea.

The action showed the perils of makeshift multinational task forces and the importance of clear tactical direction and aerial reconnaissance. In addition, the battle demonstrated the superiority of certain Japanese weapon types, particularly their faster "Long Lance" torpedoes.

FEBRUARY 4–5

▲ General Douglas MacArthur (second from left), US commander in the Philippines during the Japanese offensive.

FEBRUARY 4–5

POLITICS, *SINGAPORE*
British commanders on Singapore reject Japanese demands for the colony to surrender. The next day, the British cruise liner *Empress of Asia*, converted to a logistical role, is sunk while attempting to reach Singapore with supplies.

FEBRUARY 5

POLITICS, *US*
The US Government declares war on Thailand.

FEBRUARY 6

LAND WAR, *PHILIPPINES*
US troops mount a counterattack against Japanese reinforcements advancing on Luzon, but make little headway.

FEBRUARY 7–11

LAND WAR, *SINGAPORE*
On the night of February 7, the Japanese Guards Division makes a feint

▼ The British destroyed anything that might be of use to the Japanese at Rangoon before they evacuated the port.

attack against the island of Pulau Ubin off Singapore's northeastern coast. The next evening, the Japanese 5th and 18th Divisions cross into Singapore from the opposite direction, striking inland and taking the vital British air base at Tengeh. They are followed the next night by the Guards Division landing on the central-northern coast around Kranji. Having repaired the Johor causeway, the Japanese now pour more than 30,000 troops of the Twenty-Fifth Army, commanded by Lieutenant-General Yamashita, on to the island. These troops are supported by large numbers of armoured vehicles and ground-attack aircraft. The Japanese have

▲ *The Australian war effort swings into action: soldiers of the Australian Imperial Forces (AIF) at Freemantle in 1942.*

STRATEGY AND TACTICS

US STRATEGY FOR 1942

Though the US had believed that a war against Japan was inevitable long before Pearl Harbor, indeed air bases and other facilities were being constructed on Wake Island and the Marshall Islands in the months leading up to war, the Japanese surprise attack caught the US off guard. Therefore, the initial US strategy for 1942 was at first disorganized and lacking coherence.

The US lacked the manpower or the equipment to hold on to what Pacific territory it had, and had little way of reinforcing the Philippines nor any other islands in the face of Japanese invasion. Thus US strategy was to hold on for as long as possible, whilst US strategists came up with a plan. However, strategic thinking in 1942 was limited by several factors. Firstly, the shock of Pearl Harbor and the destruction of vital

shipping there took its toll. Secondly, superior Japanese planning in the lead-up to 1942 gave them an advantage over the Americans. Lastly, the condition of US unpreparedness could only be improved over a period of time, and not overnight. By the summer of 1942, American strategic planning began to take shape as the US reorganized its Pacific forces. Strategic goals included carrier-based attacks against the Marshall Islands and Wake Island, the daring Doolittle Raid that was designed to boost morale, and the build-up of forces in Australia. After the crucial Battle of Midway, US strategic planners could plan without Japanese carrier craft ever presenting a major threat to US operations in the Pacific. It was this fact that allowed Nimitz and MacArthur to plan aggressive counteroffensives for the second half of 1942.

complete air supremacy. Allied forces are squeezed into the southernmost tip of Singapore around Singapore City.

FEBRUARY 8

POLITICS, *PHILIPPINES*

The US Government rejects a proposal from the president of the Philippines, Manuel Quezon, that the Philippines should become entirely independent of both the Japanese and the

US so that the country can declare its neutrality in the war.

FEBRUARY 10–20

LAND WAR, *DUTCH EAST INDIES*

The Japanese Army continues its southward-moving consolidation of the Dutch East Indies. With Borneo and Celebes under Japanese control, the invaders of Western Force land on southern Sumatra on February 14, following up with parachute landings around Palembang to take its oil refinery on the 15th. Timor and Bali are the next to be invaded on the 19th and 20th, the Japanese again using paratroopers for a drop at Kupang, Timor, on February 20.

FEBRUARY 14

POLITICS, *PACIFIC*

Vice-Admiral C.E.L. Helfrich of the Royal Netherlands Navy takes over

as C-in-C Allied Naval Forces, South West Pacific, relieving Admiral T.C. Hart of the US Navy.

FEBRUARY 15

POLITICS, *SINGAPORE*

British and Commonwealth forces suffer the worst defeat in their history when Lieutenant-General Percival finally surrenders the island of Singapore to the Japanese. A total of 62,000 British, Australian and Indian soldiers fall into captivity, many of whom will die from sickness, overwork and malnutrition in Japanese prison camps. The defence of Singapore became futile when Japanese forces took control of the island's reservoirs and severed Singapore City's

▼ *P-40 Warhawk aircraft of the US 16th Fighter Squadron, 51st Fighter Group, lined up on an airfield in Burma prior to a flight to a Chinese air base.*

KEY PERSONALITIES

ADMIRAL E.J. KING

Admiral Ernest J. King was a driving force behind US Navy operations in both the Atlantic and Pacific theatres during World War II. He was born in Ohio in 1878, and under the strict discipline of a tough-minded father King soon developed the aggressive and determined personality that was to distinguish his career. He entered the US Navy during World War I, and rose quickly through the ranks by showing capable leadership. By 1938 he was a temporary vice-admiral, and in February 1941 was appointed C-in-C of the US Atlantic Fleet. In this post he gained additional combat experience and, prior to America's entry into the war, made a significant impact on U-boat operations in the Atlantic. In December 1941, King was again promoted to C-in-C of the US Fleet.

In the Pacific war he showed great aplomb, using amphibious and carrier resources to defeat the Japanese. He excelled in the Pacific by knowing every aspect of naval operations (in the 1930s he had commanded a submarine flotilla and then the Battle Fleet's aircraft carriers). More importantly, he was also instrumental in obtaining sufficient resources to conduct offensive operations against Japan. Despite his strategic excellence, King did not always get his way, and was overruled by Roosevelt on issues such as his proposed invasion of Formosa in 1944 – the president preferred MacArthur's Philippines operation. King was, however, undoubtedly one of the great architects of the Pacific victory. He retired on December 15, 1945.

water supply. Japanese losses amounted to fewer than 2000 killed. The day before the surrender, Japanese troops had killed 150 patients and staff at the Alexandra Military Hospital.

FEBRUARY 19

SEA WAR, *BADOENG STRAIT*
Dutch and US warships engage Japanese Imperial Navy vessels in the Badoeng Strait, east of Bali, the Japanese having just landed an invasion force on the coast. While one Japanese destroyer is damaged, the Dutch lose a cruiser and a destroyer.

HOME FRONT, *UNITED STATES*
Some 11,000 Japanese-Americans are moved from the Pacific coast to camps in Arkansas and Texas under new US

▼ *Soldiers from the Japanese 18th Infantry Division land on the Andaman Islands to score another easy victory.*

Government war powers. Executive Order 9066 enables the war secretary to displace people from military areas, and the Japanese-Americans, already alienated following Pearl Harbor, are the primary victims of this policy. There are fears in the US, mostly unfounded, that Japanese-Americans might provide intelligence for a Japanese attack on the US west coast. Such fears prove groundless, but more than 112,000 people are interned.

AIR WAR, *AUSTRALIA*
Darwin is bombed by Japanese aircraft in an attack that kills 172 people and damages 16 ships.

FEBRUARY 20

POLITICS, *PHILIPPINES*
The leader of the Philippines, President Quezon, and many of his officials are evacuated from Luzon by the submarine USS *Swordfish*.

▲ *Chinese troops retreat in the face of the rapid Japanese advances in Burma at the end of February.*

FEBRUARY 21

LAND WAR, *BURMA*
Allied resistance to the Japanese Army's advance through Burma crumbles at the Sittang River, 160km (100 miles) north of Moulmein. At one point, British forces crossing the river using a single bridge are forced to blow it up with large numbers of men stranded on the other side. Allied losses are heavy, many men drowning when attempting to swim the Sittang. Elements of the Japanese Fifteenth Army are now free to turn west and drive for Rangoon itself, which the British began to evacuate on February 18.

FEBRUARY 23

SEA WAR, *UNITED STATES*
Making a rare attack on the US homeland, the Japanese submarine *I-17* shells an oil refinery at Ellwood, California. In total 17 rounds are fired, inflicting only minor damage to a pier and an oil well derrick.

FEBRUARY 24

SEA WAR, *WAKE ISLAND*
Japanese forces occupying Wake Island are attacked by a US naval task force led by the carrier USS *Enterprise*.

FEBRUARY 25

POLITICS, *ALLIES*
The ABDA Command is disbanded, and its leader, General Sir Archibald Wavell, goes on to become C-in-C of India. ABDA proved to be too complicated for the effective coordination of forces and was unable to overcome national animosities and suspicions.

DUTCH EAST INDIES, *BATTLE OF JAVA SEA*
A combined force of US, Dutch, British and Australian warships is almost entirely destroyed during two nights of battle against powerful naval elements of the Japanese Eastern Force.

MARCH 1-8

SEA WAR, *DUTCH EAST INDIES*
Japanese naval power is proven in ocean manoeuvres when nine Allied warships and ten merchant ships are sunk during close-range naval engagements off the coast of the Dutch East Indies. Losses include the British cruiser HMS *Exeter* and the British destroyer HMS *Stronghold*.

LAND WAR, *DUTCH EAST INDIES*
Japanese troops land on the northern coastline of Java on March 1, occupying the important naval base at Surabaya and pushing south to conclude their conquest of the Dutch East Indies by March 8. The surrender of Allied forces in the region gives the Japanese access to invaluable stocks of natural materials, including oil, rubber, bauxite and rice, and raises the possibility of further Japanese assaults against Australia.

▲ *Admiral Sir James Somerville was created commander of the British Far East Fleet, which operated from Ceylon.*

MARCH 3

▶ US and Filipino troops surrender to the Japanese during the campaign on the Bataan Peninsula in early march.

MARCH 3

AIR WAR, *AUSTRALIA*
Seventy people are killed and twenty-four aircraft destroyed during a fifteen-minute Japanese air raid at Broome, Western Australia.

HOME FRONT, *US*
All Japanese-American citizens are prohibited from living on the eastern seaboard of the US.

MARCH 4

SEA WAR, *MARCUS ISLAND*
US carrier aircraft from the USS *Enterprise* bomb Japanese positions and installations on Marcus Island. One US aircraft is downed, but a total of 96 bombs cause damage among ammunition dumps, airfields and radio installations.

MARCH 8

LAND WAR, *BURMA*
The British garrison of Rangoon narrowly escapes as the city falls to the Japanese Fifteenth Army. The collapse follows a period of social chaos and internal support for the Japanese from Burmese nationalists. The loss of the Burmese capital results in several British command changes. The commander of the Burma Army, General Thomas Hutton, is replaced by General Harold Alexander.

LAND WAR, *NEW GUINEA*
The battle for New Guinea begins as Japanese invasion forces land two battalions at Lae and Salamaua in the Huon Gulf. Allied air attacks are directed against the Japanese two days later but, at the same time, the Japanese begin preparatory air raids on Port Moresby, the Papuan capital on the southeast coast.

▼ Victorious Japanese troops celebrate on New Guinea after being landed at Lae in early March.

► *General Jonathan Wainwright began evacuating US troops to Corregidor as the Japanese conquered Bataan.*

MARCH 10

LAND WAR, *NEW GUINEA*

The Japanese consolidate their hold of New Guinea's northern coastline by landing troops at Finschafen at the tip of the Huon Peninsula.

AIR WAR, *NEW GUINEA*

The carriers USS *Enterprise* and USS *Lexington* launch major air raids against Japanese shipping supporting the New Guinea landings. By March 18, the US Navy is reporting two enemy heavy cruisers sunk, one light cruiser and three destroyers probably sunk, one cruiser and one destroyer badly damaged, and five other transport vessels sunk.

ATROCITIES, *FAR EAST*

Anthony Eden, the British foreign secretary, gives a report to a shocked gathering of Members of Parliament in the Houses of Parliament concerning Japanese atrocities in the Far East. The

▼ *Japanese tanks, with air support overhead, close in on Rangoon. In 1942 neither Britain nor the US was prepared to commit significant forces to save Burma. For its part, Japan deployed the Fifteenth Army to take the country.*

report reveals horrific details of torture, murder and rape against Allied prisoners of war and indigenous peoples.

MARCH 12

US COMMAND, *PHILIPPINES*

General Douglas MacArthur is flown out of the beleaguered Bataan Peninsula, and Lieutenant-General Jonathan Wainwright takes over command. MacArthur's parting words are, "I shall return".

LAND WAR, *BURMA*

US General Joseph Stilwell is appointed commander of the Chinese Fifth and Sixth Armies in the China-Burma-India theatre (particularly the eastern Shan States and around Mandalay), with the main objective of keeping the Burma Road open in China. Air support is provided by a volunteer force of around 30 US airmen known as the "Flying Tigers" and an RAF squadron.

SEA WAR, *PACIFIC*

Giving an early indication of how significant submarine warfare will be in the Pacific, a single US submarine sinks three Japanese freighters and one troop ship in Japanese home waters.

MARCH 13-24

▶ *Japanese troops on the outskirts of a Burmese oil field during their triumphant advance in March.*

MARCH 13-24

LAND WAR, *BURMA*
British forces establish a defensive line across from Prome, Toungoo and Loikaw around the Salween River, with Major-General William Slim in command of the Burma Corps, an ill-equipped force of one Indian and one Burmese division.

MARCH 14

HOME FRONT, *AUSTRALIA*
US troops begin to arrive in Australia, the first convoy to arrive disembarking 30,000 American soldiers. Since March 2, all physically fit Australian adult male civilians have been eligible for war service.

MARCH 16-18

AIR WAR, *NEW GUINEA*
Combined US and Australian air units attack Japanese shipping and shore installations around Lae and Salamaua, New Guinea. Two Japanese heavy

cruisers are sunk and 10 other ships are either sunk or damaged. Allied losses are light, only one aircraft being shot down.

MARCH 21

LAND WAR, *PHILIPPINES*

US forces trapped in the Bataan Peninsula begin to occupy the heavily fortified island of Corregidor, 3.2km (2 miles) off the coast. The island features a labyrinth of bomb-proof underground tunnels and food stocks sufficient to feed 10,000 men for six months (the garrison numbers 15,000 Americans and Filipinos). Its strategic position astride Manila Bay makes its occupation a vital war aim for the Japanese.

▼ *Striking back – a US B-25 bomber takes off from the deck of the USS* Hornet *during the Doolittle Raid against Japan.*

MARCH 21–28

POLITICS, *INDIA*

The British Government announces that post-war India will achieve a semi-independent status from the British Empire. Sir Stafford Cripps, the Lord Privy Seal, visits India and discloses that it will have dominion status following the conflict. The move is a result of pressure put on Winston Churchill by the Labour Party, and also because Indian troops are being so heavily committed as combatants on behalf of the British.

MARCH 22

LAND WAR, *BURMA*

Allied forces abandon the airfield at Magwe, just over 160km (100 miles) east of Akyab. The capture of the airfield allows the Japanese to fly tactical air operations as far as Mandalay.

MARCH 23

LAND WAR, *ANDAMAN ISLANDS*

The Japanese occupy the Andaman Islands in the Bay of Bengal in the face of no resistance.

MARCH 24–30

LAND WAR, *BURMA*

The Chinese Fifth and Sixth Armies engage the Japanese around Taung-gyi in central Burma, but are defeated. British forces to the west at Prome withdraw farther up Burma, as the Chinese defeat and renewed Japanese assaults leave them in danger of being outflanked.

MARCH 26

POLITICS, *WASHINGTON*

Admiral E. J. King takes over from Admiral H. R. Stark as US Chief of Naval Operations, in addition to his role as C-in-C of the US Fleet.

MARCH 27

MILITARY APPOINTMENTS, *BRITAIN*

The Far East Fleet in Ceylon receives a new commander, Admiral Sir James Somerville.

POLITICS, *AUSTRALIA*

Australian forces come under the command of General Sir Thomas Blamey. Supreme command of Allied forces in the theatre is in the hands of MacArthur, who comes to hold Blamey

KEY PERSONALITIES

ADMIRAL ISOROKU YAMAMOTO

As C-in-C of the Combined Fleet from July 1939, Isoroku Yamamoto (1884–1943) was Japan's greatest wartime naval strategist. Born in 1884 in Nagaoka, he joined the naval academy shortly after the turn of the century, gaining combat experience in the Russo-Japanese War of 1904. He went to the US in 1919 to study English, and also to learn about US naval and industrial strengths.

Yamamoto returned to Japan in 1921 and rose quickly through a series of influential positions. Most significantly, he became an expert in the new art of naval aviation warfare, something he later put to devastating effect as architect of the Pearl Harbor attack. However, Yamamoto was not a supporter of Japanese aggression, correctly believing that US industrial power would triumph in a sustained campaign. But once war was inevitable he committed himself to Japanese victory. Pearl Harbor ably demonstrated the forward-thinking and tactical capabilities of Yamamoto, and it fulfiled all his claims for naval aviation being the future of war at sea.

Respect for Yamamoto grew as the initial Japanese Pacific campaign went from victory to victory. He experienced his first criti-

cal defeat at Midway, by which time ULTRA intelligence was giving the US warning of Japanese naval movements. After Midway, Yamamoto's combined fleet remained potent, but increasingly disadvantaged by US technology, intelligence, tactics and numbers. In the end, it was the US mastery of the principles of naval aviation that helped force the Japanese navy into submission. On April 18, 1943, Yamamoto was killed when he flew to inspect bases in the Solomon Islands. The itinerary of his aircraft was intercepted by ULTRA and the admiral was shot down by US fighters.

▲ *Japanese troops at Mandalay railway yard. The British had stocked a series of depots in the Mandalay–Meiktila area, which were captured by the Japanese.*

in little regard. However, Blamey upholds Australia's interests against British and American strategic demands.

MARCH 30

POLITICS, *PACIFIC*
Meetings between the US and British divide up the operational responsibilities of World War II. The US takes command of the Pacific theatre. Its territorial responsibilities include Australia and New Zealand.

The Pacific theatre is separated into two commands. Admiral Nimitz takes command of the Pacific Ocean Areas, with its sub-divisions of North, Central and South Pacific areas. General MacArthur is the commander of the special Southwest Pacific area. The territories stretching from Singapore westwards to the Mediterranean are under British command.

LAND WAR, *BURMA*
The Japanese occupy Toungou in central Burma after ejecting the Chinese Fifth Army, which held out for a violent 10 days. Toungou provides the Japanese with another useful air base.

MARCH 31

POLITICS, *INDIA*
The nationalist Indian Congress Party makes demands for immediate independence from the British Empire.

APRIL 1

LAND WAR, *NEW GUINEA*
Japanese forces assaulting New Guinea mount two more landings: one is at Hollandia on the north coast; the other on the west coast at Sorong.

LAND WAR, *SOLOMON ISLANDS*
The Japanese occupy Buka Island in the Solomon Islands.

SEA WAR, *INDIAN OCEAN*
A Japanese naval raiding group led by the carrier *Ryujo* sets out from Burma to conduct operations against Allied shipping along the Orissa coast. In the next 10 days it will sink 28 Allied merchant vessels.

◄ *General Stilwell (right) and his staff in the Burmese jungle. After rescuing the encircled Chinese garrison at Toungoo, Stilwell and his men retreated to India, travelling on foot.*

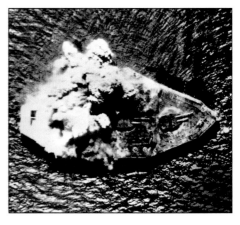

▲ Corregidor under Japanese attack. The island had nine major batteries mounting twenty-five coast artillery weapons, with full support facilities.

APRIL 6

LAND WAR, *SOLOMON ISLANDS/ADMIRALTY ISLANDS*
Japanese forces make amphibious landings at Bougainville in the Solomon Islands and also on the Admiralty Islands.

SEA WAR, *CEYLON*
The Japanese Navy launches a major air and sea attack against Colombo harbour. However, the harbour is practically empty of Allied shipping, most of it having been moved to Addu Atoll west of Ceylon two days earlier. The Japanese do find the destroyer USS *Tenedos* and the cruisers HMS *Dorsetshire* and HMS *Cornwall*, however, which are subsequently sunk. Also in the vicinity is the dated British carrier HMS *Hermes* and the destroyer HMAS *Vampire*. Twenty-six Allied aircraft are shot down during the attack.

APRIL 6

AIR WAR, *INDIA*
The east coast of India faces Japanese air attacks at Vizagapatam and Cocanada on April 6. The India Congress Party leader subsequently pledges full military support for the Allied resistance.

APRIL 8

LAND WAR, *PHILIPPINES*
US soldiers are ordered to destroy their equipment in preparation for their surrender to the Japanese.

APRIL 2

AIR WAR, *PACIFIC*
US Army Air Force (USAAF) B-17 Flying Fortress bombers attack the Japanese fleet around the Andaman Islands.

APRIL 2

LAND WAR, *BURMA*
The Japanese Fifteenth Army continues to push back the Allied Burma Army. Two key positions fall to the Japanese today: the town of Prome, located on the Irrawaddy River north of Rangoon; and the vital port island of Akyab. This latter conquest brings the entire territory of the Arakan in western Burma under Japanese control.

APRIL 5–7

LAND WAR, *PHILIPPINES*
On April 5, the Japanese begin a fresh offensive to take enemy positions on Bataan. They are reinforced by the 4th Division, and inflict heavy US casualties after a five-hour bombardment. By April 7, the US I and II Corps are in retreat.

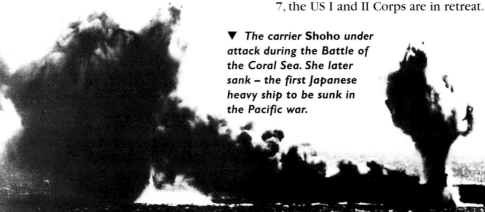

▼ The carrier Shoho under attack during the Battle of the Coral Sea. She later sank – the first Japanese heavy ship to be sunk in the Pacific war.

APRIL 9

▶ *A Nakajima B5N Kate bomber trails smoke after being hit during the Battle of the Coral Sea.*

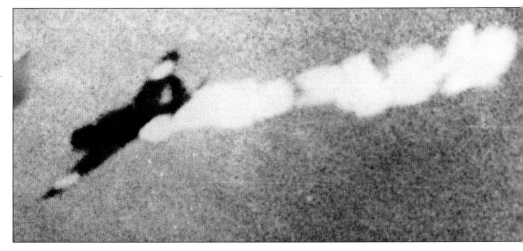

APRIL 9

POLITICS, *PHILIPPINES*

The remaining US forces in the Bataan Peninsula finally surrender. Their commander, Major-General Wainwright, has escaped with 2000 men to Corregidor to continue resistance there. The 78,000 US and Filipino troops who fall into Japanese hands on Bataan are subsequently made to walk 104km (65 miles) in the most dreadful conditions. Around one in three men die in what will become known as the "Bataan Death March". On April 10, the Japanese put ashore another 12,000 men on Cebu Island, consolidating their hold over the Philippines.

AIR WAR, *CEYLON*

Eighty-five Japanese carrier aircraft attack Trincomalee harbour, but find no Allied shipping there. Eight Allied aircraft and fifteen Japanese aircraft are shot down in aerial combat. However, a Japanese scout plane spots the carrier HMS *Hermes* and the destroyer HMAS *Vampire*. The subsequent air strike sinks HMS *Hermes* in only 10 minutes after 40 bomb hits, and the *Vampire* goes down after suffering 13 explosions. The Japanese attacks of the last four days have effectively finished the British Pacific Fleet as a significant force in the region.

APRIL 10

POLITICS, *PACIFIC*

The US Pacific Fleet is reorganized into type commands: Battleships (Rear-Admiral W.S. Anderson); Aircraft Carriers (Vice-Admiral W.F. Halsey); Cruisers (Rear-Admiral F.J. Fletcher); Destroyers (Rear-Admiral R.A. Theobald); Service Force (Vice-Admiral W.L. Calhoun); Amphibious Force (Vice-Admiral W. Brown); Submarine Force (Rear-Admiral T. Whiters); and Patrol Wings (Rear-Admiral H.S. McCain).

APRIL 10–16

LAND WAR, *BURMA*

The Japanese continue their northward advance through Burma. The retreating "BurCorps" destroys the oil facilities at Yenangyaung (the largest oil field in the Far East) on April 16 as the unit is pushed up against the Irrawaddy valley. The Chinese Fifth and Sixth Armies are unable to halt the onslaught.

APRIL 12

POLITICS, *INDIA*

Despite the British rejection of Indian proposals for post-war independence, Pandit Nehru, the leader of the Indian Congress Party, pledges to cooperate with the Allies in bringing about the full defeat of Germany and Japan.

APRIL 16

LAND WAR, *PHILIPPINES*

The Philippine island of Panay is invaded by 4000 Japanese troops (41st Infantry Regiment).

APRIL 18

AIR WAR, JAPAN

Sixteen US B-25 Mitchell bombers flying from the aircraft carrier USS *Hornet* and led by Colonel James Doolittle strike a major propaganda victory by bombing the Japanese capital, Tokyo. The planes operate at the extremes of range, so fly on to China after the mission rather than return to the carrier. Although the damage inflicted is militarily insignificant, the Japanese Government is shocked. Japanese forces will now go all out to destroy US airpower.

APRIL 19

LAND WAR, BURMA

Allied troops fall back to Meiktila, a crucial town in central Burma on the main Rangoon to northern Burma rail route. The capture of Meiktila would be of crucial advantage to Japanese logistics in the Burma campaign.

APRIL 23

LAND WAR, BURMA

Troops of the Chinese Expeditionary

▼ The crew of the USS **Lexington** abandons ship during the Battle of the Coral Sea. The destroyer at right is taking off the sick and wounded.

Force hold off Japanese advances around Twingon, allowing thousands of Allied troops around Yenangyaung to escape the Japanese net.

APRIL 25

LAND WAR, NEW CALEDONIA

US troops land on the Free French colony of New Caledonia. The island's capital, Nouméa, becomes a major US naval base.

APRIL 29

LAND WAR, BURMA

The Japanese 56th Division pushing through Burma reaches as far north as Lashio, having defeated the Chinese 55th Division. Elements of the Japanese

Army now turn southwest to begin the attack on Mandalay, in support of the 18th Division heading directly up from the south. More worryingly, on April 29, the Japanese cut the Burma Road, thus making Chinese Nationalist forces entirely dependent on air supplies.

APRIL 30

LAND WAR, BURMA

General Stilwell, commander of the "BurCorps" in Burma, receives permission to withdraw his troops into India.

SEA WAR, PACIFIC

Three of Japan's most formidable carriers – *Shoho*, *Shokaku* and *Zuikaku* – begin to deploy for operations against Port Moresby, New Guinea.

DECISIVE WEAPONS

USS ENTERPRISE

The USS *Enterprise* was one of the most influential warships of World War II. A "Yorktown" class aircraft carrier that joined the Pacific Fleet in 1938, the USS *Enterprise* was immediately sent into action following the Japanese attack on Pearl Harbor. The ship made its first successful engagement of the war on December 11, 1941, when its aircraft sank the Japanese submarine *I-170*. The USS *Enterprise*'s defining engagement came in June 1942 during the Battle of Midway. Aircraft flying from the USS *Enterprise*, particularly the redoubtable Douglas SBD Dauntless dive-bomber, sank the Japanese carriers *Kaga* and *Akagi*, assisted in the sinking of the carrier *Hiryu*, and later sank the heavy cruiser *Mikuma*.

After Midway, the USS *Enterprise* was to be found wherever action was thickest, from providing air cover for the Guadalcanal landings to participating in the huge air engagements during the Battle of the

Philippine Sea, known as "The Marianas Turkey Shoot", in June 1944. The USS *Enterprise* suffered critical battle damage. She was hit by three bombs during the Battle of the Eastern Solomon Islands in August 1942, and by another three bombs the following October during the Battle of Santa Cruz. In 1945, Japanese kamikaze attacks nearly destroyed the great ship, and in May she returned to the US for major repairs, sitting out the rest of the war.

SPECIFICATIONS:

CREW: 2919 officers and enlisted men
DIMENSIONS: length 246.7m (810ft); beam 34.75m (114ft); draught 8.84m (29ft)
DISPLACEMENT: 25,908 tonnes (25,500 tons)
SPEED: 33 knots
ARMAMENT: eight 12.7cm AA guns; four quadruple 28mm AA guns; 16 12.7mm Browning machine guns in AA mounts
AIRCRAFT: (1942) 15 torpedo bombers; 37 dive-bombers; 27 fighters

◀ **US Douglas Dauntless dive-bombers at the Battle of Midway. Each aircraft could carry a bomb load of 544kg (1197lb) over a range of 730km (456 miles).**

MAY 1–8

LAND WAR, *BURMA*

The Japanese advance through Burma continues. Mandalay falls to the 18th and 56th Divisions on May 1, while the 33rd Division takes Monywa to the west. The Japanese then drive up the Irrawaddy valley against the Chinese Fifth Army's futile defensive positions around Myitkyina. General Stilwell personally leads the 241km (150-mile) retreat of a group of 100 men and civilians from the River Irrawaddy to Imphal, India.

MAY 3

LAND WAR, *SOLOMON ISLANDS*

Japanese forces land on the island of Tulagi in the Solomons. The island is subsequently turned into a major Japanese seaplane base.

MAY 4–6

SEA WAR, *CORAL SEA*

The Battle of the Coral Sea, the first major carrier battle of the war, is ignited as three US task forces head to intercept a Japanese invasion group from Rabaul bound for Port Moresby. A Japanese covering group, including the carriers *Shoho*, *Zuikaku* and *Shokaku*, is heading around the Solomon Islands in the hope of surprising US naval forces from the rear. The US has been forewarned of Japanese intentions through its ULTRA intelligence, but throughout the 5th and 6th the two carrier forces are unable to locate one another.

MAY 6

LAND WAR, *PHILIPPINES*

The US-held fortress island of Corregidor off the coast of Bataan finally falls after a Japanese landing preceded by a massive bombardment. This brings to an end the Philippines campaign, which has cost the Allies 140,000 lives. With the surrender on May 10, nearly 12,500 US and Filipino soldiers become prisoners of the Japanese.

MAY 6

LAND WAR, *CHINA*

Chinese forces led by General Chiang Kai-shek begin a major offensive along a 640km (400-mile) front against Japanese occupiers in seven major cities, including Shanghai and Nanking.

MAY 7

SEA WAR, *CORAL SEA*

Japanese carrier aircraft attack Allied Task Force 44, the unit of cruisers and destroyers set to intercept the Japanese Invasion Group heading for Port Moresby. However, Task Force 44, commanded by Rear-Admiral Crace of the Royal Navy, manages to turn back the Japanese invasion force. Meanwhile, Japanese carrier aircraft to the south of the Solomon Islands bomb and sink the US destroyer USS *Sims* and the fleet oiler USS *Nesho*. The US carriers have already located the Japanese covering group, and a massive air assault by carrier aircraft from the USS *Lexington* and USS *Yorktown* hits the *Shoho* with 1000lb bombs and seven torpedoes. The *Shoho* sinks at 11:35 hours.

MAY 8

SEA WAR, *CORAL SEA*

US and Japanese carriers exchange major air strikes throughout the day at a range of only 320km (200 miles). The *Shokaku* is badly damaged after bomb hits from US dive-bombers. On the US side, the USS *Yorktown* receives substantial bomb damage while the USS *Lexington* is critically damaged by torpedo and bomb strikes, precipitating huge onboard fires that force the carrier to be abandoned at 17:00 hours (enemy bombs rupture a number of her gasoline tanks; gasoline vapour then seeps out of the bulging tanks). She is later sunk by US ships. Most of the 1200 crew are saved.

LAND WAR, *BURMA*

The Japanese capture Myitkyina, an important rail terminus and air base in northern Burma. In a futile attempt to stem the Japanese Burma offensive, the Chinese Fifth Army had been sent to occupy defensive positions around the town, but was unable to halt the Japanese Fifteenth Army.

MAY 9

SEA WAR, *CORAL SEA*

US and Japanese carrier forces break off contact in the Battle of the Coral Sea. Although the losses of shipping on both sides are roughly equivalent, the Battle of the Coral Sea halts Japanese expansion plans in Papua and the Solomon Islands, and signals the first major Japanese reverse in the war. Japan has also suffered heavy loss of pilots and aircraft.

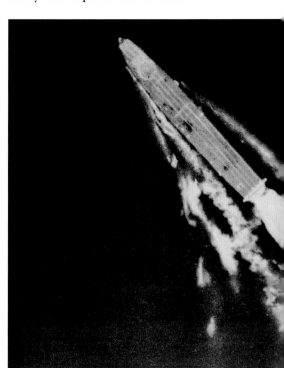

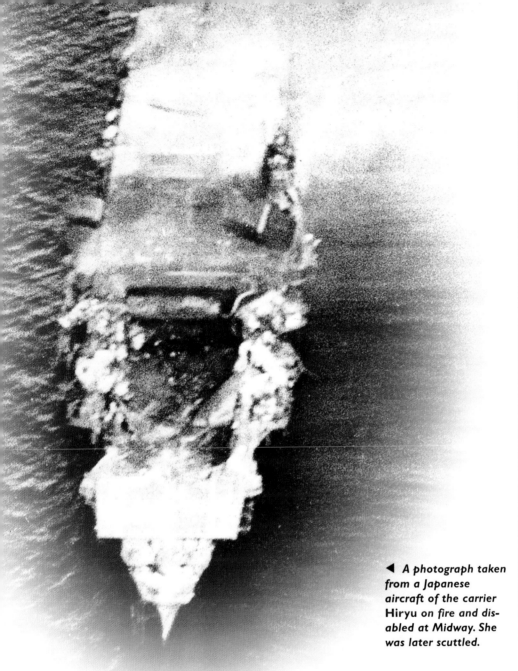

◄ *A photograph taken from a Japanese aircraft of the carrier Hiryu on fire and disabled at Midway. She was later scuttled.*

STRATEGY AND TACTICS

MIDWAY– THE PLAN

The Japanese plans for the Battle of Midway centred around their efforts to lure the US Pacific Fleet into the open and destroy it. However, as was common in Japanese strategic planning, the operation was over complex, made unjustified assumptions about how US naval forces would react, and failed to concentrate force. Indeed, even the choice of Midway Island was flawed, and deeply unpopular with Imperial Japanese Navy captains. A diversionary force would be sent to the Aleutians to draw off part of the US fleet, whilst the Japanese forces under Admiral Yamamoto would capture Midway. This would force the Americans to try to retake the island, which would give Yamamoto the opportunity to destroy Nimitz's carriers with his carrier-based aircraft, aided by land-based bombers stationed on the newly captured island. This would leave the west coast of America at the mercy of the Japanese and force the US to negotiate a peace, or so the theory went (a rather bizarre idea that took no account of the vast military and economic resources of the United States). What Yamamoto did not know was that the US Navy was well aware of his plans through communications intercepts, and had devised its own plan to destroy his forces, despite the odds being stacked against the Americans. Nimitz divided his forces into two, Task Force 16 with the carriers *Hornet* and *Enterprise*, and Task Force 17 with the USS *Yorktown*. Putting faith in his forces' ability to strike at extreme ranges, he planned to knock out the Japanese Carrier Striking Force under the command of Admiral Nagumo. It was with this simple plan in mind that Nimitz set sail for Midway.

MAY 12

LAND WAR, *BURMA*
Japan's steady advance through Burma slows substantially under extremely heavy monsoon rains, which turn jungle trails into almost impassable quagmires.

MAY 14

SEA WAR, *PACIFIC*
US intelligence code-breakers obtain details of Japanese plans to destroy the US Pacific Fleet by fighting a decisive carrier engagement around Midway.

MAY 15

ATROCITIES, *CHINA*
In retaliation for the US Doolittle air

◄ *As seen from a US bomber, the Japanese carrier Akagi takes evasive action at Midway. She was later hit and scuttled.*

raid on Tokyo, Japanese troops kill 100 Chinese families.

MAY 20

LAND WAR, *BURMA*
The Japanese conquest of Burma is completed, with the Japanese having suffered around 7000 casualties against 13,463 British, Indian and Burmese dead. Allied troops are now arriving in Imphal.

MAY 22

SEA WAR, *PACIFIC*
US intelligence reveals Japanese plans for attacks on Midway Island and the Aleutian Islands.

MAY 22

► *Heavy anti-aircraft fire erupts around Japanese torpedo-bombers as they endeavour to sink US ships at the Battle of Midway in early June.*

MAY 22

POLITICS, *MEXICO*
The Mexican Government announces its declaration of war on the Axis powers.

MAY 23

LAND WAR, *BURMA*
Lieutenant-General Stilwell and a small group of men reach safety at Dimapur after a 241km (150-mile) retreat through the Burmese jungle.

MAY 27

SEA WAR, *PEARL HARBOR*
The damaged carrier USS *Yorktown* reaches safety. Navy repair teams restore the carrier (she had been dam-

▼ *Midway cost the Japanese four aircraft carriers, a cruiser and 332 aircraft. The US lost one carrier and 137 aircraft.*

aged by bombs at the Battle of the Coral Sea) and return her to combat readiness in only four days.

MAY 28–29

LAND WAR, *CHINA*
The Japanese penetrate Yunnan Province using the Burma Road. In Chekiang Province, Japanese forces take the capital, Kinhwa, having suf-

fered heavy losses from Chinese resistance. In one action, the Japanese lost 1500 men in a minefield.

MAY 29

TECHNOLOGY, *AUSTRALIA*
Australia's first home-produced wartime aircraft, the Commonwealth CA-12 Boomerang, makes its first flight. Although designed in only five months,

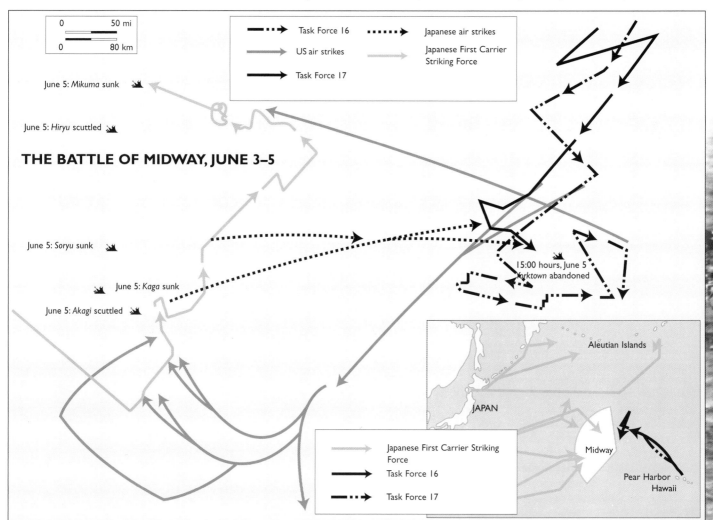

THE BATTLE OF MIDWAY, JUNE 3–5

- - -► Task Force 16	• • • • ► Japanese air strikes
──► US air strikes	──► Japanese First Carrier Striking Force
──► Task Force 17	

June 5: *Mikuma* sunk

June 5: *Hiryu* scuttled

June 5: *Soryu* sunk

June 5: *Kaga* sunk

June 5: *Akagi* scuttled

15:00 hours, June 5 Yorktown abandoned

Aleutian Islands

JAPAN

Midway

Pear Harbor Hawaii

──►	Japanese First Carrier Striking Force
──►	Task Force 16
- - -►	Task Force 17

the Boomerang proves to be a tough and manoeuvrable fighter.

JUNE 1

SEA WAR, *AUSTRALIA*

Three Japanese midget submarines are sunk during an attack on shipping in Sydney harbour. The Australians lose the logistics vessel HMAS *Kuttabull* and with it 16 sailors. Fears are raised that the attack signals a full-scale Japanese invasion.

AIR WAR, *MIDWAY ISLAND*

Japanese carrier aircraft make a heavy raid against US installations located on Midway Island.

JUNE 2

POLITICS, *CHINA*

The US and China sign a lend-lease agreement. Thereafter US begins channelling large amounts of military equipment through to Chinese forces via Indian ports.

JUNE 3

SEA WAR, *MIDWAY*

The Battle of Midway begins, effectively the turning point in the Pacific War. Almost the entire Japanese Combined Fleet under Admiral Isoroku Yamamoto sets sail with several key objectives, including the capture of the Aleutian Islands and Midway Island with its important air base. By taking these objectives, the Japanese hope to draw the remaining US aircraft carriers into battle, to be destroyed by Vice-Admiral Chuichi Nagumo's First Carrier Striking Force comprising the carriers *Akagi*, *Kaga*, *Hiryu* and *Soryu*. The US face this threat with Task Force 17 commanded by Rear-Admiral Fletcher and containing the carrier USS *Yorktown* (patched up from the Coral Sea action), and Rear-Admiral Spruance's Task Force 16 with the carriers USS *Hornet* and USS *Enterprise*.

From June 3–7, the Japanese occupation of the Aleutian islands of Kiska and Attu is completed successfully, but Admiral Nimitz keeps his Pacific forces concentrated around Midway, having been informed through US intelligence of the Japanese battle plan to divert US warships northwards.

▼ *The Japanese heavy cruiser* **Mikuma,** *photographed from an SBD aircraft during the afternoon of June 5, 1942, after she had been bombed by US aircraft.*

▲ *Japanese troops on Attu Island during their invasion of the Aleutian Islands, a diversionary move in conjunction with their strike against Midway.*

AIR WAR, *ALASKA*

Dutch harbour in Alaska is attacked by a force of four Japanese bombers and about fifteen Japanese fighters. The raid results in minimal damage to shore installations.

JUNE 4-5

SEA WAR, *MIDWAY*

Japanese carrier aircraft begin a bombardment of Midway Island, although Nagumo does not know the locations of US naval positions and he believes there are no US carriers in the area. An

initial US attack by aircraft based on Midway Island fails, resulting in heavy losses. Around 09:30 hours, a wave of 150 aircraft from the carriers USS *Enterprise*, USS *Yorktown* and USS *Hornet* roll into action against the Japanese carriers. Again, the attack by the vulnerable Devastator torpedo-bombers is smashed by Japanese Zero fighters. A subsequent flight of US dive-bombers cannot find Nagumo's ships, which have changed course. Finally, at around 10:30 hours, US dive-bombers locate the Japanese carriers, fortuitously catching them when their decks are packed with aircraft, munitions and aviation fuel. In a

◄ *A Japanese observation post outside a base for maritime attack aircraft on New Guinea. The post was used to spot the approach of Allied aircraft.*

blistering attack, three Japanese carriers – *Kaga*, *Akagi* and *Soryu* – are sunk in only five minutes.

Remaining Japanese carrier aircraft retaliate and cripple the USS *Yorktown* – the great ship is sunk two days later by a Japanese submarine while under tow. But the US then repeats its success after aircraft from the USS *Enterprise* create a devastating fire aboard the *Hiryu*, which is scuttled the next day.

The Battle of Midway ends with the balance of power dramatically altered in the Pacific theatre, with the Japanese having lost half of its carrier fleet and 275 aircraft. The US and Japanese navies now face each other with virtual parity.

JUNE 5

LAND WAR, *INDIA*

A huge British convoy of men and materials reaches India intact, substantially raising India's defensive capability against the Japanese.

JUNE 5–7

ALEUTIAN ISLANDS, *KISKA*

The Japanese make an unopposed landing on Attu in the Aleutians on June 5, taking Kiska two days later. US forces

▶ *The US war economy gets into full swing: President Roosevelt (left) and magnate Henry Kaiser watch the launch of a new cargo ship.*

will not discover the Japanese military presence on these islands for another five days.

JUNE 8

SEA WAR, *AUSTRALIA*

Japanese submarines shell the Australian cities of Newcastle and Sydney. The bombardment is ineffectual, with little significant material damage and no casualties.

JUNE 21

SEA WAR, *US*

Fort Stevens on the Oregon coast is

JUNE 27

AIR WAR, *WAKE ISLAND*
Japanese positions on Wake Island are bombed by US aircraft.

JULY 4

SEA WAR, *ALEUTIANS*
US submarines torpedo four Japanese destroyers around the Aleutian Islands, three at Kiska and one at Agattu. Three of the destroyers are sunk.

JULY 7–12

LAND WAR, *NEW GUINEA*
Australian troops make a five-day march across the Owen Stanley Mountains in southern Papua. They take up defensive positions along the Kokoda trail, which snakes from coast to coast across southern Papua.

JULY 21

SEA WAR, *ALEUTIAN ISLANDS*
US submarines sink a further three Japanese destroyers around Kiska in the Aleutians.

shelled by a Japanese submarine. Seventeen shells are fired in total, but they cause no damage.

▲ **Men of the 1st US Marine Division storm ashore on Guadalcanal in the Solomons. They met little initial resistance.**

JUNE 24

POWS, *THAILAND*

Six hundred Allied POWs begin work on what will be a 470km (294-mile) extension to the Singapore–Bangkok railway. The Japanese intend to connect the existing rail line with Rangoon in southern Burma, and are relying on vast numbers of Allied POWs and Asian slave workers to perform the manual labour. This is acceptable under the Geneva Convention, but not the brutal regime they will work under.

▼ **The USS George F. Elliot burns off Tulagi after a Japanese air attack.**

KEY MOMENTS

BURMA–THAILAND RAILWAY

The Burma–Thailand railway was one of the greatest, and most appalling, engineering feats of World War II. In mid-1942, the Japanese were faced with chronic problems in supplying their forces fighting in Burma, particularly as shipping routes to Rangoon were increasingly interdicted by Allied aircraft, ships and submarines. The solution was to build a railroad extension between Thanbyuzayat in Burma and Nong Pladuk in Thailand, which, when linked to existing rail routes, would provide a logistical lifeline throughout Burma and give better access to shipping supplies running up through the Gulf of Siam.

The main challenge, however, was that the rail route stretched over 321km (200 miles) of mountainous jungle terrain. Tropical temperatures would easily exceed 100 degrees F, humidity approached 100 percent, and tropical diseases (particularly malaria) abounded.

To achieve this feat, the Japanese used 61,000 Allied POWs and more than 270,000 labourers from Japanese-occupied territories. The work was done under the most inhumane conditions. The labourers were forced to work 14-hour days or more on starvation rations, with little water and no medical attention. Beatings, executions and torture were constant, and anyone who fell through illness was likely to be bayoneted or shot on the spot. The railway extension ultimately stretched 420km (240 miles) and cost an estimated 12,000 POW lives and the lives of 90,000 other labourers – an average of 425 deaths for every mile of track laid.

The Burma–Thailand railway did not improve Japanese logistics in Burma as significantly as expected. Allied aerial bombing managed to cut the infamous bridge over the Kwai Yai in 1944; and, by early 1945, the stretch of railway was abandoned in the face of Allied advances.

JULY 21–29

LAND WAR, *NEW GUINEA*

Units of the Japanese Eighteenth Army land at Buna on the northern coast of Papua in a renewed Japanese attempt to take Port Moresby, following the defeat of the previous invasion force during the Battle of the Coral Sea. Major-General Tomitaro Horii's "South Seas Force" intends to push across the Kokoda trail and take the town. On July 29, the Japanese take Kokoda itself, halfway along the trail, after a shock night attack.

JULY 30

POLITICS, *US*

The industrial magnate Henry J. Kaiser is "enlisted" by the US Government to galvanize US war production. Kaiser has previously revolutionized production of the US Liberty cargo vessels (nicknamed "American ugly ducklings") using assembly line techniques of construction (one ship could be produced in only 80 hours), and the US Government hopes he can achieve similar results in the production of aircraft, armoured vehicles and warships.

▼ *A US Marine Corps LVT-1 Alligator amphibious assault vehicle hits the beach on Guadalcanal. Each vehicle could accommodate up to 24 soldiers.*

STRATEGY AND TACTICS

JAPANESE STRATEGY ON GUADALCANAL

After the setback at the Battle of Midway in June 1942, the Japanese concentrated their efforts on defence of their territorial gains – what they euphemistically called the Greater East Asia Co-Prosperity Sphere – basically the areas of Asia that gave Japan the raw materials and resources it needed to fight the war. This strategy of defence included building an airfield on Guadalcanal (later renamed Henderson Field by the Americans) as a way of using land-based aircraft in support of carrier-borne units against any US attack.

For the US, the assault on Guadalcanal was a mission of denial rather than of long-term occupancy, preventing the airfield from falling into Japanese hands and allowing it the chance to use its bombers against the US Pacific Fleet. Once entrenched on Guadalcanal, the Japanese planned to use the "Tokyo Express" (essentially a naval supply chain of ships) to keep the island re-supplied and reinforced by sea from the base at Rabaul. When the US attacked the vital shipping routes they fought fiercely to keep these lanes open, resulting in a number of relatively large naval battles off the coast of the Solomon Islands. The overall Japanese strategy once Henderson Field had been seized by the Americans shortly after they landed on August 7, 1942, was to wrest control of the airfield and use it to attack the US fleet, though in this venture they were unsuccessful as the US Marines had secured victory on Guadalcanal by early February 1943. The Japanese lost thousands of troops in futile attacks on the perimeter of the airfield.

JULY 31

AIR WAR, *SOLOMON ISLANDS*

Japanese airfields on Tulagi and Guadalcanal are bombed by US aircraft.

AUGUST 7–8

LAND WAR, *GUADALCANAL*

On August 7, units of the 1st Marine Division land on Guadalcanal in the Solomon Islands. It is the first major US offensive operation of the war, expedited by Japanese construction of an airfield (Henderson Field) on Guadalcanal, and is composed of a 19,000-strong amphibious task force under Rear-Admiral Turner, with operational

 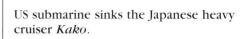
US submarine sinks the Japanese heavy cruiser *Kako*.

AUGUST 12

LAND WAR, *CHINA*

Japanese forces in central Shantung Province launch a massive new offensive against Chinese Nationalist troops. The Japanese are taking advantage of internecine warfare raging between Communist and Nationalist soldiers.

AUGUST 17

COMMANDO RAID, *GILBERT ISLANDS*

US troops of the 2nd Raider Battalion, US Marine Corps, attack Japanese coastal installations on Makin Island during a night-time raid. The commandos are transported to their objective by the submarines USS *Nautilus* and USS *Argonaut*, with USS *Nautilus* providing offshore gunfire support as the 2nd Raiders go ashore in small landing craft.

AUGUST 18–19

LAND WAR, *NEW GUINEA*

The main pass across the Owen Stanley Mountains is now in the hands of the Japanese Eighteenth Army. On the 19th, troops from the Australian 7th Division begin amphibious reinforcement of Port Moresby.

▼ *A US SBD Dauntless dive-bomber lies wrecked on Henderson Field following a Japanese air attack. The airfield was originally constructed by the Japanese.*

▲ *After a heavy naval bombardment (seen here), landings began on Tanambogo, spearheaded by a pair of tanks. By nightfall the island was in US hands.*

command falling to Rear-Admiral Fletcher. The initial landings on Guadalcanal are unopposed, but stiff resistance is encountered during subsequent landings at Tulagi and Gavutu. By August 8, Henderson Field is secured by the Allies, but the Japanese begin a major naval and aerial bombardment of US positions.

AUGUST 8–11

LAND WAR, *NEW GUINEA*

Kokoda is temporarily recaptured from the Japanese by a mixed force of Australian and Papuan troops, but by August 11 the Allies are driven 8km (5 miles) back towards Port Moresby.

AUGUST 8–9

SEA WAR, *BATTLE OF SAVO ISLAND*

A force of Allied cruisers under Rear-Admiral Crutchley fights a brutal night action north of Savo Island against a Japanese cruiser force attempting to destroy US transport vessels supplying operations on Guadalcanal. The Japanese force, led by Vice-Admiral Mikawa, demonstrates total superiority in night-fighting, sinking four Allied cruisers for no losses in only 90 minutes, killing more than 1000 Allied seamen. The Allied resistance, however, prevents the Japanese attacking the vital logistics shipping; and the day after the battle, a

AUGUST 18-22

LAND WAR, *GUADALCANAL*
The Japanese land a regiment at Taivu, 32km (20 miles) east of Henderson Field. The regiment, under Colonel Ichiki, is around 900-men strong and advances westwards and attacks the US perimeter around the air base on August 21-22. All attacks are repulsed, the US having constructed a solid defensive perimeter around Henderson Field since the initial landings. Ichiki's force is decimated on the Tenaru River, and Ichiki himself commits suicide.

AUGUST 20-24

AIR WAR, *GUADALCANAL*
US forces on Guadalcanal receive their first contingent of land-based aircraft (31 fighters) for use from Henderson Field. The aircraft will provide much needed close-support and naval interdiction operations over the coming weeks. On August 24, a Japanese air at-

tack suffers 21 aircraft downed against 3 US losses.

AUGUST 23-25

SEA WAR, *EASTERN SOLOMON ISLANDS*
A Japanese supply convoy, protected by the aircraft carriers *Ryujo*, *Zuizaku* and

▲ *Japanese premier Hideki Tojo (front row, second from left) with his war cabinet in Tokyo. He took over the office of foreign minister in early September.*

Shokaku, attempts a resupply mission to Guadalcanal, but is intercepted by Vice-Admiral Fletcher's Task Force 61,

▲ Australian troops, supported by a US M2A2 light tank, assault a Japanese position on New Guinea. Note how the wartime censor has masked any unit identification markings on the tank.

also containing three carriers (USS *Saratoga*, USS *Wasp* and USS *Enterprise*). On the 24th, US and Japanese carrier aircraft deal mutual blows, the US sinking the *Ryujo* and the Japanese damaging, although not critically, the USS *Enterprise*. The carrier forces separate, but the next day US Marine dive-bombers flying from Henderson Field sink two Japanese transporters (*Jintsu* and *Kinryu Maru*) and the destroyer *Mutsuki*. Japanese supply runs to Guadalcanal are now to be made under more awkward night conditions.

▲ US Marines on the island of Guadalcanal photographed just after they had stormed a Japanese camp. The enemy left in a hurry, leaving their food on the table.

AUGUST 25

LAND WAR, *GILBERT ISLANDS*
Japanese forces occupy Nauru in the Gilbert Islands and Goodenough Island off the coast of New Guinea.

AUGUST 25-26

LAND WAR, *NEW GUINEA*
Milne Bay, in the southeastern corner of Papua, is invaded by a Japanese unit of 1200 men. They are attempting to occupy land suitable for a Japanese forward air base to support the army's drive on Port Moresby. The landing is heavily resisted by Australian troops occupying coastal positions, who kill numerous Japanese and destroy several landing craft.

AUGUST 28

AIR WAR, *SOLOMON ISLANDS*
USAAF aircraft attack a Japanese reinforcement convoy heading for Guadalcanal. The Japanese destroyer *Asagiri* is sunk and two other destroyers are damaged, with the convoy unable to put ashore its troops.

◀ Troops of the US 1st Marine Division with an M1918 155mm howitzer on Guadalcanal. This artillery piece was based on a French World War I design.

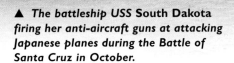

▲ *The battleship USS* South Dakota *firing her anti-aircraft guns at attacking Japanese planes during the Battle of Santa Cruz in October.*

AUGUST 30

LAND WAR, *ALEUTIAN ISLANDS*
US Navy and Army troops occupy Adak in the Aleutian Islands, intending to use it as an air and naval operating base in the North Pacific area.

AUGUST 31

SEA WAR, *SOLOMON ISLANDS*
The carrier USS *Saratoga* is damaged by a torpedo launched from the Japanese submarine *I-25* 418km (260 miles) southeast of Guadalcanal. She is then towed part of the way to Pearl Harbor for repairs.

SEPTEMBER 1

LAND WAR, *GUADALCANAL*
Troops of the Naval Construction Battalion – otherwise known as "Seabees" – are landed on Guadalcanal to assist in developing the US base there. The Seabees are known for ingenious and fast engineering work under combat conditions.

SEPTEMBER 3

POLITICS, *JAPAN*
The Japanese war minister and premier, Hideki Tojo, takes over the office of foreign minister after the resignation of Shigenori Togo. There are now

▼ *Two Japanese aircraft are shot down during the Battle of Santa Cruz. Both had been attempting to attack the US cruiser seen in the background.*

no civilian personnel in the Japanese cabinet.

SEPTEMBER 3–7

LAND WAR, NEW *GUINEA*
The Japanese land 1000 reinforcements at Buna to reinforce the flagging New Guinea campaign. On September 5–7, the Japanese Special Navy Landing

▼ *US Marine Corps pilots race to their Corsair aircraft on Guadalcanal. The first deliveries of this excellent aircraft to combat units began in July 1942.*

◄ *The USS Hornet on fire at the Battle of Santa Cruz. During the engagement she was hit by two kamikaze attacks, seven bombs and two torpedoes in one assault, followed by another assault by torpedo bombers. She later was abandoned and eventually sunk.*

Force is compelled to withdraw from Milne Bay by the violent defence of the Australian 7th Brigade and the 18th Brigade of the Australian 7th Division. The Japanese lose around 1000 men in the action, the first defeat for a Japanese amphibious invasion force.

SEPTEMBER 7/8

LAND WAR, *GUADALCANAL*

A force of Marine Raiders conducts a night-time assault against Japanese positions at Taivu, obtaining intelligence about Japanese campaign plans and inflicting damage on Japanese logistics.

SEPTEMBER 11

AIR WAR, *NEW GUINEA*

The Japanese destroyer *Yayoi* is sunk by a combined force of British and US aircraft flying from Normandy Island, D'Entrecasteaux Islands, off New Guinea.

▶ *The fighting around Henderson Field was particularly savage, with the Japanese launching mass infantry attacks against US positions, to no avail.*

SEPTEMBER 12–14

LAND WAR, *GUADALCANAL*
The 6000-strong Japanese 25th Brigade launches a major attack against Henderson Field around "Bloody Ridge". The US Marines, forewarned by intelligence gathered from Taivu Field, put up a ferocious defence. After two days of fighting and more than 1200 losses, the Japanese commander, General Kawaguchi, orders his men to withdraw.

SEPTEMBER 14–15

LAND WAR, *NEW GUINEA*
By September 14, Japanese forces advancing across the Kokoda trail are only 50km (30 miles) from Port Moresby. The capital, however, is receiving heavy reinforcements in the shape of US infantry.

SEPTEMBER 15

SEA WAR, *GUADALCANAL*
The carrier USS *Wasp* and a US destroyer are sunk by Japanese submarines while running convoy protection duties for transport ships bound for the island of Guadalcanal.

▼ *Smoke rises from a Japanese bomber shot down in the Guadalcanal area, just as its pilot attempted to ram the ship whose rail can be seen in the foreground. The puffs of smoke are from anti-aircraft fire.*

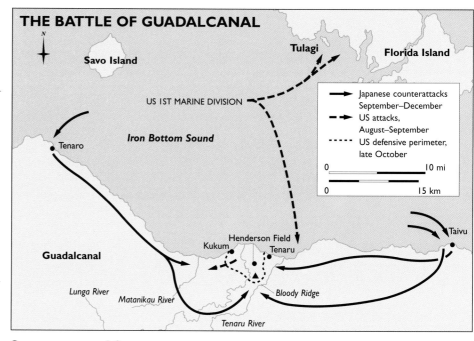

THE BATTLE OF GUADALCANAL

N

Savo Island

Tulagi

Florida Island

US 1ST MARINE DIVISION

Iron Bottom Sound

Tenaro

→ Japanese counterattacks
September–December

--▶ US attacks,
August–September

···· US defensive perimeter,
late October

0   10 mi
0   15 km

Guadalcanal

Henderson Field
Kukum   Tenaru

Taivu

Lunga River

Matanikau River

Bloody Ridge

Tenaru River

SEPTEMBER 18

LAND WAR, *GUADALCANAL*
US forces on Guadalcanal are reinforced by the 7th Marine Regiment.

SEPTEMBER 21

LAND WAR, *BURMA*
Allied forces in Burma attempt to go on the offensive against Japanese units in the Arakan around the Bay of Bengal. The offensive fails, and the 14th Indian Division suffers heavy losses.

SEPTEMBER 23–31

LAND WAR, *NEW GUINEA*
The 7th Australian Division launches a major counteroffensive against the Japanese in the Gona/Buna area of Papua, attacking the Japanese at the very point where they made their initial landings the previous July. The Japanese, now starving and struck with tropical diseases, are forced into retreat from Port Moresby by the Australians, and by the end of the month are driven as far back as Wairopi.

SEPTEMBER 24–27

LAND WAR, *GILBERT ISLANDS*
Japanese forces make three landings throughout the Gilberts, putting troops ashore at Maiana, Beru and Kuria.

SEPTEMBER 27

ALEUTIAN ISLANDS, *ATTU*
The Japanese forces on Attu begin secretly transferring to Kiska to strengthen the garrison there.

OCTOBER 1

SEA WAR, *CHINA*
The Japanese ship *Lisbon Maru* carrying 1816 Allied POWs is torpedoed by the US submarine USS *Grouper* off the coast of China. Japanese seamen close the hatches on the prisoners, and 840 go to the bottom. Many of those who manage to escape

▶ *The cruiser USS Boise arrives at the Philadelphia Navy Yard for repairs following damage suffered at the Battle of Cape Esperance.*

▲ *Sailors from the cruiser USS* Boise *admire their battle score after service in the Solomons: two heavy cruisers, a light cruiser and three destroyers sunk.*

▲ *Japanese troops in retreat on New Guinea following the counterattack by the 7th Australian Division at the end of September, which saved Port Moresby.*

are machine-gunned on the surface. Japanese prison ships did not display the red cross to signify prisoners aboard, and conditions were so horrifying that more than 22,000 Allied POWs died on Japanese ships during the war.

OCTOBER 3–4

AIR WAR, *GUADALCANAL*
US and Japanese aircraft trade blows over Guadalcanal. On the 3rd, 30 Japanese Zeros attack US positions, but 7 Navy Wildcat fighters manage to shoot down 9 of the attackers while anti-aircraft batteries destroy another 2. In the

night, US Navy and Marine Corps aircraft bomb a Japanese convoy landing troops on Guadalcanal, hitting one cruiser.

OCTOBER 5

AIR WAR, *SOLOMON ISLANDS*
US carrier aircraft strike at a concentration of Japanese ships massing around Shortland Island, south of Bougainville. Six vessels are damaged, and around ten Japanese aircraft are destroyed.

OCTOBER 7–9

LAND WAR, *GUADALCANAL*
US Marine forces at Henderson Field

make westward attacks against nearby Japanese forces, fighting heavy engagements on the Matanikau River. Shortly after the battles, the US Marines receive their first US Army reinforcements in the form of the 164th Infantry Regiment of the Americal Division.

OCTOBER 11–12

SEA WAR, *CAPE ESPERANCE*
A US cruiser force under Rear-Admiral Scott intercepts a Japanese supply convoy, covered by a Japanese cruiser squadron under Rear-Admiral Goto, heading for Guadalcanal between the

OCTOBER 14

East and West Solomon Islands. Despite some inefficient communications and poor tactical manoeuvring by the US ships, US radar provides an advantage and the initial clash sees the Japanese lose the destroyer *Fubuki*, while the cruisers *Furutaka* and *Aoba* are seriously damaged. The Japanese retaliate by crippling the USS *Duncan* and USS *Boise*, but are forced into retreat. The action shows how US advances in shipboard radar might deprive the Japanese of their tactical supremacy in night fighting.

OCTOBER 14

SEA WAR, *GUADALCANAL*
Henderson Field suffers a heavy bombardment from the Japanese battleships *Kongo* and *Haruna* and an assortment of other vessels. US battery fire damages two Japanese destroyers.

OCTOBER 23–26

LAND WAR, *GUADALCANAL*
Henderson Field suffers another major Japanese attack by 20,000 soldiers under the command of General Maruyama. Wave after wave of Japanese troops assault the US Marines' southern positions, concentrated along the Mananikau, Lunga and Tenaru rivers, over the next three days, but each attack is defeated and the offensive collapses with 3500 Japanese casualties.

OCTOBER 25–26

SEA WAR, *SANTA CRUZ*
The Japanese Combined Fleet moves towards Guadalcanal in support of General Maruyama's offensive against the US Marines on the island. US Task Forces 16 and 17, containing the carriers USS *Hornet* and USS *Enterprise*, are sent to intercept the Japanese around Santa Cruz Island. A strike force of US carrier aircraft miss their target on the 25th, and at first light on the 26th both the US and Japanese put flights of attack aircraft into the sky. Over the course of a four-hour battle, the Japanese carriers *Zuiho* and *Shokaku* are badly damaged, while the USS *Enterprise* suffers a smashed flight deck and the USS *Hornet* is destroyed by two tor-

▶ *The battleship* USS New Jersey *is launched at the Philadelphia Naval Shipyard. It took a year to train her crew before she was ready for duty.*

pedo and six bomb strikes and has to be abandoned. The Japanese claim victory in the battle, but have lost more than 100 pilots and aircraft, unacceptably high losses that render many of the carriers almost inoperable.

OCTOBER 30

LAND WAR, *ALEUTIAN ISLANDS*
The Japanese land a second invasion force on the island of Attu in the Aleutian Islands.

▲ *Japanese troops in a firefight with Australians during the retreat from the Port Moresby area. Japanese forces were desperately short of food by this time.*

NOVEMBER 1–30

LAND WAR, *GUADALCANAL*

US forces on Guadalcanal continue to pressure Japanese units. On November 3, six US battalions trap a Japanese unit near Point Cruz and kill 300 enemy troops. In addition, the 7th Marines and units of the 164th Infantry Division attack a 1500-strong Japanese force landed as reinforcements near Koli Point, inflicting heavy losses and pushing the Japanese inland. Following these actions, the Japanese abandon their two-front strategy on Guadalcanal. The US keeps receiving reinforcements, including the 2nd Raider Battalion, 8th Marines and 182nd Infantry, so the Japanese have little respite.

NOVEMBER 2

LAND WAR, *NEW GUINEA*

Australian forces in New Guinea retake Kokoda, having pushed the Japanese halfway back across the Kokoda trail.

NOVEMBER 7

AIR WAR, *GUADALCANAL*

US aircraft flying from Henderson Field bomb and damage two Japanese destroyers off the coast of Guadalcanal.

NOVEMBER 11–13

LAND WAR, *NEW GUINEA*

The disease-ravaged and exhausted Japanese suffer another defeat on Papua, losing 600 men in an Australian flanking action at the town of Oivi. Japanese troops on the Kokoda trail are pushed back beyond the Kumusi River, ensuring the safety of Port Moresby. Advancing Australian troops find evidence of cannibalism among the starving Japanese.

NOVEMBER 12–13

SEA WAR, *SOLOMON ISLANDS*

A Japanese convoy of transport ships, supported by 11 destroyers and carrying

▶ *An Australian mortar crew on New Guinea. By the end of 1942, many Australians were sick with malaria and their units were understrength.*

13,000 infantry reinforcements, heads for Guadalcanal, while a large force of 18 Japanese warships (including two battleships and two cruisers) under Admiral Tanaka bombards Henderson Field as a covering action. Japanese carriers provide air cover from the northern Solomon Islands. A US force of eight destroyers and five cruisers, commanded by Rear-Admiral Callaghan, moves to intercept, guided by ship-borne radar.

Tanaka's and Callaghan's forces clash in the early hours of the morning around "Ironbottom Sound" between the coast of Guadalcanal and Savo Island. The action is bloody, the Japanese suffering two cruisers sunk and one battleship (the *Hiei*) crippled, while the US loses one cruiser and four destroyers. Almost all vessels participating in the battle are damaged, and Callaghan is killed. The action is broken off, and the Japanese supply convoy is unable to reach Guadalcanal.

NOVEMBER 13

SEA WAR, *SOLOMON ISLANDS*

The crippled battleship *Hiei* is sunk by a US air attack north of Savo Island. Meanwhile, the Japanese attempt once again to run the reinforcements convoy into Guadalcanal.

NOVEMBER 14–15

SEA WAR, *SOLOMON ISLANDS*

US dive-bombers and torpedo aircraft sink six transports and two cruisers of the con-

▲ *A Japanese machine gunner on Guadalcanal. By the end of the year the Imperial Army had lost over 20,000 dead trying to dislodge US forces from the island.*

voy heading for Guadalcanal. A rescue force of 14 Japanese warships under Admiral Kondo is sent into battle and is met by US Task Force 64 under Admiral Lee, comprising two battleships and four destroyers. They fight around midnight on November 14/15. Task Force 64 loses four warships in quick succession, leaving the battleship USS *Washington* to destroy the Japanese battleship *Kirishima* and one destroyer with its radar-controlled guns. By 00:30 hours, the Japanese are in retreat, and the attempt to reinforce the Japanese Guadalcanal garrison is

NOVEMBER 17–19

▲ *Australian tanks and infantry flush out Japanese troops in pillboxes in the final assault on Buna. In the foreground, a soldier is reloading his rifle.*

curtailed, although Japanese destroyers still manage to put ashore around 10,000 men (most rescued from the sunken transports).

NOVEMBER 17–19

LAND WAR, *NEW GUINEA*
The Japanese on the Kokoda trail are forced back into defensive positions in the Buna/Gona area, reinforced by some 1000 extra troops on November 17. A US-led attack against Buna on November 19 is beaten off.

NOVEMBER 24

LAND WAR, *SOLOMON ISLANDS*
The Japanese land troops at Munda Point, New Georgia.

NOVEMBER 30

SEA WAR, *SOLOMON ISLANDS*
The Japanese 2nd Destroyer Flotilla under Admiral Tanaka attempts to run a supply convoy to Guadalcanal through Ironbottom Sound under the cover of darkness. A large force of destroyers and cruisers under Rear-Admiral Wright engages the Japanese with gunfire, sinking the destroyer *Takanami*, before losing one cruiser and suffering three badly damaged cruisers by a nimble Japanese torpedo counterattack. Despite the failure of the supply convoy, the action again demonstrates Japanese excellence in naval night-fighting.

DECEMBER 2

LAND WAR, *GUADALCANAL*
US Marines ambush a Japanese patrol around the Lunga River, killing 35 of the 60 enemy soldiers.

DECEMBER 3

AIR WAR, *NEW GEORGIA*
US bombers concentrate attacks on Munda Point in an attempt to prevent the construction of a Japanese air base there.

DECEMBER 7

SEA WAR, *US*
The USS *New Jersey* is launched, the largest battleship in the US Navy

◄ *The corpses of Japanese soldiers, shattered ammunition boxes and debris litter a beach near the port of Gona, New Guinea, in late 1942.*

with a displacement of 55,767 tonnes (54,889 tons), and featuring a main armament of nine 16in guns set in three triple turrets.

DECEMBER 9

LAND WAR, *GUADALCANAL*
Major-General Alexander M. Patch takes over command of the US Guadalcanal forces from General Vandegrift. The 1st US Marine Division begins to leave Guadalcanal as reinforcements arrive. During December, the US forces on Guadalcanal will reach 58,000 men, as opposed to 20,000 poorly equipped Japanese.

LAND WAR, *NEW GUINEA*
Australian troops of the 21st Brigade take Gona, sealing the Japanese entry

point to the Kokoda trail. More than 630 Japanese are killed in the close-quarters battle, while the Australian victory is bought at the heavy price of 530 casualties.

DECEMBER 17–31

LAND WAR, *BURMA*

The 14th Indian Division begins to take the Allied war back into Burma. It crosses the Indian border and advances 241km (150 miles) to positions just north of the Maungdaw–Buthidaung line extending out from the western coast of Burma. The goal of the advance is Akyab, around 96km (60 miles) to the south, but the 14th Indian Division faces nimble Japanese delaying tactics and is eventually halted by the 55th Division. Allied penetration, how-

▼ *Jeeps loaded with military equipment on their way to supply US forces fighting Japanese troops in New Guinea.*

KEY PERSONALITIES

ADMIRAL CHESTER NIMITZ

Admiral Chester W. Nimitz was one of the most gifted naval commanders of World War II. Born in 1885 in Texas, Nimitz first set his sights on a career in the US Army, but owing to a lack of places at West Point he began attendance at the Naval Academy Class in 1905.

Nimitz excelled academically, athletically and in leadership skills. He first took to sea in the USS *Ohio*, before commanding the gunboat USS *Panay* then the USS *Decatur*. Between 1907 and 1918, Nimitz was assigned to service in submarines: he commanded a number of vessels and, for one year, the Atlantic Submarine Flotilla. In 1919, he returned to service on board surface vessels for one year; and, during the 1920s, he occupied more strategic-level roles in the US Navy, including Chief of Staff to the Commander Battle Forces and Chief of Staff to the C-in-C, US Fleet. The late 1920s and 1930s saw Nimitz take various ship and submarine commands, including the heavy cruiser USS *Augusta*, before moving on to naval division commands and also becoming the Chief of the Bureau of Navigation in 1939.

Nimitz's crowning achievement came when he replaced Rear-Admiral Kimmel as

C-in-C of the US Pacific Fleet after the attack on Pearl Harbor, Nimitz being promoted to full admiral. Throughout the Pacific campaign, Nimitz demonstrated an aggressive defensive attitude combined with a deep practical understanding of naval warfare, and an affable personality that made him popular and respected. Nimitz presided over the great naval battles of the Pacific War, and had an excellent grasp of how to support amphibious land campaigns. It is a sign of his capabilities that, in November 1945, he was made Chief of Naval Operations on the retirement of Admiral King.

ever, resumes southwards; and, on December 31, Rathedaung is taken.

DECEMBER 19

LAND WAR, *NEW GUINEA*

Australian troops overwhelm the Japanese defences at Buna, signalling the end of the Japanese campaign in New Guinea.

DECEMBER 26–31

LAND WAR, *GUADALCANAL*

US XIV Corps faces a bloody Christmas battling with desperate Japanese forces on Guadalcanal. Despite being half-starved, stricken with malaria and running out of ammunition, the Japanese on Mount Austen still put up a tenacious defence. However, on December 31, the Japanese imperial general staff orders the abandonment of Guadalcanal.

DECEMBER 27–28

LAND WAR, *NEW GUINEA*

Recognizing the futility of resistance in New Guinea, the Japanese high command orders troops at Napopo and Buna to begin retreating to Giruwa.

1943

LAND WAR, *GUADALCANAL*
The Japanese high command gives the orders for a phased withdrawal of Japanese forces from Guadalcanal. US strength on the island is now around 50,000 troops, with massive air, artillery and naval resources, while Hyakutake's Seventeenth Army consists of fewer than half that number, has limited ammunition and rations, and little hope of resupply. General Patch's XIV Corps pushes outwards from the Lunga perimeter.

▼ *Two US soldiers prepare to enter a Japanese dugout on New Guinea, January 3, 1943. Their weapons are M1 Garand semi-automatic rifles.*

A s the US war economy switched into high gear, more ships and aircraft became available for the Pacific theatre. With resources to hand, the Allies, with the US as the major player, were able to mount sustained offensives in the central and southwest Pacific. The Japanese were forced back in New Guinea and the Solomons, while US forces won hard-fought victories in the Gilbert Islands.

▼ *A Japanese Zero fighter, its fuselage riddled with machine-gun rounds, lies wrecked on Guadalcanal in January 1943.*

JANUARY 2

LAND WAR, *GUADALCANAL*
US troops attack Japanese positions on Mount Austen, a piece of high ground dominating the landscape between the Lunga and Matanikau rivers. However, the Japanese beat off the attack.

JANUARY 2-13

LAND WAR, *NEW GUINEA*
Allied forces achieve total control over the Kokoda trail, having engaged in fierce fighting along its length for 10 months. The Japanese do not go easily, and a US assault against Buna on January 2 meets heavy resistance: there are 2870 Allied casualties, but the settlement is finally taken.

JANUARY 3-55

AIR/SEA WAR, *NEW GEORGIA*
US fighter and bomber aircraft attack Japanese targets around the New Geor-gia group, concentrating on the Japanese airfield at Munda and several Japanese destroyers anchored off Rendova Island. On the 5th, US surface vessels bombard Munda.

JANUARY 5

LAND WAR, *GUADALCANAL*
US troops manage to capture high-ground positions on Mount Austen, and

▲ *Surrounded by tall kunai grass, a US Army sergeant drinks from his canteen during a lull in the fighting around Buna in New Guinea in early January.*

see off six enemy counterattacks with 150 Japanese soldiers dead.

JANUARY 6-9

SEA WAR, *HUON GULF*
The US demonstrates its increasing su-premacy in sea power during the Battle

▲ *A photograph taken from a US aircraft shows bombs bursting on a Japanese airfield at Lae on New Guinea.*

STRATEGY AND TACTICS

JAPANESE STRATEGY FOR 1943

By 1943, it was becoming apparent to a number of Japanese commanders that they were fighting a losing battle. After failing to knock out the US carriers at Pearl Harbor, the hope for 1942 had rested on securing a perimeter wide and deep enough to protect its territories. Yamamoto, commander of the Combined Fleet, felt that the qualitative difference in national strength between Japan and the US was patently obvious, and that any prolonged war between the two countries could only end in defeat for Japan. He hoped that the rapid destruction of the main force of the US fleet and the strategy of continually seeking decisive engagements would weaken the morale of both the US Navy and the people, forcing the government to seek peace at the negotiation table.

But, by 1943 the Japanese had suffered a series of serious setbacks, such as the Battle of Midway in mid-June 1942. They therefore set about devising another way of holding back the American tide. They were determined to hold what they could, and this meant vigorously fighting for and reinforcing New Guinea and the neighbouring islands. By using the fortified base at Rabaul, the Japanese hoped to strike at the Americans with air- and sea-based power. Meanwhile, in Burma and on the Indian border, the Japanese went ahead with Operation U-Go, the assault on Imphal, and Operation Ha-Go, a diversionary attack on the Arakan Peninsula. By striking into India, the Japanese planned to take the communication centres of Imphal and Kohima and thus deliver a crippling blow against the British build-up for operations to retake Burma.

---

of Huon Gulf. Waves of US aircraft attack Japanese supply convoys destined for Papua New Guinea, sinking three Japanese transports and downing eighty Japanese aircraft with few losses.

JANUARY 9

POLITICS, *CHINA*
The Japanese puppet government established in China declares war on the US and Britain. In response, Japan reduces the extent of its claims on Chinese territory and hostility towards Chinese sovereignty.

LAND WAR, *NEW GUINEA*
Troops of the Australian 17th Brigade

are airlifted into Wau, landing under Japanese fire. The landing prevents 2500 Japanese troops from capturing Wau airfield, and fighting continues as the Allies attempt to regain control of the airfield and the surrounding jungle.

JANUARY 12–19

LAND WAR, *ALEUTIAN ISLANDS*
At the northern extremity of the Pacific War, US troops start to claw back Japanese conquests in the freezing Aleutian Islands. On January 12, a US amphibious force deploys 2000 men on the island of Amchitka, losing 14 soldiers after the destroyer USS *Worden* sinks in severe weather. On January 18/19, a force of six US warships bombards Japanese-held Attu Island.

JANUARY 14

LAND WAR, *GUADALCANAL*
In a clear signal of Japanese intentions,

◀ *The heavy cruiser USS* Chicago *(in the foreground), which was sunk by Japanese aircraft in the Solomon Islands at the end of January.*

DECISIVE WEAPONS

GRUMMAN F6F HELLCAT

In early 1943, the Grumman F6F Hellcat carrier-borne fighter began its operational deployment to the Pacific theatre, having first flown in prototype form in June 1942. The Hellcat had the manoeuvrability, power and armament to take on and surpass the best of Japanese aircraft, and its kill rate was formidable – 5156 Japanese aircraft destroyed between 1943 and 1945. Some 480 F6Fs of US Task Force 58 were at the frontline of the slaughter of more than 400 Japanese aircraft during the Battle of the Philippine Sea; and, in total, F6Fs accounted for three-quarters of all Japanese aircraft downed during the war. The F6F was produced in a number of forms, including the radar-equipped F6F-3E and F6F-3N and the F6F-5 fighter-bomber. Total production of F6Fs was 12,275.

SPECIFICATIONS: (F6F-5)

CREW: one

POWERPLANT: one 1419kW (2000hp) Pratt & Whitney R-2800-10W radial piston engine

DIMENSIONS: wingspan 13.05m (42.8ft); length 10.24m (33.6ft); height 3.99m (13ft)

PERFORMANCE: max speed 612kmh (380mph); range 1521km (945 miles); service ceiling 11,396m (37,300ft)

ARMAMENT: two 20mm cannon and four 12.7mm machine guns, wing-mounted (alternatively, six 12.7mm machine guns); underwing provision for two 454kg bombs

▲ *US motor torpedo boats. During the Solomons campaign they operated against Japanese shipping in the "Slot".*

Japanese troops are landed at Cape Esperance on the far northwestern tip of the island to prepare landing zones for evacuation shipping.

SEA WAR, *GUADALCANAL*
US motor torpedo boats make torpedo runs against Japanese destroyers attempting to deliver supplies to army units on Guadalcanal. Three destroyers are hit and the enemy force withdraws.

JANUARY 16–18

LAND WAR, *BURMA*
The Indian 14th Division suffers heavy losses during the continued Allied offensive into the Arakan. A stern Japanese resistance beats off attacks against Rathedaung and Donbaik.

JANUARY 21–30

LAND WAR, *NEW GUINEA*
The Allied advance through New Guinea is now directed towards Salamaua and Lae in the Huon Gulf, driving the Japanese towards New Guinea's western coastline. Victory is now complete in Papua with the fall of Sanananda, though at the cost of more than 7000 US/Australian casualties. An estimated 13,000 Japanese have been killed in the Papuan campaign. In northern New Guinea, 3000 Japanese troops begin a three-pronged offensive against Allied positions around the mining town of Wau in northern Papua, forcing 700 Australian troops into a localized offensive withdrawal. Heavy rains and airlifted reinforcements permit the Allies to stop the Japanese advance by the end of the month.

JANUARY 23

LAND WAR, *GUADALCANAL*
US forces on Guadalcanal take the Japanese base at Kokumbona after a three-day naval bombardment and a final assault. The Japanese are now being driven into the northwestern corner of Guadalcanal as Japanese shipping prepares to evacuate remaining troops.

JANUARY 27

LAND WAR, *GUADALCANAL*
During the US westward advance across Guadalcanal, a major enemy command post is captured, with 37 Japanese soldiers killed and 3 taken prisoner. Significant amounts of arms, ammunition and supplies are also captured.

JANUARY 30

SEA WAR, *SOLOMON ISLANDS*
The heavy cruiser USS *Chicago* of Rear-Admiral Robert Giffen's Task Force 18 is sunk following an air raid by 31 Japanese G4M bombers 80km (50 miles) north of Rennell Island. Tactical errors by Giffen aggravate the attack, which also damages a US destroyer.

FEBRUARY 1

LAND WAR, *NEW GUINEA*
Australian forces manage to hold off Japanese attempts to take Wau airfield, even though the Japanese advance

FEBRUARY 1–9

comes within 350m (1148ft) of the air-field's centre.

FEBRUARY 1–9

LAND WAR, *GUADALCANAL*

The final 11,000 Japanese troops on Guadalcanal are evacuated from the northern sector of the island around Cape Esperance. Ejecting the Japanese from Guadalcanal is a crucial land victory for the US, giving it a base from which to penetrate Japan's Pacific conquests and providing security for Australia and New Zealand. The Japanese leave more than 20,000 dead on the island.

FEBRUARY 1–3

LAND WAR, *BURMA*

A major British offensive in the Arakan around Donbaik and Rathedaung ends without success, as the Japanese hold on to extremely strong defensive positions in the area.

▼ *A US Marine 155mm howitzer in action on Guadalcanal during the final phase of the campaign to eject the Japanese from the island.*

FEBRUARY 4

AIR WAR, *GUADALCANAL*

US aircraft attack a large force of Japanese destroyers around Guadalcanal. One Japanese destroyer is sunk and four others badly damaged. In aerial combat during the incident, the US loses four torpedo planes, four fighters and two bombers, while twenty-two Japanese aircraft are shot down.

▲ *US Marine Raiders deploy into rubber boats during the seizure of Russell Island. The Japanese evacuated the island before the US Marines arrived.*

FEBRUARY 6

AIR WAR, NEW *GUINEA*

The Allies begin to demonstrate their air superiority over New Guinea when 37 Allied fighters shoot down 26 Japanese aircraft out of a raiding force of 70.

FEBRUARY 7

POLITICS, *CHINA*

The Chinese Nationalist leader Chiang Kai-shek consents to the use of Chinese military forces in the future Burmese campaign. Chiang usually shows interest only in the Chinese theatre, but the promise of US aid has brought concessions.

FEBRUARY 8–15

LAND WAR, *BURMA*

General Orde Wingate leaves Imphal in India to conduct guerrilla warfare behind Japanese lines with the newly formed 77th Indian Brigade, known as the "Chindits". Named after the stone lions seen guarding Buddhist temples, the 3000-strong Chindits are created for deep-penetration incursions into northern Burma, operating in eight self-contained units (known as "Columns") supplied only by air drops. Their mission is to disrupt Japanese communications and tactical deployments, and so open more opportunities for conventional offensives. On February 14/15, the Chindits cross the Chindwin River.

FEBRUARY 10–11

POLITICS, *INDIA*

Mahatma Gandhi, the Indian leader, begins a 21-day hunger strike, having been interned by the British along with all other members of the All-India Congress Party. The action puts considerable pressure on British policy in India,

▼ *Chindits lay explosive charges on a railway bridge deep behind Japanese lines in Burma. The Chindits relied on airdrops for their supplies during operations.*

STRATEGY AND TACTICS

ALLIED STRATEGY FOR 1943

The strategic outlook for 1943 could not have been more different from the previous year. Compared with the position of weakness after Pearl Harbor, the planning for 1943 was aggressive, bold and determined. Operation Cartwheel, the two-pronged assault on the Japanese stronghold at Rabaul on New Britain, began in earnest. This called for large-scale attacks on New Guinea and the Solomon Islands. Within the highest levels of the US command there had been disagreement about what kind of strategy to take (two independent, coordinate commands, one in the Southwest Pacific under General of the Army Douglas MacArthur, and the other in the Central, South, and North Pacific Ocean Areas under Fleet Admiral Chester W. Nimitz, were created early in the war). Except in the South and South-

west Pacific, each conducted its own operations with its own ground, air, and naval forces in widely separated areas.

The argument centred on whether to move through the southwest Pacific towards the Philippines (the plan favoured by General MacArthur), or to strike at Formosa through the central Pacific (the method favoured by Admiral Nimitz). It was the endorsement of MacArthur's plan that saw Operation Cartwheel launched.

Meanwhile, on the Asian mainland, Allied plans to strike back at the Japanese forces in Burma and China were formulated and launched. This included a disastrous attack on the Arakan Peninsula as well as the use of the Chindit long-range guerrilla troops to attack the Japanese behind their lines. US strategy also saw immense efforts being put into keeping China in the war.

especially as Indian troops are dying for the Allied cause in places such as Burma and North Africa.

FEBRUARY 12

LAND WAR, *NEW GUINEA*

The Allies initiate the Elkton Plan, the campaign to eject Japanese forces from New Guinea, New Britain and the Solomon Islands and isolate the Japanese base at Rabaul. In response to Allied victories in Papua and Guadalcanal, the Japanese begin pouring reinforcements into New Guinea, including the Eighteenth Army under Lieutenant-General Adachi Hatazo and the Fourth Air Army.

FEBRUARY 17

LAND WAR, *BURMA*

Attacks by the 47th and 55th Indian Brigades against Japanese positions at Donbaik in the Arakan are repulsed.

FEBRUARY 18

LAND WAR, *BURMA*

The Chindits encounter the Japanese in action for the first time as part of "Operation Longcloth". On February 18, the

▼ *General Orde Wingate (left), the commander of the Chindits. The man to his left holds a device used to signal aircraft.*

FEBRUARY 21

▶ *Chinese Nationalist troops repair the damage caused by a landslide on the Burma Road, which ran through treacherous mountain country.*

Southern Group advancing towards Kyaikthin engages in a firefight around Maingnyaung, also cutting the railway line between Mandalay and Myitkyina.

FEBRUARY 21

LAND WAR, *SOLOMON ISLANDS*
A force of US assault battalions takes the diminutive Russell Island to the northwest of Guadalcanal in "Operation Cleanslate". The occupation is the first in a series of US campaigns to reclaim the Solomon Islands, and looks to cut off the Japanese naval and air base at Rabaul, New Britain, in a wider pincer operation called "Operation Cartwheel". Cleanslate is also the first element in General MacArthur and Admiral Nimitz's plan to re-conquer the Pacific by working up from the south and east through Japanese-occupied territory in a systematic island-hopping strategy.

FEBRUARY 22

LAND WAR, *BURMA*
Numbers Three, Seven and Eight Columns of the Northern Group of Chindits advancing towards Naungkan raid a Japanese camp at Sinlamaung.

FEBRUARY 25

HOME FRONT, *NEW ZEALAND*
One New Zealand soldier and 48 Japanese POWs are killed after the POWs make an attempted breakout from their prison camp.

▼ *Two US bombers about to attack a Japanese ship during the Battle of the Bismarck Sea. Moments after this photograph was taken the ship was hit and sunk. Another Japanese ship can be seen burning on the horizon.*

KEY PERSONALITIES

GENERAL DOUGLAS MACARTHUR

General Douglas MacArthur (1880–1964) is probably the defining figure of the US land campaign in the Pacific. MacArthur's associations with the Far East began in 1922 when, as a brigadier-general, he was sent to command the military district of Manila. He returned there in 1935, and the following year the Philippine president, Manuel Quezon, made MacArthur field marshal in the Philippine Army. The next year MacArthur retired from army life, becoming a military adviser in the Philippines. However, in July 1941 President Roosevelt recalled him to the forces, making him a lieutenant-general in command of US forces in the Far East.

In 1942, with the US now at war with Japan, MacArthur became supreme commander of the Southwest Pacific Area. His war record in the Pacific is patchy. His defence of the Philippines in 1941–42 was disastrous, and he subsequently showed a tendency towards costly tactics. However, he later took as his own the idea of island hopping – bypassing heavily defended Japanese positions in favour of taking weaker ones – and used it to good effect, isolating Rabaul and advancing his way towards mainland Japan from the southern Pacific. His most controversial act was insisting on the recapture of the Philippines, opposing the plan of Admiral King (MacArthur was generally at odds with the US Navy) and others to isolate Japan by taking Formosa. MacArthur's strategy won over Roosevelt, who probably felt it politically expedient to support him, and MacArthur executed a brilliant campaign to retake the Philippines in 1944. In April 1945, MacArthur was placed in command of all US Army forces in the Pacific, and in September he presided over the Japanese surrender aboard the USS *Missouri*. He then administered Japan for five years.

FEBRUARY 28

LAND WAR, *BURMA*

Completion of a new Burma Road allows Chinese forces in northern Burma to receive supplies by land rather than by laborious air drops and landings, the Japanese having originally cut the road in early 1942. The road runs 428km (300 miles) from Ledo to southern China, and was constructed by US Army engineers with more than 14,000 indigenous labourers.

MARCH 1

LAND WAR, *NEW GUINEA*

Allied forces make steady progress pushing the Japanese back towards the northern coastline of New Guinea. The main offensive to clear the territory is scheduled for June 1943.

MARCH 2–5

SEA WAR, *BISMARCK SEA*

A Japanese convoy (eight transports and eight destroyers), attempting to reach the Lae-Salamaua area of New Guinea with the 7000 men of the 51st Division, is devastated by 355 US and Australian aircraft and US torpedo boats, the US having been forewarned of the convoy by ULTRA intelligence. The US attacks begin on the night of March 2 with one transport sunk and two damaged. Thereafter, the Japanese suffer constant waves of aircraft employing dive-bombing, skip-bombing, torpedo runs and strafing attacks with superb accuracy, with US PT boats finishing off crippled survivors on March

▲ *A Japanese Zero fighter burns on the ground at Lae during the Battle of the Bismarck Sea. Japanese losses included 72 aircraft; the Allies lost 4 aircraft.*

5. In total, all the transports and four destroyers are sunk, with 3660 Japanese soldiers killed and only 950 making it to New Guinea.

MARCH 3–6

LAND WAR, *BURMA*

The Chindits continue their incursion deep into Japanese territory. On March 3, the Southern Group crosses the Mu River and once again blows up the Mandalay–Myitkyina railway line. Three days later, the Northern Group attacks rail and bridge systems between Bongyaung and Nankan. Despite these successes, the Chindits are suffering casualties as the Japanese mobilize to take on the guerrilla force. Between March 2 and 4, Four Column and Two Column are dispersed in heavy fighting.

MARCH 4

LAND WAR, *BURMA*

The campaign towards Akyab grinds to a halt in the face of very heavy Japanese resistance.

MARCH 6

SEA WAR, *SOLOMON ISLANDS*

Japanese airfields at Munda and Vila are bombarded by US Navy gunfire. During the action, two Japanese destroyers are also hit and sunk.

MARCH 8–13

LAND WAR, *CHINA*

Japanese forces in China renew their offensive drive against much weakened

▼ *Major-General Claire Chennault (standing, in centre), the commander of the US Fourteenth Army Air Force in China.*

▲ *The heavy cruiser USS Salt Lake City fires her guns during the Battle of the Bering Sea in late March.*

Chinese Nationalist troops. On March 8, the Japanese push across the Yangste River, although the Chinese repel the invaders by March 13.

MARCH 10

AIR WAR, *CHINA*

To expand Allied air cover for Burmese and eastern Pacific operations, the US Fourteenth Army Air Force is created and stationed in China, commanded by Major-General Claire Chennault.

MARCH 17–18

LAND WAR, *BURMA*

The Japanese launch a major offensive to repel the Allies from the Arakan. The Japanese 55th Division and other units make a two-pronged assault against the Allies; attacking from the front along the Arakan coastline and also swinging against the Allied left flank around Htizwe. Indian troops pull back from Buthidaung and Rathedaung and discontinue attacks on the Japanese at Donbaik.

MARCH 24–31

LAND WAR, *BURMA*

The battered Northern and Southern Groups of the Chindits meet up around Baw, combining forces for an attempt to cut the Mandalay–Lashio railway line. Subsequent fighting results in a defeat for the Chindits as the Japanese mass against them; and, on February 24, General Wingate receives orders to return his forces to India. The Chindits now break up into various groups and begin one of the epic retreats of history, each man marching more than 1600km (1000 miles) through the jungle to return to safety, the Chindits losing 500 men in the process.

MARCH 26

SEA WAR, *BERING SEA*

A US Task Force, consisting of two cruisers and four destroyers under Vice-Admiral Charles McMorris, engages Vice-Admiral Hosogaya Boshiro's escort force of four cruisers

◀ Dropping supplies from a transport aircraft to Chindit forces operating in Burma. By late March, the Japanese had forced the Chindits to retreat to India.

all resources will be directed to Japan's defeat following Germany's downfall. In the meantime, Pacific forces have the immediate strategic goal of isolating Rabaul through a two-pronged offensive through New Guinea and the Solomon Islands. The long-term objectives are a sweep through the Gilbert, Marshall and Mariana Islands, although in March 1943 Pacific commanders agree that resources are not present to accomplish such tasks, or even strike all the way to Rabaul.

MARCH 31

LAND WAR, *NEW GUINEA*
A force of US infantry, commanded by Colonel Archibald MacKechnie, makes an amphibious landing at the mouth of the Waria River.

LAND WAR, *ALEUTIAN ISLANDS*
The US invasion of Attu in the Aleutian Islands is scheduled for May 7. The Aleutians have little tactical significance to the Pacific campaign, apart from drawing US and Japanese forces into the north of the ocean.

APRIL 5

LAND WAR, *BURMA*
The British military disaster in the Arakan continues to unfold. The Japanese have by now pushed the British forces halfway back up the Mayu Peninsula, and today they capture the British brigade headquarters.

and four destroyers in the Bering Sea, about 1600km (1000 miles) south of the Komandorskiye Islands in the north Pacific, as the Japanese attempt to run reinforcements to the Aleutian Islands. The four-hour gun battle results in

▼ At the Casablanca Conference, Allied leaders discussed strategic war plans. Prime Minister Churchill (seated, third from left) and President Roosevelt (seated, fourth from left) reiterated the Germany First policy.

both sides suffering one damaged cruiser, and eventually the Japanese withdraw owing to fuel and ammunition shortages.

MARCH 28

POLITICS, *CASABLANCA*
The strategic priorities of the entire war are fixed at the Casablanca Conference of Allied leaders. The Germany First policy is reiterated, with Pacific commanders given the assurance that

▲ *Lieutenant-General Shojiro Iida, commander of Japanese forces in Burma, who was replaced in early April.*

▲ *The general who replaced Iida – Masakazu Kawabe. His forces were reorganized as the Burma Area Army.*

APRIL 7–13

AIR WAR, *SOLOMON ISLANDS*
The Japanese Air Force launches Operation I, a programme of bombardment against Allied shipping in the Solomon Islands and New Guinea. More than 200 Japanese aircraft attempt to weaken the Allies' grip on their new conquests and reclaim air superiority, attacking US, British and Commonwealth shipping and airfields around Guadalcanal, Port Moresby and Milne. Three Allied transports, one destroyer and one corvette are sunk, as well as seven Allied aircraft destroyed. The Japanese lose 19 aircraft, and the offensive is a disappointment, indicating Japanese problems in making good the loss of well-trained pilots in recent campaigns.

APRIL 8

POLITICS, *JAPAN*
The commander of Japanese forces in Burma, General Iida, is replaced by General Kawabe. With the Allied offensive in the Arakan stalled, and the Chin- dit incursion into northern Burma reversed, Kawbe takes over the command at a favourable juncture.

APRIL 13

AIR WAR, *ALEUTIAN ISLANDS*
US carrier aircraft launch 10 separate attacks on Kiska in the Aleutians, assaulting the airfield and military barracks.

APRIL 18–21

POLITICS, *JAPAN*
On April 18, the Japanese Commander-in-Chief of the Combined Fleet and the tactician behind the Pearl Harbor attack, Admiral Isoroku Yamamoto, is killed after US Lockheed P-38 Lightning fighters (of the US Army Thirteenth Air Force, 339th Squadron) intercept his aircraft in the southwest Pacific. Allied code breakers alerted Allied commanders in advance that Yamamoto was travelling among key bases, allowing them to prepare an ambush and demonstrate the increasingly vital role ULTRA intelligence is playing in the Allied war effort. Yamamoto's death is a major military and psychological blow to the Japanese (he was considered Japan's greatest military leader).

▼ *Japanese troops advance during the large-scale offensive launched in Hunan Province in early May. In the same month the Chinese Nationalists counterattacked along the Yangtze River.*

▲ *A US pilot rushes to his P-38 Lightning in New Guinea. It was P-38s that shot down the aircraft carrying Yamamoto.*

APRIL 20

POLITICS, *TOKYO*
Mamoru Shigemitsu becomes the new Japanese foreign minister.

APRIL 20–21

AIR WAR, *SOUTH PACIFIC*
On April 20, US aircraft attack the Japanese base on Nauru; the Japanese retaliate the next day by bombing US positions in the Ellice Islands.

APRIL 21

POLITICS, *US*
Increasing evidence of Japanese atrocities against US and Allied POWs leads President Roosevelt to declare that all war criminals will be tried following an Allied victory.
POLITICS, *JAPAN*
Admiral Mineichi Koga takes over command of the Japanese Combined Fleet following the death of Yamamoto.

APRIL 23

AIR WAR, *GILBERT ISLANDS*
US bombers attack the Japanese airfield on Tarawa in the Gilbert Islands.

APRIL 30

LAND WAR, *BURMA*
The survivors of General Wingate's first ill-fated Chindit expedition cross into British India and safety. Emaciated and fatigued, the troops have covered more than 1609km (1000 miles) to reach safety, and the campaign has cost 1000 British lives. A question mark now hangs over the future use of the Chindits.

MAY 2

AIR WAR, *AUSTRALIA*
The Australian port of Darwin is bombed by Japanese aircraft.

MAY 5

LAND WAR, *CHINA*
Japanese forces in central China begin a huge offensive into Hunan Province in an attempt to extend territorial gains and seize additional rice fields. Since 1941, the China conflict has been a mixture of savage localized campaigns by the Japanese, often involving the slaughter of whole village populations, and de facto truces between the Japanese, the Chinese Nationalists under Chiang Kai-shek and the Chinese Communists under Mao Tse Tung. US commanders wanting to station air bases in China have been particularly disappointed by the intermittent Chinese co-existence with the Japanese invaders.

MAY 7–14

LAND WAR, *BURMA*
The Allied offensive into the Arakan

▼ *The Trident Conference in Washington. From left to right: Brigadier-General John Deane, Admiral William Leahy and Admiral Ernest King.*

▲ *A US Navy reconnaissance photograph of A6M2-N floatplane Zeroes in the Aleutians, prior to the US invasion.*

▲ *US bombs drop on Attu in the Aleutians from aircraft of the Eleventh United States Army Air Force.*

finally collapses. The Japanese retake Maungdaw and Buthidaung, driving the Allies northwards and back to the original start positions of the offensive. The disastrous campaign is a salutary reminder of British offensive limitations in the theatre.

MAY 8

AIR WAR, *SOLOMON ISLANDS*
US Dauntless and Liberator aircraft bomb Japanese shipping and installations throughout the Solomon Islands. Three Japanese destroyers are damaged, one severely. The next stage of Operation Cartwheel, the invasion of New Georgia, is planned for the following month, and the US commanders are eager to soften up Japanese naval resources throughout the Solomon Islands.

MAY 11

LAND WAR, *ALEUTIAN ISLANDS*
Following a huge aerial and naval bombardment, a US amphibious force lands 11,000 men of the 7th US Infantry Division on Attu, beginning the land campaign to retake the Aleutian Islands. The US troops go ashore in the northern and southern sectors of Attu's southeastern coastline, and from the outset they encounter a ferocious defence from the 2400-strong Japanese garrison commanded by Colonel Yamazaki Yasuyo.

MAY 12–25

POLITICS, *WASHINGTON*
British Prime Minister Churchill and US President Roosevelt attend the Trident Conference of Allied war leaders in Washington. Despite a unified confirmation of the Germany First strategy, including setting a date for the Allied

invasion of occupied Western Europe, British concerns are raised that the Pacific war is diverting too many resources away from European operations.

MAY 15

SEA WAR, *AUSTRALIA*
The Australian hospital ship HMAS *Centaur* is torpedoed and sunk by a Japanese submarine off the coast of Brisbane, despite being clearly marked as a medical vessel. More than 260 people are killed, with only 63 survivors.

MAY 16

LAND WAR, *ALEUTIAN ISLANDS*
The campaign to take Attu has become a war of attrition, with both sides taking heavy losses. The US land forces commander even states his belief that the island will take six months to liberate, a comment that costs him his job. However, the Japanese are steadily being pushed out of their fortified positions and retreat to Chichagof harbour as the southern and northern US groups combine into a single thrust against them.

MAY 17

ESPIONAGE, *US AND BRITAIN*
The US and Britain arrive at a cooperation agreement in the code-breaking

▼ *Troops of the US 7th Infantry Division land on Attu on May 11. A US-occupied Attu would isolate the Japanese on Kiska between US bases on Attu and Adak, making Kiska easier to capture.*

STRATEGY AND TACTICS

ALLIED INTELLIGENCE
There were two forms of Allied intelligence in the Pacific theatre, known as ULTRA and MAGIC. ULTRA referred to the decryption of military communications, whereas MAGIC related to diplomatic sources. Both were part of the massive Allied code-breaking effort which hit a high spot when the British deciphered German Enigma machine codes. As the war progressed, the British and US intelligence communities began to combine their efforts to decipher Japanese equivalents. On May 17, 1943, the BRUSA (Britain and the United States of America) agreement formed a working intelligence partnership, the US Army overseeing decryption of Japanese military codes and ciphers, while the British concentrated mainly on the European theatre. MAGIC codes – which were produced on the formidable "Purple" coding machine – were actually being broken before December 1941, giving the US an indication of the outbreak of war, but not telling it where the first attack would

come. Such was typical of MAGIC intelligence, and it proved more useful as a general guide to future Japanese intentions than as a script to future Japanese operations.

ULTRA intelligence was much harder to acquire. The Japanese naval code, JN-25, was never fully overcome during the war, but the portions of some messages read gave the US a crucial combat advantage at the battles of the Coral Sea and Midway. Japanese Army codes were not read at all until April 1943, but in 1944 – following the capture of Japanese code books on New Guinea – they were readily deciphered to assist victory in the New Guinea and Marshall Islands campaigns.

The deciphering of Japanese military signals was a cat-and-mouse game that neither side lost entirely during the war. US code breaking was certainly not helped by some caustic inter-service intelligence rivalries, but intelligence did give US forces critical advantages at crucial moments in the Pacific campaign.

war against the Axis. From now on, the two countries will actively share the burden of unravelling the ciphers produced by the German Enigma, the Japanese Purple and the Italian C38M machines. The Allies will share not only technical knowledge, but also the intelligence gleaned, to be known as

ULTRA. US intelligence analysts are to spend more time on Pacific theatre intelligence, while Britain focuses on German and Italian ciphers.

LAND WAR, *ALEUTIAN ISLANDS*
US forces take significant Japanese positions on high ground overlooking Holtz Bay.

MAY 19

▶ *Chinese Red Cross nurses attend to wounded Nationalist soldiers during the Japanese offensive in Hunan Province in mid-May 1943.*

MAY 19

LAND WAR, *ALEUTIAN ISLANDS*
US troops on Attu clear the Sarana Pass on the approaches to Chichagof harbour, where much of the remainder of Attu's Japanese garrison is confined.

MAY 21–24

LAND WAR, *ALEUTIAN ISLANDS*
Attu Village, a key Japanese defensive position, is completely wiped out by a massive US assault supported by ground-attack P-38 Lightning fighter-bombers. Lightnings are playing a key role in the US campaign on Attu, despite the appalling Arctic weather. As well as supporting ground units, they are intercepting and shooting down Japanese bombers in the air. On the 24th, Chichagof Valley is cleared of Japanese troops, often by recourse to hand-to-hand fighting.

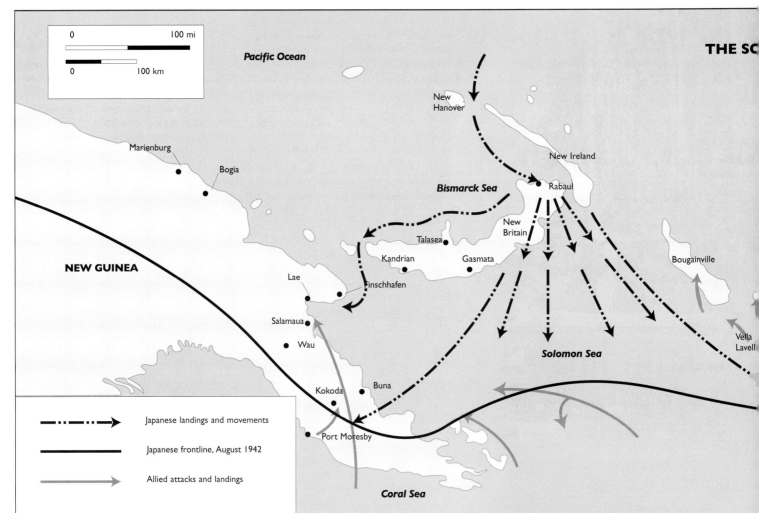

THE SC

Pacific Ocean

New Hanover

Marienburg

Bogia

New Ireland

Bismarck Sea

Rabaul

NEW GUINEA

New Britain

Talasea

Bougainville

Kandrian

Gasmata

Lae

Finschhafen

Salamaua

Wau

Solomon Sea

Vella Lavell

Kokoda

Buna

Port Moresby

Coral Sea

0   100 mi
0   100 km

▪–▪–▪–▶   Japanese landings and movements

━━━━   Japanese frontline, August 1942

━━━▶   Allied attacks and landings

tens of thousands of Japanese civilians (Germany honours him with the award of the Knight's Cross with Oakleaves and Swords).

JUNE 7

AIR WAR, *RUSSELL ISLANDS*
In a major air action around the Russell Islands, South Pacific, US fighter aircraft shoot down 19 Japanese fighters out of a total of 40 attackers.

JUNE 7-16

AIR WAR, *SOLOMON ISLANDS*
Japanese air sorties over the Solomon Islands become increasingly costly in terms of aircraft and pilots. On 7 June, a Japanese air attack against Guadalcanal results in 23 Japanese aircraft lost for only 9 US aircraft destroyed. On June 12, the US kill-to-loss ratio widens, downing 31 Japanese bombers while losing just 6

▼ *A US mortar team in action on Arundel Island, west of New Georgia, in the Solomon Islands.*

MAY 29-30

LAND WAR, *ALEUTIAN ISLANDS*
Japanese troops on Attu launch a final suicidal charge around Chichagof in an attempt to drive US forces from the island. The attack makes some progress, overrunning two US command posts,

▼ *Operation Cartwheel was designed to destroy Japanese power in New Guinea and the Solomon Islands.*

▲ *US B-25 Mitchell bombers drop para-fragmentation bombs on a Japanese airstrip in New Georgia.*

but US firepower proves decisive and Japanese survivors are forced to retreat, whereupon many commit suicide. The Attu campaign costs the Japanese 2351 lives – only 28 soldiers surrender. US losses are also heavy: 561 dead and 1136 wounded.

MAY 31

AIR WAR, *CHINA*
US and Chinese aviators shoot down 20 Japanese fighters in a short aerial combat over Ichang, Hunan Province.

JUNE 5

HOME FRONT, *JAPAN*
Admiral Yamamoto receives a full state funeral in Tokyo. He is mourned by

▼ *An unidentified American seaplane overflies troops landing on Rendova Island in the Solomons in June 1943.*

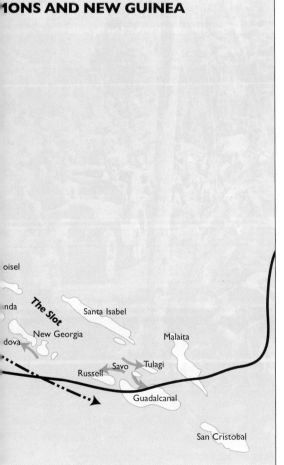

MONS AND NEW GUINEA

oisel

The Slot

nda   Santa Isabel

New Georgia
dova   Malaita
Russell   Savo   Tulagi
Guadalcanal

San Cristobal

JUNE 8

The Axis countries hope that Bose will be able to mobilize practical Indian resistance to the British war effort.

LAND WAR, *CHINA*
Chinese forces in western Hupeh have now recaptured all territory lost to the Japanese during the recent offensive towards Chungking (the headquarters of Nationalist forces and government). In a two-week push, the Chinese lose more than 70,000 troops.

fighters. On June 16, the slaughter reaches unsustainable levels when 107 out of 120 Japanese aircraft attacking Guadalcanal are destroyed.

JUNE 8

POLITICS, *JAPAN*
The Japanese high command gives orders that Kiska, one of the Aleutian Islands, be evacuated. A US blockade of the island, plus the fall of Attu and the strategic irrelevance of the Aleutians, leads the Japanese to abandon this northern Pacific outpost.

JUNE 14

POLITICS, *JAPAN*
The pro-Axis Bengali leader Subhas Chandra Bose is feted by Japanese officials in Tokyo. Bose was forced to flee India in 1939 because of anti-British activities, making his way to Germany by 1941 and then setting off to Japan in February 1943 (he made the journey by German then Japanese submarine).

JUNE 18

POLITICS, *AUSTRALIA*
With the Japanese defence having collapsed in Guadalcanal and Papua, the Australian prime minister, John Curtin, declares that there is no longer the risk of a Japanese invasion of the Australian mainland.

POLITICS, *ALLIES*
The supreme commander of the South West Pacific and C-in-C India, Sir Archibald Wavell, is replaced by Sir Claude Auchinleck following British Prime Minister Churchill's dissatisfaction with progress in the Burma theatre.

▼ A US mortar team on Rendova fires at Japanese positions on the island. The men are crouching down to avoid the muzzle blast.

JUNE 20

LAND WAR, *NEW GUINEA*
The US Sixth Army establishes a head-quarters at Milne Bay.

JUNE 21

LAND WAR, *NEW GEORGIA*
The US begins its offensive to retake New Georgia – Operation Toenails. An

▲ *Craft of the 9th Defense Battalion, US Marine Corps, are shelled by Japanese artillery off the island of New Georgia in July 1943.*

air and naval bombardment pounds Japanese positions, while the waters around New Georgia are mined to prevent Japanese reinforcements. Meanwhile, soldiers of the 4th Marine Raider Battalion take Segi Point at the southern tip of New Georgia and begin an advance towards Viru harbour.

JUNE 23

LAND WAR, *SOUTH PACIFIC*
US forces make an unopposed landing on the Troubriand Islands to the southeast of New Guinea.

JUNE 24

POLITICS, *JAPAN*
Subhas Chandra Bose, leader of the Indian National Army, makes a radio broadcast to India, imploring Indian soldiers and civilians to turn against the British.

JUNE 29

SEA WAR, *SOLOMON ISLANDS*
US warships shell Bougainville and Kolombangara in the Solomon Islands.

JUNE 30

LAND WAR, *NEW GEORGIA*
The US 43rd Division has taken the island of Rendova, within artillery range of the New Georgian mainland and the important airfield at Munda. The occupation of Munda is vital to enabling the next

▲ *An Australian infantry officer from the 3rd Division directs fire from a US light tank against Japanese positions at Mumbo in New Guinea.*

"hop" up the Solomon Islands towards Bougainville. Other US landings are made at Wickham, Viru and Segi Point.

JUNE 29/30

LAND WAR, *NEW GUINEA*
A battalion of the US 32nd Division is landed 32km (20 miles) south of Japanese positions at Salamaua. Forces of the Australian 3rd Division are making an overland advance towards Salamaua from Wau, but it will be more than a month before the Japanese are ejected from the town.

JULY 1–7

LAND WAR, *SOLOMON ISLANDS*
The harbour at Viru falls to the US Marines on July 1. The US 43rd Division

▶ *Roosevelt (third from left) and Churchill (third from right) with their advisers behind them at the Quebec Conference in August. They decided to bypass the main Japanese base at Rabaul.*

and elements of the 37th Division are landed at Zanana, about 8km (5 miles) east of Munda, on July 2, while US infantry and Marines make a further landing north of Munda at Rice Inlet on July 5. The next few days are an appalling baptism of fire for the inexperienced US troops, who face brutal and jungle-wise Japanese opposition commanded by Major-General Noboru Sasaki – the rate of psychological evacuations rockets. By July 7, the advance on Munda has stalled.

JULY 5–6

SEA WAR, *SOLOMON ISLANDS*
The Battle of Kula Gulf erupts when US warships, acting on ULTRA intelligence, intercept a convoy of Japanese destroyers and transports heading for New Georgia. Despite sinking one Japanese destroyer, the US warships do not stop the convoy and lose one of their own cruisers. The convoy adds a further 850

▼ *General Sir Claude Auchinleck, C-in-C India (centre, in peaked cap), argued that land operations in Burma should be suspended in favour of aiding the Chinese.*

troops to the 10,000-plus already defending the Munda area.

JULY 7–13

LAND WAR, *NEW GUINEA*
Australian troops take the Japanese stronghold at Mumbo on the inland approaches to Salamaua. The action is part of a general Allied campaign pushing the Japanese into the northeastern corner of New Guinea.

JULY 12–13

SEA WAR, *SOLOMON ISLANDS*
A Japanese "Tokyo Express" supply convoy fights a night-time naval en-

gagement with US Task Force 18 off Kolombangara Island. The Japanese once again use their skill in night combat, along with new technologies for detecting US radar signals, and succeed in sinking one Allied destroyer and damaging three cruisers. US warships manage to sink one Japanese vessel – the cruiser *Jintsu*, flagship of Rear-Admiral Tanaka, commander of the Japanese Transport Group. Over the

◀ When the island of Munda was taken by US forces, the airfield was repaired for use by Allied aircraft, such as this Douglas C-47.

last week, the Tokyo Express has managed to reinforce the New Guinea garrison with an additional 2000 men.

JULY 15

AIR WAR, *NEW GEORGIA*
Forty-five Japanese aircraft are shot down over Rendova. Such is the superiority of US pilots that only three US aircraft are lost.

JULY 17

AIR WAR, *SOLOMON ISLANDS*
More than 200 Allied aircraft, including Boeing B-17 Flying Fortress four-engined bombers, make a 12-hour attack on Japanese shipping and military positions in and around Bougainville. The action is a major success. Forty-nine Japanese aircraft are shot down, and many others destroyed at the devastated airfield at Kahili. Dauntless dive-bombers and Avenger torpedo-bombers sink seven ships in Buin-Faisi harbour,

▶ John F. Kennedy, the future president of the United States, seen in his PT boat during World War II in the Pacific.

including a light cruiser and a destroyer, losing only six aircraft.

JULY 22–30

SEA/AIR WAR, *ALEUTIAN ISLANDS*
US forces continue to pound Japanese positions on Kiska from the sea and air. The US is not aware that Japan is in the process of abandoning Kiska, and it maintains a daily bombardment of the

island, with US aircraft flying constant bombing runs from nearby Adak. The 5200-man Japanese garrison on Kiska is evacuated under cover of fog on July 28; such is the skill of the evacuation that the US is still pounding the island two days later.

JULY 25–31

LAND WAR, *NEW GEORGIA*
US forces begin a new drive to take Munda. Despite the backing of huge firepower, the attack once again stalls after bloody assaults on key features such as Horseshoe Hill, which the US soldiers take, then lose, on July 31. On July 29, the commander of the US 43rd Division, Major-General John Hester, is replaced by the Guadalcanal veteran Major-General John Hodge.

AUGUST 1

SEA WAR, *SOLOMON ISLANDS*
The Japanese destroyer *Amagiri* rams a US Navy fast patrol boat, number *PT-109*. All the crew members are reported missing, including its commander, the future president of the US, John F. Kennedy.

POLITICS, *BURMA*
In an attempt to advance the development of the their Greater East Asia

AUGUST 1–2

Co-Prosperity Sphere, Japan announces that Burma is to be an independent nation led by the nationalist leader Dr Ba Maw. Ba Maw's administration immediately declares war on the Allies.

AUGUST 1–2

POLITICS, *CHINA*
The president of the Chinese National Government, Lin Sen, passes away and is replaced by acting president Chiang Kai-shek.

AUGUST 4

SEA WAR, *SOLOMON ISLANDS*
The US Navy rescues Lieutenant John F. Kennedy and 10 other surviving crew members from *PT-109*. Two crew members die when rammed by the *Amagiri*, and the survivors spend the next three days swimming among minor islands off the Solomons attempting to attract help. Two natives with a canoe take a coconut shell, inscribed with a plea for help, to US naval forces on Rendova, who send a PT boat to rescue the crew.

AUGUST 5

LAND WAR, *SOLOMON ISLANDS*
The vital Japanese base at Munda is finally conquered by US forces of the 43rd Division. It is a major milestone in

▲ *US and Canadian flags fly over Kiska Island following its capture. The barges in the background are bringing in supplies.*

the taking of New Georgia, and US engineers set about making the airfield fit for US aircraft to use as a forward base for the Solomon Islands campaign.

AUGUST 6–7

SEA WAR, *SOLOMON ISLANDS*
A Japanese supply convoy heading for Kolombangara suffers a heavy defeat at the hands of six US destroyers in the Vela Gulf. For no US losses, three Japanese destroyers are sunk and 1210 Japanese troops and sailors killed.

AUGUST 7–15

LAND WAR, *CHINA*
Fighting erupts between Communist and Nationalist Chinese forces in Shantung Province. Taking advantage, the Japanese launch an offensive against the Nationalist LI Corps and are nearly destroyed in the subsequent action.

AUGUST 13

POLITICS, *INDIA*
General Sir Claude Auchinleck, C-in-C India, proposes that there should be no more British offensive land operations in Burma. Instead, he argues, efforts should be concentrated on the air supply of Chinese forces in the north.

AUGUST 13–24

POLITICS, *ALLIES*
Allied leaders, including British Prime Minister Winston Churchill and US President Franklin Roosevelt, attend a war planning conference, codenamed "Quadrant", in Quebec, Canada. Regarding the Pacific theatre, Britain states its intention to re-deploy the Chindits in their insur-

▼ *A US reconnaissance photograph showing the aftermath of an air raid against a Japanese airfield at Lae, New Guinea.*

▲ *US troops make use of a bridge built from felled trees during their advance against Japanese forces in northern New Guinea. Judging by their cloth headgear, the frontline is some way off.*

gency role in Burma. Vice-Admiral Lord Louis Mountbatten becomes the head of the new South East Asia Command (SEAC), with Joseph Stilwell as his deputy. The geographical remit of SEAC is Burma, Malaya, Sumatra, Thailand and French Indochina. SEAC's main objectives are to draw more Japanese away from the Pacific theatre and support Chinese military efforts to the north of the zone. The decision is also made to bypass the fortified port of Rabaul, previously a key objective of Operation Cartwheel.

AUGUST 14

AIR WAR, *SOLOMON ISLANDS*
The air base at Munda, captured from the Japanese, is now in full working order. The base makes the movement of Japanese transport shipping down "the Slot" between the Solomon Islands much more precarious.

DECISIVE WEAPONS

M1 GARAND

The .30in-calibre M1 Garand rifle was the first self-loading rifle issued as a standard firearm to an army. It was actually accepted into military service in 1932, but had a long technical gestation period in which its designer, John C. Garand, refined it into a first-class combat weapon. The M1 was a gas-operated rifle fed by an internal magazine holding eight rounds, refilled by pushing an eight-round clip down through the opened bolt. If anything, the magazine system proved to be the only practical flaw of the M1; the rifle could only be loaded when empty, and the magazine could not be topped up with individual rounds. Also, the empty clip was ejected with an emphatic "ping", signalling to enemy soldiers that the infantryman had to reload. However, in other respects the M1 was a superb weapon. It was extremely rugged, and provided utterly dependable service to US soldiers in all theatres of war. Its semi-automatic action allowed units to generate the heavy firepower so essential in the jungle combat of the Pacific War, and its .30in round had decisive stopping power. The M1 was also accurate, though only in trained hands, explaining why two later sniper versions – the M1C and M1D – never saw large-scale production.

SPECIFICATIONS:

CALIBRE:	0.30in
MAGAZINE CAPACITY:	8 rounds
LENGTH:	1.107m (43.6in)
WEIGHT:	4.313kg (9.5lb)
MUZZLE VELOCITY:	855mps (2805fps)

◄ *Examples of the Garand. One of America's finest military leaders, General George S. Patton, described the M1 Garand as "the greatest battle implement ever devised".*

▲ *US Vought F4U Corsair fighter-bombers ready for take-off prior to a raid against enemy positions on Marcus Island at the beginning of September.*

AUGUST 15

LAND WAR, *ALEUTIAN ISLANDS*
After pounding the island of Kiska for weeks with air and naval bombardment, US and Canadian amphibious troops finally make a landing, but find the island deserted.

LAND WAR, *SOLOMON ISLANDS*
US forces of the 25th Division land on the island of Vella Lavella, north of Kolombangara, against little resistance. The landings bypass the heavy Japanese defences of Kolombangara, with its important airfield. It is the intention to build a new airstrip on Vella Lavella, thus rendering the southerly airfield irrelevant.

AUGUST 17

AIR WAR, *NEW GUINEA*
US aircraft launch a startling raid on the Japanese Fourth Air Army base at Wewak on the northern coast of New Guinea. The attack shocks the Japanese, who believed that US aircraft were outside the combat radius for a raid on Wewak. However, US engineers covertly constructed a forward air base 95km (60 miles) west of Lae, putting Wewak only 640km (400 miles) away from the USAAF aircraft of Lieutenant-General George C. Kenney. The attack by 200 US aircraft results in three-quarters of the Japanese air base being rendered unusable and only 38 Japanese aircraft left operational.

◀ *Destroyed Japanese aircraft on New Guinea. By mid-August, US aircraft were operating from an airfield only 95km (60 miles) west of Lae.*

AUGUST 19

LAND WAR, *NEW GUINEA*

Four Australian divisions and one US division begin a major offensive up through northern New Guinea, enjoying the decline in numbers of Japanese ground-attack aircraft following the air raids of August 17. The Japanese-fortified stronghold on Mount Tambu falls on the 19th.

AUGUST 23

AIR WAR, *CHINA*

Chungking, the home of the Chinese Nationalist Government, is bombed by the Japanese. The city has not been bombed since 1941.

▼ *Soldiers of the 14th New Zealand Brigade come ashore on Vella Lavella Island. The 35th Infantry Regiment, US 25th Division, had originally occupied the island.*

AUGUST 25

LAND WAR, *SOLOMON ISLANDS*

Operation Toenails, the US campaign to take New Georgia, now ends, with all Japanese resistance cleared from the island. The Japanese rearguard survivors are finally evacuated from northern New Georgia to the neighbouring island of Kolombangara on August 22. Reinforcements from the US 25th Division assist the battle-toughened US 43rd Division in finishing the task. The next major American operation in the Solomon Islands chain is an amphibious offensive against Bougainville and Choiseul, planned for October/November.

AUGUST 28

LAND WAR, *ELLICE ISLANDS*

US forces land at Nanomea in the Ellice Islands. The Ellice Islands campaign is the beginning of US penetration into the southeastern corner of Japanese conquests. The Gilbert Islands and the

▲ *A squad of US soldiers from the 25th Division halts during a patrol on Vella Lavella Island.*

SEPTEMBER 1

▶ *US Marines examine the wreckage of a Japanese aircraft abandoned on an airstrip on Kolombangara Island. It appears to have been stripped for spares.*

Marshall Islands are the next objectives in this sector.

SEPTEMBER 1

AIR WAR, *MARCUS ISLAND*
Japanese positions on the mid-Pacific Marcus Island receive an early morning raid by US Navy dive-bombers. US reports state that 85 percent of the island's military installations have been destroyed, including two airstrips severely damaged and seven Japanese aircraft destroyed on the ground. US losses total two fighters and one torpedo-bomber.

SEPTEMBER 4

LAND WAR, *NEW GUINEA*
The Australian 9th Division lands just north of Lae in the Huon Gulf, opening a new front in the advance up New Guinea. The next day, the US 503rd Parachute Regiment is dropped over Nadzab (the first Allied parachute deployment in the Pacific theatre), and the Australian 7th Division is airlifted into the area. While these forces make an advance on Lae – an important coastal position for the Japanese – farther south the Australian 3rd Division and 17th Brigade strike out from Wau towards Salamaua and Nassau Bay.

▼ *Japanese infantry in New Guinea in September 1943. By this time the initiative in the southwest Pacific had passed to the Allies, specifically the sizeable US forces in the area.*

SEPTEMBER 12–16

LAND WAR, *NEW GUINEA*

The Allies take Salamaua on September 12, and Lae falls four days later. With an important port and airfield now in Allied hands, the New Guinea offensive splits into two lines of advance: one closely following the line of the coastline; the other cutting inland on a northwest bearing towards Kaiapat. The two-pronged offensive threatens to encircle the Japanese in the Huon Peninsula.

SEPTEMBER 13

AIR WAR, *PARAMUSHIRU*

A flight of B-24 Liberator and B-25 Mitchell bombers attacks enemy shipping and ground installations at Paramushiru in the north Pacific. Four enemy vessels are damaged, but ten US aircraft are lost after they are attacked by twenty-five Japanese fighters.

SEPTEMBER 13

POLITICS, *CHINA*

Chiang Kai-shek becomes chairman and president of the National Government of China. Chiang has proved to be a mercurial war leader, and shows little interest in the general Allied war against Japan except when US, British and Commonwealth efforts affect his own campaign. His relationship with General Stilwell, Allied chief-of-staff in the Burma-India-China theatre, is particularly troubled, especially as Stilwell recommends an alliance between the Nationalists and Communists to defeat Japan.

KEY PERSONALITIES

GENERAL SIR WILLIAM SLIM

General Sir William Slim (1891–1970) was an important Allied leader in the Far Eastern war. Slim had long-standing experience of soldiering in the Far East, having moved from the British Army to the Indian Army in 1919 and risen to the rank of brigadier by 1939. This experience was to stand him in good stead with his men, who appreciated both his tough yet personable character, and his ability to talk in Urdu and Gurkhali as well as English.

His first campaigns in World War II were fought in East Africa and Syria, but in March 1942 he was transferred to Burma to oversee the Allied retreat from Rangoon as commander of BurCorps (Slim was by this time ranked lieutenant-general). Burma was to be his battleground for the rest of the war. He led XV Indian Corps during its disastrous campaign into the Arakan, but offset this defeat by steering the Fourteenth Army

to victories in the Arakan and also the crucial defeat of the Japanese offensive at Imphal. In July 1945, Slim rose to the position of C-in-C Allied Land Forces Southeast Asia after the dismissal of General Sir Oliver Leese from the position.

SEPTEMBER 18–19

AIR WAR, *SOUTH PACIFIC*

The US widens its air campaign against Japanese targets in the southeast Pacific, bombing Tarawa, Makin and Apamama Islands in the northern Gilberts, and Nauru Island, west of the Gilbert group. Over 200 land- and carrier-based aircraft participate in the attack, causing severe damage to enemy installations.

SEPTEMBER 19–22

LAND WAR, *NEW GUINEA*

With Japanese forces retreating northwards across the Huon Peninsula towards Sio, the Allies maintain their advance. On the 19th, Kaiapat falls to

▼ *Japanese shipping try to evade US bombs while under aerial assault in Rabaul harbour. The aircraft involved are US B-24 Liberators and B-25 Mitchells.*

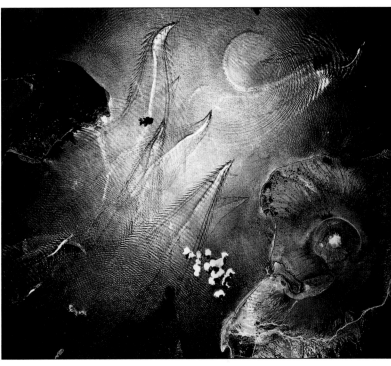

Australian forces, and on the 22nd other Australian units make an amphibious landing at positions just north of Finschhafaen, roughly 80km (50 miles) west of Lae on the easterly tip of the peninsula.

SEPTEMBER 20

LAND WAR, *SOLOMON ISLANDS*
New Zealand troops finally clear the island of Vella Lavella of all remaining Japanese opposition. Japanese troops on Vella Lavella numbered around 600, but the greatest threat to the Allies came from air attack.

SEPTEMBER 24

AIR WAR, *SOLOMON ISLANDS*
Allied air operations begin from the new airstrip on Vella Lavella, giving air

▶ *A US cruiser bombards enemy positions on Wake Island. Targets on the island included ammunition dumps, fuel stores, aircraft hangers and shore batteries.*

◄ *Japanese troops march through a town in the Philippines. Though accorded independent status by Tokyo, the Philippines were still under Japanese occupation.*

cover for the northerly Solomon Islands operations.

SEPTEMBER 26

LAND WAR, *NEW GUINEA*
Japanese troops launch an attack against Australian positions around Finschhafaen, but are unable to dislodge the defenders.

AIR WAR, *NEW GUINEA*
The Japanese airstrips at Wewak are struck once again by US aircraft. More than 60 Japanese aircraft are destroyed on the ground and, offshore, 6 Japanese ships are sunk.

SEPTEMBER 26–27

SEA WAR, *SINGAPORE*
Using canoes for covert night-time deployment, six Australian Special Forces soldiers led by Major Ivan Lyon penetrate Japanese shipping in Singapore harbour and place limpet mines on select vessels. Two Japanese transports are sunk, and a further five are damaged.

OCTOBER 2

LAND WAR, *NEW GUINEA*
Australian forces take Finschhafaen, consolidating Allied positions on the coastline of the Huon Peninsula.

OCTOBER 4

SEA/AIR WAR, *WAKE ISLAND*
The isolated Japanese outpost of Wake Island comes under a heavy naval and aerial bombardment from the large US Navy Task Force 14, commanded by Rear-Admiral Alfred E. Montgomery. B-24 Liberator bombers drop more

▼ *Tightening the stranglehold on Japan. A Japanese merchant ship sinks stern first after being torpedoed by a US submarine.*

than 325 tonnes (320 tons) of bombs. Some 61 Japanese aircraft are destroyed, comprising 30 on the ground and 31 in aerial combat. US forces lose 13 aircraft.

OCTOBER 4

LAND WAR, *NEW GUINEA*
The Australian 7th Division and 21st Brigade advancing northwest up the Huon Peninsula reach Dumpu, only 48km (30 miles) from the northern coast. Japanese forces are now confined along the northern coastline of the peninsula.

OCTOBER 4–6

LAND WAR, *SOLOMON ISLANDS*
The final elements of the Japanese garrison on New Georgia are evacuated

▲ *New Zealand troops unload supplies from Landing Craft Personnel (LCP) amphibious vehicles on Treasury Island following its capture in October.*

from Kolombangara. Japanese forces now have no air base in the central Solomon Islands, and US air superiority is demonstrated by the destruction of 27 Japanese aircraft during the final air battles. The fighting for the Vila airfield region has cost the US nearly 5000 casualties, including 1094 dead. Japanese casualties include 2500 fatalities.

OCTOBER 6

POLITICS, *BURMA*
The Allied Eastern Command receives a new C-in-C, General Sir William Slim,

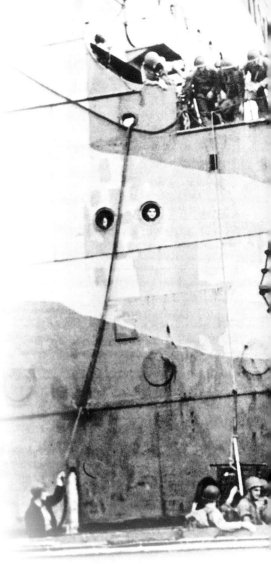

who also takes command of the newly formed Fourteenth Army.

OCTOBER 12

AIR WAR, *RABAUL*

The crucial Japanese air and naval base at Rabaul is hit by a massive air strike of 349 US bombers. In total, the Allies were to drop 20,913 tonnes (20,584 tons) of bombs on the heavily fortified port.

OCTOBER 15

LAND WAR, *SOLOMON ISLANDS*

Orders are given for "Operation Good-

▲ *US troops land on Bougainville. The absence of enemy shells and small-arms fire suggests that they are reinforcements, landed after the main assault forces.*

time", the next "hop" up through the Solomon Islands. Marines of US Task Force 311 will land on Bougainville at the beginning of November. Possession of the island is a crucial step towards the Allied dominance of the Japanese base at Rabaul.

OCTOBER 18

AIR WAR, *SOLOMON ISLANDS*

The Allies continue preparatory bombardments of Japanese positions around

Bougainville. Today, the Japanese air base at Buin is severely damaged.

OCTOBER 19

SEA WAR, *PACIFIC*

A US Navy communiqué reveals that, since December 7, 1941, US submarines

▼ *The objective of the Allied Solomons campaign was to isolate Rabaul, which made the capture of air bases imperative. This is a US air base in the Russell Islands.*

◀ *US Marines of the 3rd Marine Division clamber down the side of a transport ship into landing craft off Bougainville. The invasion forces consisted of 14,321 troops.*

have sunk or damaged more than 400 Japanese vessels (319 confirmed sinkings). The tally would have been higher had it not have been for defective torpedoes, which often did not explode on hitting a vessel.

OCTOBER 21

POLITICS, *PHILIPPINES*
The Philippines are given independent status by the Japanese Government, although the independence has little real value as the islands remain under Japanese jurisdiction.

OCTOBER 22

AIR WAR, *RABAUL*
The Japanese lose 123 aircraft during another massive US air raid on air facilities around Rabaul.

OCTOBER 25

BURMA, *POWS*
At a cost of 12,000 Allied POWs and 90,000 other slave labourers, the Burma–Thailand rail link is completed. Despite the massive construction project, the railway delivers much less capacity than originally intended.

OCTOBER 27

LAND WAR, *SOLOMON ISLANDS*
"Operation Blissful" is launched, the US 2nd Marine Para Battalion being landed on Choiseul Island, as a diversion away from the main invasion of Bougainville planned for November 1 and codenamed "Cherryblossom". Also today, New Zealand troops capture Treasury Island, just off Bougainville's southern coast. Treasury Island is subsequently used as a build-up point for the Bougainville invasion forces.

POLITICS, *JAPAN*
Emperor Hirohito acknowledges that the war in the Pacific is entering a crucial phase, with the Allies poised to reclaim much of the south Pacific from the Japanese. As early as 1942, Hirohito attempted to persuade the Japanese Government to negotiate a settlement with the Allies, correctly believing that Japan could not sustain a long-term campaign against the US.

NOVEMBER 1

LAND WAR, *SOLOMON ISLANDS*
The US offensive against Bougainville begins with the landing of the 3rd Marine Division, part of I Marine

▼ *A North American B-25 Mitchell bomber swoops low over the harbour at Rabaul during a heavy US air raid.*

Amphibious Corps, under Lieutenant-General A.A. Vandegrift, at Cape Torokina on the western coastline of the island. The landings go reasonably smoothly, but most of Bougainville's 60,000-strong Japanese garrison is concentrated in the south of the island.

NOVEMBER 2

SEA WAR, *SOLOMON ISLANDS*

A US task force of four light cruisers and eight destroyers battles with four Japanese cruisers and six destroyers around Empress Augusta Bay off Bougainville. The Japanese ships are intending to destroy landing craft and supply vessels supporting the Bougainville landings. The US task force, commanded by Rear-Admiral A.S. Merrill, suffers five ships

▼ *A US cruiser shells Makin Island. The naval bombardment raised a large pall of smoke and dust that obscured the island completely from the assault craft.*

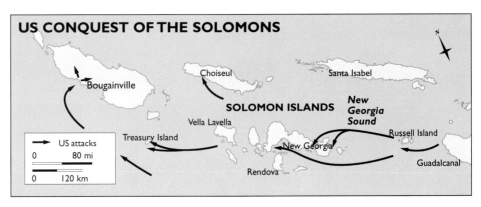

US CONQUEST OF THE SOLOMONS

▲ *During the Solomons campaign US forces displayed a mastery of amphibious warfare techniques.*

badly damaged, but sinks one Japanese light cruiser and a destroyer, and damages two heavy cruisers and two destroyers. The Japanese commander breaks off the attack.

NOVEMBER 5–11

AIR WAR, *RABAUL*

US aircraft from Rear-Admiral Frederick C. Sherman's Task Forces 38 subject Rabaul to six days of intense bombardment. The

US attacks are concentrated against shipping in the attempt to limit naval support available to the Japanese defence of the Solomon Islands. Aircraft from carriers including the USS *Saratoga*, USS *Bunker Hill*, USS *Essex*, USS *Independence* and USS *Princeton* sink two Japanese warships, severely damage 11 other vessels and destroy 55 Japanese aircraft.

NOVEMBER 13

LAND WAR, *SOLOMON ISLANDS*

US troops levels on Bougainville now reach 34,000 men, but the pace of advance through the island's jungle swamps is painfully slow. A priority is

▲ LVTs of the 2nd Marine Division make their way towards Tarawa. The LVTs were used to traverse the reef and Japanese man-made obstacles.

to establish an airstrip at Torokina to provide the advance with air cover.

NOVEMBER 13-20

AIR/SEA WAR, GILBERT ISLANDS
US forces begin the preparatory bombardments of Makin and Tarawa in the Gilbert Islands. The build-up for the US offensive against the Gilbert and Marshall Islands began back in January with the assembly of troops, ships and aircraft in Hawaii, the Fijian Islands and New Hebrides. The force now arraigned against Japanese forces in the Marshall Islands is enormous, and includes eight aircraft carriers and more than 100,000 troops. The first operations, against the Gilbert Islands, are under the overall command of the Commander Central Pacific Force, Vice-Admiral R.A. Spruance.

NOVEMBER 20-23

LAND WAR, GILBERT ISLANDS
US troops of the 27th Infantry Division go ashore at Makin, but find the atoll poorly defended and clear it easily over the next three days.

LAND WAR, GILBERT ISLANDS
In striking contrast to the operations on Makin, US Marines of the 2nd Marine Di-

DECISIVE WEAPONS

◄ A flamethrower Sherman tank on Okinawa, April 1945. The US Marines had eight Sherman flame tanks on Okinawa, which were ideal against caves and fortifications.

FLAMETHROWERS

Flamethrowers were among the prolific support weapons used by both Japanese and US soldiers during the Pacific war. They were ideal for flushing out enemy troops from fortified jungle and coastal bunkers, working either through burning the troops out or suffocating them as the flames used up all available oxygen around the position. The two basic Japanese flamethrowers were the Type 93 and Type 100, essentially the same weapon with only minor variations. Both types had a three-cylinder configuration (two cylinders for the fuel, one for the compressed-gas propellant), a burn duration of about 10 seconds and a range of around 30m

(99ft). US flamethrowers came in three man-portable versions – the M1, M1A1 and M2-2. All had better performance than the Japanese models, having similar burn durations but ranges of between 35m and 45m (114ft and 148ft). Even more effective were the US tank-mounted flamethrowers. These were usually fitted in place of a bow machine gun or, in light tanks, in place of the main armament. These systems could throw flame 70m (230ft) in a concentrated arc. Tactics included spraying unburned fuel on to a bunker before igniting it all in one explosive fireball and, on Okinawa, pumping the fuel down into caves through a series of pipes before igniting and incinerating the occupants.

vision attacking the atoll of Tarawa face appalling levels of resistance. Although the atoll is cleared by the 23rd, nearly 4500 Japanese are killed and the US Marines lose 1000 dead and 2000 wounded out of a total force of 18,600. Offshore, the US Navy suffers comparable heavy attacks. The light carrier USS *Independence* is damaged by torpedoes, while five other vessels are hit, including the destroyer USS *Frazier* which is rammed by the Japanese submarine *I-35*.

NOVEMBER 22-26

POLITICS, ALLIES
Allied war leaders, including the Chinese Nationalist leader Chiang Kai-shek, meet in Cairo, Egypt, to discuss post-war plans for the Far East. Known as the "Sextant Conference", it lasts until the 26th, after which British Prime Minister Churchill and US President Roosevelt fly on to meet with the Soviet leader Joseph Stalin in Tehran, Iran, to discuss overall Allied war strategy.

November 24

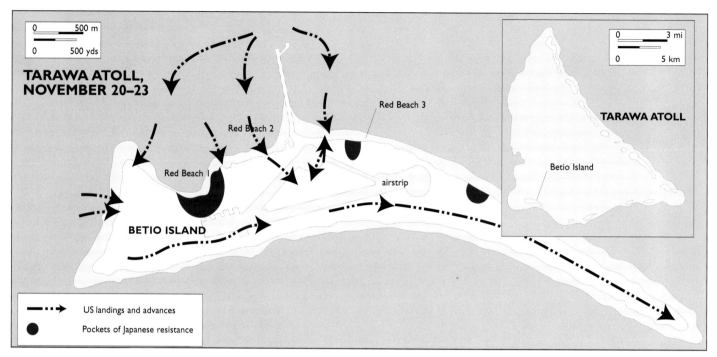

TARAWA ATOLL, NOVEMBER 20–23

BETIO ISLAND

Red Beach 1

Red Beach 2

Red Beach 3

airstrip

0 500 m
0 500 yds

TARAWA ATOLL

Betio Island

0 3 mi
0 5 km

- - -▸ US landings and advances
● Pockets of Japanese resistance

▲ *The Americans flew over 1000 sorties against Betio on November 18–19 to soften up the island's defences and to inflict fatalities on the 4500 defenders.*

NOVEMBER 24

SEA WAR, *GILBERT ISLANDS*
The US escort carrier USS *Liscombe Bay* is torpedoed and sunk off Makin Atoll in the Gilbert Islands, with 644 men killed.

NOVEMBER 24–29

INDUSTRY, *USA*
Two new modern aircraft carriers are commissioned in the US, the USS *Wasp* and the USS *Hornet*, both named after US vessels sunk at earlier actions in the war. In 1943 alone, the US commissioned nine new aircraft carriers; the Japanese, suffering from severe industrial shortages, commissioned only two, these being conversions from existing vessels.

NOVEMBER 25

SEA WAR, *CAPE ST GEORGE*
Five US destroyers intercept five Japanese destroyers near Cape St George, off the coast of New Ireland, as the Japanese ships make their way

▼ *Troops of the 2nd Battalion, 155th Infantry Regiment, wade ashore on Yellow Beach Two on Makin Atoll. The assault barge on the right is grounded on the reef.*

▲ A dead Japanese soldier on Tarawa. Only 17 Japanese and 129 Korean labourers surrendered at Tarawa. The rest of the garrison and construction workers died.

back from the supply drop at Buka, near Bougainville. The Japanese destroyers *Onami*, *Makinami* and *Yugiri* are sunk, and another destroyer is damaged in the resulting naval action. US forces suffer no sunk or damaged vessels.

DECEMBER 1

POLITICS, ALLIES
After three days of negotiations, the conference of Allied leaders in Tehran finally comes to a close. Most of the

discussions have focused on the Allied invasion of occupied France, with Stalin pushing hard for the opening of a second front to relieve some of the pressure on the Soviet Union.

DECEMBER 1–8

LAND WAR, *NEW GUINEA*
Australian troops continue to make a good overland advance across New Guinea, capturing Huanko on the 1st and Wareo on the 8th, before pushing on towards Wandokai.

▲ Smashed vehicles and US Marine dead on Tarawa. Some 5000 Marines had stormed the landing beaches of Betio on November 20 – 1500 were dead, wounded or missing by nightfall.

DECEMBER 1–31

LAND WAR, *BURMA*
Britain's XV Corps builds up forces in northern Burma ready for a renewed offensive down towards Akyab. It is faced by the Japanese Fifteenth Army, which is preparing for an offensive into eastern India.

KEY MOMENTS

THE TARAWA EXPERIENCE
The US operation against Tarawa in the Gilbert Islands in November 1943 was among the bloodiest actions of the entire Pacific war. Tarawa Atoll was a little over 16km (10 miles) long, but the bulk of Japanese defences were concentrated on the islet of Betio, around 3.2km (2 miles) long and 0.8km (0.5 miles) wide. The 4500 Japanese troops on Betio, commanded by Rear-Admiral Shibasaki, had created dense networks of fortified bunkers, trenches and pillboxes, in which they sat out the US Navy's preliminary bombardment of 3048 tonnes (3000 tons) of shells in only two-and-a-half hours (bunkers constructed of sand-packed palm-tree logs proved especially durable).

The first troops of the US 2nd Marine Division went ashore at Betio on November 20, straight into a hail of bullets and shells. Beach reconnaissance had been inaccurate, and many of the "Amtrac" amphibious vehicles grounded on a shallow reef, leaving the occupants to wade ashore under blistering small-arms and artillery fire. On the beach itself, the soft sand made it difficult for the US soldiers to dig in. Radio communications between US units broke down, resulting in 1500 US Marine casualties by the end of the day. However, a beachhead was established through sheer US firepower, and over the next two days the Marines fought their way across Tarawa, the entrenched defenders contesting every metre of ground to the death. A final suicidal charge by the Japanese on the 22nd signified that resistance was finally crumbling,

▲ *A US Marine throws a grenade at a Japanese pillbox from a sandbagged position on Tarawa on November 20.*

and on the 23rd the fighting finally stopped. The fanatical defence of Tarawa shocked US leaders. For this tiny scrap of land, the Japanese had sacrificed nearly 4500 men – only 17 Japanese soldiers surrendered, along with 129 Korean labourers.

DECEMBER 4

▶ *A US Consolidated B-24 Liberator lies smashed on the ground following a Japanese air raid against Allied airfields in Hunan Province, China.*

DECEMBER 4

SEA WAR, *MARSHALL ISLANDS*
Kwajalein and Wotje Atolls in the Marshall Islands are bombed by US aircraft from six carriers, destroying seventy-two Japanese aircraft on the ground and sinking six Japanese transport vessels. In a return attack by the Japanese, the carrier USS *Lexington* is damaged by an aircraft torpedo.

DECEMBER 5–8

AIR WAR, *INDIA*
Using forward air bases in Burma, the Japanese increase the level of air raids on the Indian mainland, attacking Allied air bases and coastal positions. On the 5th, Calcutta port is bombed with 350 people killed, and on the 8th the airfield at Tinsukia is attacked by nearly 70 Japanese warplanes.

DECEMBER 9

AIR WAR, *BOUGAINVILLE*
US engineers on Bougainville bring the airstrip at Torokina, on the island's central-west coast, up to full operational capacity (though it is still shelled by enemy artillery). The air base is used to provide air cover for Allied troops advancing across Bougainville, but is also only 241km (150 miles) from Rabaul, New Britain, well within the operational radius of even fighter aircraft.

▼ *The "Big Three" in December at the Tehran Conference (seated, from left to right): Joseph Stalin, Franklin D. Roosevelt and Winston Churchill.*

LAND WAR, *CHINA*
With Japanese forces increasingly over-stretched in the Pacific theatre, Chinese Nationalist forces make significant gains within their own country. In a major urban battle which costs the Nationalists more troops than the Japanese, Chinese troops reclaim the important city of Changteh, previously held on two occasions by the enemy.

▲ *The US airstrip at Torokina, Bougainville, which achieved operational status in early December and provided air cover for US forces on the island.*

DECEMBER 11

POLITICS, *INDIA*

Air Chief Marshal Sir Richard Edmund Charles Peirse (1892–1970) becomes overall commander of Allied air units, including USAAF forces, within South East Asia Command (SEAC). The air units will now be operating under a new entity, the Eastern Air Command.

AIR WAR, *CHINA*

Forty USAAF and Chinese aircraft are destroyed in a surprise night attack against Allied airfields in Hunan Province, China. The Japanese are hoping to sever the highly efficient air supply services relied on by Chinese Nationalist troops assaulting the city of Kung-an.

DECEMBER 15

LAND WAR, *NEW BRITAIN*

US Army troops of the 112th Cavalry Division are landed on Arawa Peninsula in southern New Britain. The landings are intended as a diversion from the forthcoming main landings on New Britain at Cape Gloucester on the other side of the island. The army soldiers subsequently occupy the airfield at Arawa, and then dig in to face heavy Japanese attacks over the next few weeks. Though determined, the attacks are all repulsed.

KEY PERSONALITIES

GENERAL JOSEPH STILWELL

General Joseph Stilwell (1883–1946) – known to many as "Vinegar Joe" because of his aggressive and difficult personality – rose to command all US and Chinese forces in the China-Burma-India theatre. As a young man he graduated from West Point in 1904, before serving in the Philippines and as an intelligence officer (with the rank of colonel) in France during World War I. Stilwell's suitability for the Asian post came from four military tours of China in the 1920s and 1930s, during which time he learnt to speak Chinese (he also spoke French and Spanish) and gained a genuine understanding of Chinese culture. General George Marshall, the US Army Chief of Staff, noted Stilwell's qualities and gave him command of the 7th Infantry Division in 1940, then III Corps. In 1942, Stilwell returned to China as a lieutenant-general, and commanded two Chinese armies in Burma. He personally headed the retreat of Chinese soldiers and Burmese refugees across 225km (140 miles) of jungle from Burma to India, refusing to take the aircraft provided to him and his staff. Stilwell

subsequently became Chiang Kai-shek's Allied chief of staff, and he invested much effort into turning the Chinese Army into an effective fighting force and organizing the flow of US aid. During 1944, Stilwell's Chinese soldiers had significant success in northern Burma, retaking Myitkyina in August. Stilwell was promoted to general but, two months later, Chiang Kai-shek had him recalled to the US for political reasons.

ALLIES, *SOLOMON ISLANDS*

A US naval operating base is established in the Treasury Islands. The Solomon Islands are now effectively within US control, and US commanders are planning the final operations to encircle Rabaul.

DECEMBER 18

AIR WAR, *CHINA*

Japanese aircraft bomb targets in the southern Chinese province of Yunnan. Southern China is mainly in Nationalist hands, with the Allies using the territory to establish air bases. The Japanese

DECEMBER 24

▶ *A transport ship loaded with supplies for the US 1st Marine Division's landing at Cape Gloucester. The ship is part of the Seventh Amphibious Force.*

are planning a major offensive into northern India for 1944, so need to gain a stronger hold over the southern Chinese states that border Burma and India.

POLITICS, *CHINA*

US General Joseph Stilwell takes command of all Chinese troops operating in the India/northern Burma region.

DECEMBER 24

SEA WAR, *SOLOMON ISLANDS*

A US Task Force of three cruisers and four destroyers under Rear-Admiral A.S. Merrill conducts a heavy bombardment of Japanese positions in the Buka-Bunis area of northern Bougainville.

LAND WAR, *BURMA*

In northern Burma, Chinese and US forces in Joseph Stilwell's Northern Combat Area Command push forward through the Hukawng Valley as part of an offensive aimed at retaking Myitkyina. The town has a vital airfield and needs be taken to establish an Allied overland supply route between India and China.

DECEMBER 25

LAND WAR, *CHINA*

Chinese troops recapture the city of Kung-an in northern Hunan Province after weeks of costly and bitter fighting.

DECEMBER 26–29

LAND WAR, *NEW BRITAIN*

The US 1st Marine Division under Major-General W.H. Rupertus, comprising the 1st, 5th and 7th Marine Infantry Regiments and the 11th Marine

KEY PERSONALITIES

HIDEKI TOJO

Hideki Tojo (1885–1948) was the political power behind the Pacific war. The son of a Japanese Army general, he entered the military and quickly rose through the ranks. Political rather than operational appointments beckoned. Within the army he served as the chief of police affairs and chief of staff before becoming the vice minister of war then finally minister of war in 1941, the same year he became Japanese prime minister. Tojo took Japan to war in December of that year by giving the order to attack Pearl Harbor, and he advocated a strategy of total military and economic warfare on the Allies, which helped make the Pacific war the merciless fight it became. After the Japanese defeat on Saipan in July 1944, he was forced to resign; he made a failed attempt at suicide after the final Japanese surrender. In 1948,

he was condemned to death for war crimes by the International Military Tribunal in Tokyo, and hanged.

STRATEGY AND TACTICS

THE TOKYO EXPRESS

"Tokyo Express" was the Allied nickname for the Japanese supply convoys running between Rabaul in New Britain and the Solomon Islands. The Japanese ships usually travelled via the Slot, the narrow stretch of water south of Bougainville that attracted violent naval battles. In early 1943, the Japanese had naval and air superiority over the northern parts of the Solomon sea lanes, but entered more dangerous waters farther south where US carriers were within striking distance. Most of the convoys were part of Rear-Admiral Raizo Tanaka's Transport Group, and featured powerful escorts of cruisers and destroyers, which inflicted significant losses on US shipping. However, in 1943–44, the balance of power tilted towards the Allies as they steadily reclaimed territory in the Solomon Islands. Radar, ULTRA intelligence and coastwatchers – indigenous people trained to provide intelligence on Japanese shipping movements along the coastlines – meant Japanese ships could rarely move undetected (picture

shows Japanese ships under attack). Increased US air superiority and more effective US submarine patrols also meant that the levels of attrition among transport vessels became appalling. The interdiction of the Tokyo Express was an important factor in strangling Japanese resistance throughout the Solomons.

◄ *Troops of the US 1st Marine Division wade ashore at Cape Gloucester. The amphibious landing took place following a heavy bombardment and bombing by naval gunfire and aircraft.*

Artillery Regiment, is landed at Cape Gloucester in New Britain by the 7th Amphibious Force. The action opens the land campaign to take New Britain and isolate the vital Japanese naval and air facilities at Rabaul in the north. Japanese aircraft attempt to repel the invasion fleet, sinking the destroyer USS *Brownson* and damaging three other destroyers and a landing ship. On the 29th, the US troops advance out to seize Cape Gloucester airfield, which will give the Allies air control over the vital corridor between New Britain and New Guinea. Japanese efforts to retake the airfield are unsuccessful.

DECEMBER 31

LAND WAR, *BOUGAINVILLE*

The year ends with the US having established strong positions on Bougainville, despite determined Japanese opposition in the island's interior. Empress Augusta Bay is now a fully operational US Navy base with three airstrips on land.

1944

This was the year when the Allies won substantial victories against the Japanese. The Imperial Navy was effectively destroyed at the Philippine Sea and Leyte Gulf, while US forces landed on the Gilbert and Marshall Islands and the Philippines during their march across the central Pacific. The Japanese were also defeated in Burma, and from airfields in the Philippines B-29s began to bomb Japan itself.

▼ *The final moments of a Japanese cargo ship, as seen through the periscope of the US submarine that torpedoed her.*

JANUARY 1

AIR WAR, *NEW IRELAND*
US aircraft from Rear-Admiral F.C. Sherman's carrier task force bomb a Japanese convoy of transports, destroying several cruisers off Kavieng in New Ireland.

JANUARY 2

LAND WAR, *NEW GUINEA*
Troops of the 126th Regiment, US 32nd Division, launch "Operation Dexterity", a large-scale landing at Saidor on the northeastern coast of New Guinea. The invasion is roughly at the midway point between the Allied advances on New Guinea from the west and east, and severs Japanese rearguard forces from their main base 88km (55 miles) farther up the coastline at Madang. However, Japanese troops of the 20th and 51st Divisions escape entrapment; around 20,000 Japanese soldiers are now forced into the jungle-covered interior of the Huon Peninsula.

◄ *By 1944 US submarines were taking a heavy toll of Japanese shipping. These submariners display a flag that shows their vessel has sunk 13 Japanese ships.*

JANUARY 6–9

LAND WAR, *NEW BRITAIN*

US troops at Cape Gloucester on the northern edge of southern New Britain begin an advance to the Aogiri River, taking the Aogiri ridge after three days of heavy fighting.

JANUARY 9

LAND WAR, *BURMA*

The British Fourteenth Army, part of XV Corps, takes the port of Maungdaw on the Bay of Bengal, having advanced 32km (20 miles) from around Bawli Bazar near the Indian border. The offensive is part of a renewed Allied attempt to take Akyab, and Maungdaw is an important supply port for the Japanese. Despite the success, the Allied troops have

▼ *A group of US Marine Raiders pose in front of a Japanese dugout they have just knocked out on Cape Totkina, Bougainville, January 1944.*

an exposed left flank, against which huge Japanese forces are massing.

JANUARY 11

SEA WAR, *SOLOMON ISLANDS*

The Japanese cruiser *Kuma* is sunk by the British submarine HMS *Tally Ho*. By 1944, Allied submarines are tightening the stranglehold on Japanese shipping travelling to and from the mainland. On January 8 alone, a US Navy communiqué states that US submarines have sunk 10 Japanese vessels, including an oil tanker.

▲ *A US bomber peels away after dropping its ordnance on the Mu River Bridge, Burma. One bomb has fallen wide, but a second bomb is in midair over the bridge.*

AIR WAR, *MARSHALL ISLANDS*

US B-24 Liberator aircraft make a low-level attack on Japanese shipping around Kwajalein Atoll, sinking two vessels and damaging four others. The raid is just one of the many taking

JANUARY 13-22

▶ *US Marines on Namur Island, February 2. Note how artillery and small-arms fire has stripped the trees of their foliage.*

place around the Marshall Islands during January as the US prepares for a land offensive there.

JANUARY 13-22

LAND WAR, *BURMA*
Stilwell's Chinese troops maintain a solid advance. By January 30, the Chinese 22nd Division has taken Taro, 160km (100 miles) to the northwest of Myitkyina.

JANUARY 15

LAND WAR, *NEW GUINEA*
Australian troops finally take Sio. There is now a gap of only 80km (50 miles) between Australian troops at Sio and US forces at Saidor, and the Japanese

defence of the Huon Peninsula is in complete disarray.

JANUARY 16

LAND WAR, *NEW GUINEA*
Australian forces take over the Finisterre range in the north of the Huon Peninsula.

JANUARY 16-17

LAND WAR, *NEW BRITAIN*
Japan launches a series of counter-attacks against US forces in southern New Britain but, by the 17th, the Allies have consolidated Arawe and are securing their hold on the southern parts of the island.

JANUARY 22-26

LAND WAR, *NEW GUINEA*
Australian troops of the 18th Brigade capture the Kankiryo Saddle, an important Japanese position crossing the western tip of the mountainous Finisterre range. The capture of the position puts the Australians only 32km (20 miles) from the coast.

LAND WAR, *MARSHALL ISLANDS*
"Operation Flintlock", the US invasion of the Marshall Islands, starts to roll as the invasion forces set sail.

JANUARY 24

AIR WAR, *RABAUL*
A 200-aircraft raid launched from US carrier groups destroys 83 Japanese aeroplanes. Japan is suffering unsustainable aviation losses in the Pacific, both of aircraft and pilots, and the US is coming to rely more and more on achieving theatre air supremacy.

JANUARY 29

AIR WAR, *MARSHALL ISLANDS*
US carrier aircraft begin a systematic one-week campaign against Japanese airpower and shipping around the Marshall Islands.

◀ *A US patrol on New Britain. The lead soldier carries a Thompson submachine gun equipped with a 50-round drum magazine.*

▲ *A B-25 Mitchell medium bomber of the Seventh US Army Air Force strikes Japanese targets on Wotje Island.*

JANUARY 31

LAND WAR, *MARSHALL ISLANDS*
Operation Flintlock begins with landings on Majuro Atoll and Kwajalein Atoll by US Army and Marine Corps troops. The attack is supported by large numbers of US land-based and carrier-based aircraft. The Majuro landing proceeds smoothly, putting the troops ashore on an undefended island. By contrast, Japanese forces on Kwajalein Atoll resist ferociously, and US casualties are heavy.

FEBRUARY 1–7

LAND WAR, *MARSHALL ISLANDS*
The US expands its invasion of the Marshall Islands by landing Marines on Roi and Namur Islands. The two islands take two days to occupy and cost US forces 737 casualties. On Kwajalein Atoll, the battle results in 372 US

casualties but, by the 7th, the island is declared secure. The Japanese lose 11,612 soldiers during the 8-day battle in the Marshall Islands.

FEBRUARY 4

LAND WAR, *BURMA*
The Japanese 55th Division, commanded by Lieutenant-General Hanaya Tadashi, counterattacks the advancing forces of Lieutenant-General Christison's British XV Corps in Operation Ha-Go. British and Commonwealth troops have a tremendously exposed left flank and an extremely vulnerable supply and administrative centre near Sinzweya, about 10km (6 miles) from the Burmese coastline, subsequently known as "Admin Box" because of its 1000m (3280ft) square layout.

FEBRUARY 5

LAND WAR, NORTHERN BURMA
General Wingate's Long Range Penetration (LRP) unit – the Chindits – crosses the Indian border into northern Burma. The 3000-strong unit, reformed and retrained after its earlier disastrous mission, is now under General

◀ *A Douglas Dauntless dive-bomber waits to take off during the air bombardment phase of Operation Flintlock.*

▲ *Two members of the 1st Punjab Regiment, 7th Indian Division, in northern Burma in early February.*

Stilwell's strategic command, though Wingate remains its immediate leader. The Chindits' mission is to support Stilwell's drive towards Myitkyina on the right flank, drawing Japanese troops away from advancing Chinese forces and cutting supply and communication links.

FEBRUARY 10

LAND WAR, *MARSHALL ISLANDS*
US forces begin mopping up remaining resistance throughout the Marshall Islands. On this day, US Marines are landed on Arno Atoll.

FEBRUARY 12

LAND WAR, *BURMA*
The 17th Indian Division at Sinzweya is cut off from Allied forces by a Japanese encirclement operation. There then be-

▼ *Military supplies are offloaded on Eniwetok Atoll following the US invasion on February 17.*

gins one of the greatest Allied defensive operations of the Far Eastern war. Troops inside the Box come to rely entirely on air supply, which provides them with sufficient ammunition and food to beat off numerous and increasingly desperate attacks.

LAND WAR, *NEW GUINEA*
The Australian 8th Brigade and 5th Division meet up with US troops at Saidor, having advanced around 80km (50 miles) from Sio. Now only 96km (60 miles) of the northern coastline of the Huon Peninsula remains in Japanese hands.

FEBRUARY 15

SEA WAR, *SOLOMON ISLANDS*
Ships of the US Third Amphibious Force land the 3rd New Zealand Division on Green Island, a small outcrop of land roughly halfway between Bougainville and New Ireland.

FEBRUARY 16

SEA WAR, *CENTRAL PACIFIC*
The Japanese light cruiser *Agano* is sunk by the US submarine USS *Skate*.

FEBRUARY 17

AIR WAR, *CAROLINE ISLANDS*
The US takes the war to the Caroline

▲ *Chindits, Burmese farmers and US air personnel at a Chindit base in Burma. The aircraft in the background is a C-47.*

Islands, which offer vital air and naval facilities in the central Pacific area between New Guinea and the Mariana Islands. Today, US Naval Task Force 58, which includes nine carriers and six battleships, makes a major attack on

Truk Atoll, a harbour for the Japanese Combined Fleet. US carrier aircraft sink two cruisers and three destroyers, and for the first time make a radar-guided night operation. More than 260 Japanese aircraft are also destroyed in the raid.

FEBRUARY 17–22

LAND WAR, *MARSHALL ISLANDS*

US Marines and US Army infantry are landed on Eniwetok Atoll, in the far northwest of the Marshall Islands. The first landings by units of the 22nd Marine Battalion proceed smoothly at Engebi, but subsequent landings by more Marines and troops from the 106th Regiment meet heavy resistance from 2000

Japanese defenders, all of whom are killed in the subsequent action.

FEBRUARY 19

AIR WAR, *RABAUL*

Allied air superiority over Rabaul forces the Japanese to give up aviation defence of the important base. From now on, it will rely on anti-aircraft guns.

FEBRUARY 23

SEA WAR, *MARIANA ISLANDS*

Having secured the Marshall Islands, US Pacific forces begin preparatory bombardments of the Mariana Islands, which include the islands of Saipan, Tinian, Rota and Guam. Aircraft from Rear-Admiral M.A. Mitscher's fast carrier task force attack all four islands. The mission to take the Marianas is known as "Operation Forager", and capture of the most northerly island, Saipan, will give the US a bomber base for strikes on the Japanese homeland.

FEBRUARY 24

LAND WAR, *BURMA*

The siege of the Admin Box is finally broken after Allied troops dislodge Japanese forces from the Ngakyedauk Pass, the overland approach route from the Burmese coast at Wabyin to Sinzweya. Elements of the Japanese Army's 55th Division are now cut off in western Burma.

▼ *Two members of the US 22nd Marine Regimental Combat Team, commanded by Colonel John T. Walker, on the beach at Eniwetok, February 22.*

FEBRUARY 21

▶ *Personnel of the 5318th Provisional Unit on the ground at Landing Zone Broadway, Burma, preparing an airstrip for Orde Wingate's Chindits.*

FEBRUARY 21

LAND WAR, *BURMA*
The US 5307th Provisional Regiment – codenamed "Galahad" but popularly known as "Merrill's Marauders" – assembles at Sharaw Ga in northern Burma to provide tactical flanking operations in support of Allied forces advancing down towards Myitkyina. The 5307th Regiment is a US equivalent of the Chindits, and has actually trained with Chindit units. Its nickname comes from the name of its commander, Brigadier-General Frank D. Merrill, although much of the practical leadership of the regiment is handled by his second-in-command, Colonel Charles Hunter.

FEBRUARY 29

LAND WAR, *ADMIRALTY ISLANDS*
The US 1st Cavalry Division invades Los Negros in the Admiralty Islands group. Though the operation was originally a reconnaissance-in-force, the landing is quickly exploited and the US piles in more forces. Capture of the Admiralty chain will provide northerly air bases for strikes against New Britain and New Ireland.

MARCH 1–4

LAND WAR, *ADMIRALTY ISLANDS*
Japanese forces on the Admiralty Islands make two major attacks to eject the US troops from Los Negros; both are beaten back, resulting in heavy Japanese casualties. On the 4th, US reinforcements are landed on Los Negros.

MARCH 3–7

SEA WAR, *ADMIRALTY ISLANDS*
A large Allied task force under Rear-Admiral V.A.C. Crutchley, British Royal Navy, pounds Japanese shore positions on Hauwei and Norilo Islands. The task force includes two US cruisers and four US destroyers.

MARCH 5–7

LAND WAR, *BURMA*
Chinese troops of the 22nd and 38th Divisions capture Maingkwan in the Hukawng Valley. On their left flank, the US troops of Merrill's Marauders cross the Tanai River and take Walabaum, only 97km (60 miles) from Myitkyina. The battle for Walabaum is ferocious, with troops of the Japanese 18th Division making suicidal bayonet charges, while US and Chinese troops often go without food for 24-hour periods. But losses among the Allied soldiers are relatively light.

MARCH 5

LAND WAR, *BURMA*
Chindit forces in northern Burma begin "Operation Thursday". The 77 and 111 LRP Brigades, about 9000 men, are deployed by glider in an area between Indaw and Myitkyina, and establish landing strips for future operational air supply. More Chindit brigades will be flown in over the next three weeks. The purpose of Operation Thursday is to harass Japanese forces to the south of Chinese and

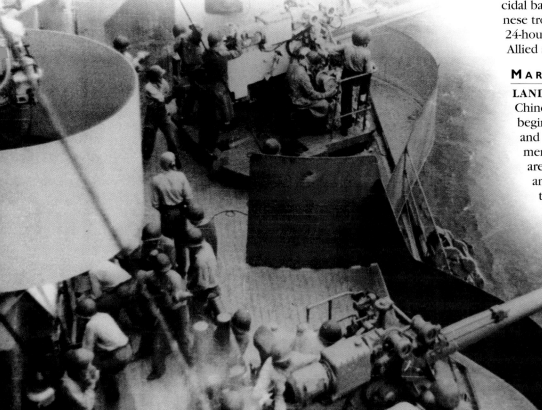

◀ *The guns of USS Phoenix open fire on Japanese positions on Los Negros in the Admiralty Islands on February 29, 1944.*

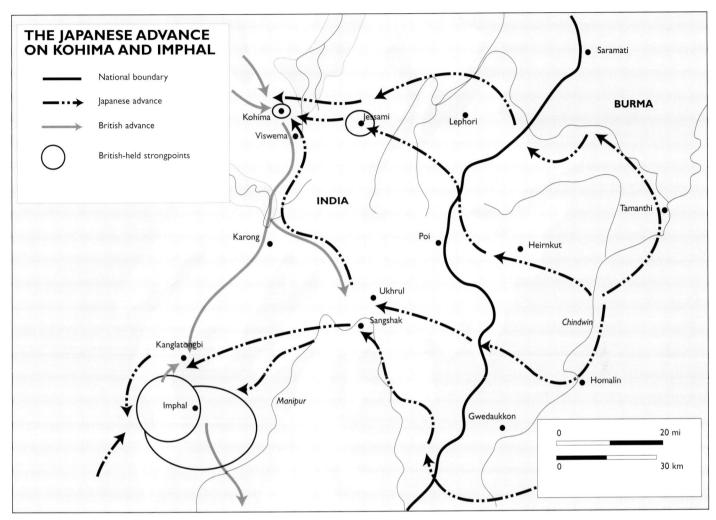

THE JAPANESE ADVANCE ON KOHIMA AND IMPHAL

——	National boundary
▬▪▪▪▶	Japanese advance
➤	British advance
◯	British-held strongpoints

US operations against Myitkyina, and cut the flow of Japanese supplies and communications heading north.

▼ *Newly arrived British reinforcements wait for orders at the Imphal airstrip.*

MARCH 7

LAND WAR, *BURMA/INDIA*
The Japanese Fifteenth Army, commanded by Lieutenant-General Renya Mutaguchi, begins "Operation U-Go" in central Burma. U-Go is a Japanese at-

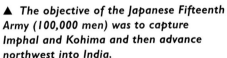

▲ *The objective of the Japanese Fifteenth Army (100,000 men) was to capture Imphal and Kohima and then advance northwest into India.*

tempt to spoil any Allied offensive moves in central Burma by crossing into India, pushing Allied forces out of Burma in the process, cutting the Assam–Burma railway used for supplying Stilwell's Myitkyina offensive, and also occupying Imphal and Kohima and the flat territory between (an ideal launch point for an Allied offensive). The first part of the offensive involves the Japanese 33rd Division advancing out and cutting the Tiddim–Imphal Road, a major Allied supply route to Imphal, and trapping the 17th Indian Division based between Tiddim and Tongzang.

MARCH 11–12

LAND WAR, *BURMA*
While the Allies in central Burma fall back under the onslaught of Operation U-Go, in the Arakan the Allies make progress by recapturing Buthidaung and the Japanese fortress at Razabil.

MARCH 13

LAND WAR, *BURMA*
The Japanese 33rd Division reaches Witok on the approaches to the Shenan Saddle.

MARCH 13

LAND WAR, *BURMA*
Forces from the Japanese Fifteenth Army attack "Broadway", one of the main Allied landing strips in the Chindits' area of operations.

MARCH 15

LAND WAR, *ADMIRALTY ISLANDS*
Troops of the US 1st Cavalry Division land on Manus, the largest island of the Admiralty chain. By taking the Admiralty Islands, the US will further isolate Japanese forces in New Britain and New Guinea.

MARCH 15–16

LAND WAR, *BURMA/INDIA*
The second part of the U-Go offensive is launched. From start positions to the east of Imphal, the Japanese 15th Division begins an advance westwards, aiming to cut the Imphal–Kohima road, cross around the north of the city and make an encirclement of Allied positions by meeting with the Japanese 33rd Division advancing from the south. Meanwhile, farther to the north, the Japanese 31st Division begins a three-pronged assault towards Kohima.

MARCH 16

SEA WAR, *JAPAN*
The Japanese destroyer *Shirakumo* is sunk by the submarine USS *Tautog* off the coast of Japan.

LAND WAR, *BURMA*
Chindit troops cut the Mandalay–Myitkyina rail link just north of the vital Japanese supply base at Indaw, thereby making Japanese resupply of the retreating 18th Division extremely difficult. However, Japanese progress in the Imphal offensive means that many

▶ *Douglas SBD Dauntless carrier-based dive-bombers return from an air strike in the Marshall Islands.*

Allied troops are now being redirected away from the Myitkyina offensive.

MARCH 18–19

SEA WAR, *PACIFIC*
A US task group that includes one aircraft carrier and two battleships bombards Mili Island in the Marshall Islands from air and sea. One US ship is damaged in the engagement, the battleship USS *Missouri*, which is hit by a shell from a Japanese coastal gun. On the 18th, US destroyers also begin a two-day bombardment of Japanese positions at Wewak on the northern coastline of New Guinea.

MARCH 20

SEA/LAND WAR, *BISMARCK SEA*
The US 4th Marine Division makes an unopposed landing on Emirau, the most easterly of the St Matthias Group of Islands just north of New Ireland. Emirau contains an airstrip useful for strikes against Japanese naval bases at Kavieng in New Ireland and Rabaul in New Britain.

MARCH 23–24

LAND WAR, *BURMA*
The 14th LRP Brigade lands at

▶ *On the airstrip at the Chindit base of Broadway, a working party takes a break during repairs to the runway. In the background is a smashed glider.*

"Aberdeen" landing zone near Manhton in support of Chindit operations.

MARCH 25

ALLIES, LEADERS
Major-General Orde Wingate, leader of the Chindits and pioneer of irregular warfare, is killed in an air crash over Burma. He is succeeded by Major-General W. Letaigne.

MARCH 25–29

LAND WAR, *ADMIRALTY ISLANDS*
US forces consolidate their hold over the Admiralty Islands. Resistance on Manus finally crumbles on the 25th;

▲ *Vice-Admiral Minechi Koga, the C-in-C of the Japanese Combined Fleet, who died in an air crash at the end of March.*

four days later, the US occupies Pityilu Island to the north of Manus.

MARCH 29

LAND WAR, *INDIA*
The Japanese 15th Division cuts the Imphal–Kohima road near Kanglatongbi. Meanwhile, in the south, the 33rd Division has ousted the 17th Indian Division from positions around Maw and Sittang and is besieging it on the Shenan Saddle, southeast of Imphal.

MARCH 30

LAND WAR, *BURMA*
Chindit operations south of Myitkyina begin to falter, the British troops being exhausted. The 16th Brigade is forced to retreat by the Japanese 53rd Division after its attempt to take the Japanese supply base at Indaw ends in failure.

MARCH 31

LEADERS, *JAPAN*
Vice-Admiral Minechi Koga, the C-in-C of the Japanese Combined Fleet from April 1943 (after Yamamoto's death), is killed in an air crash. Though a well-liked man, Koga did not have the offensive instinct of Yamamoto, or the same grasp of carrier air power.

APRIL 1

AIR WAR, *CAROLINE ISLANDS*
Three US Navy carrier groups launch a series of massive air strikes throughout

KEY PERSONALITIES

ORDE WINGATE

Orde Wingate (1903-44) was one of the great pioneers of the British Army. His formation and leadership of the Chindits in Burma were accompanied by important tactical innovations, including techniques of irregular warfare and effective use of air supply/support in tropical terrain.

Wingate was born in Naini Tal, India, on February 26, 1903. His father was an army officer, and Wingate followed him by taking a commission in the Royal Artillery in 1923. An active military career followed, including five years in the Sudan Defence Force (1928-33), working as an intelligence and combat officer in Palestine (1936) and, with the outbreak of World War II, leading units against Italian forces in Abyssinia. Wingate's next assignment was a posting to India along with a promotion to the rank of brigadier. It was in late 1942 that Wingate's commander, General Archibald Wavell, gave Wingate permission to form the Chindits, a group dedicated to insurgency style warfare that entered the Burma campaign in February 1943. Although the Chindits' first mission was essentially a failure, Wingate remained enthused by the idea of long-range

penetration, and personally presented the idea to British Prime Minister Churchill and US President Roosevelt.

It was during the Chindits' second, more auspicious, action in March 1944 that Wingate was killed. He was deeply mourned by his men, who always gave him their absolute loyalty. Wingate was undoubtedly a complex man – difficult, intelligent, ruthless and prone to severe depression. Yet he left an important military legacy relevant to any military student today.

▲ *Japanese troops attack a Stuart light tank during their advance in Burma. The Stuart was armed with a 37mm main gun.*

the Caroline Islands. Although the US loses 20 aircraft in the raids, the Japanese casualties are considerably higher: 150 aircraft destroyed and 6 warships (including 2 destroyers) and 105,664 tonnes (104,000 tons) of merchant shipping sunk.

APRIL 5–6

LAND WAR, *INDIA*
The Japanese 31st Division isolates Kohima: the 138th Regiment moves from the

north; the 58th and 124th Regiments attack from the south and west. Allied forces at Kohima are now trapped in a pocket less than 16km (10 miles) across. On the 6th, the Japanese 58th Regiment succeeds in driving through Naga Village at the northern end of Kohima and up the Imphal–Kohima road to take key positions around the centre of the settlement, but a dogged defence by the Royal West Kents stops the attack in its tracks.

APRIL 6

LAND WAR, *INDIA*
Operation U-Go completes its final objectives as the Japanese 33rd and 15th

Divisions cut off Imphal. The Allied defensive circle around Imphal is roughly 32km (20 miles) across, and contains the following IV Corps units: 17th Indian Light Division; 50th Parachute Brigade; 5th Indian Division; 23rd Indian Division; 254th Tank Brigade. Despite having been thoroughly routed, the Allied forces have made a professional retreat and conserved much of their strength and organization. Both Imphal and Kohima garrisons are now entirely dependent on air supply to maintain the defence, and their aim is to hang on until Britain's XXXIII Corps reaches them and breaks the siege.

APRIL 6–11

LAND WAR, *BURMA*
The Japanese Army's 53rd Division takes the supply base known as "White City" in the south of the Chindits' area of operations.

APRIL 7

LAND WAR, *INDIA*
To consolidate its gains around Kohima, the Japanese 138th Regiment encircles the

◀ *Japanese infantry move towards Kohima in Burma past two abandoned British Bren Gun Carriers of the Fourteenth Army.*

 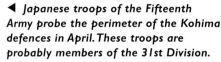
◀ *Japanese troops of the Fifteenth Army probe the perimeter of the Kohima defences in April. These troops are probably members of the 31st Division.*

1500 Allied troops (mostly from the Assam Rifles and 4th Royal West Kents) beats back the Japanese, who also suffer heavy casualties from 3.74in howitzer fire from Jotsoma.

APRIL 14

LAND WAR, *INDIA*
Allied XXXIII Corps begins its relief operations around Kohima. The 5th Brigade, 2nd Division, smashes the Japanese road block at Zubza and also breaks the Japanese grip around the 161st Indian Brigade at Jotsoma. The Jotsoma position is useful for the Allies as an ideal location for bringing

161st Indian Brigade around Jotsoma to the west of Kohima, then establishes a road block at Zubza, cutting the main Dimapur–Kohima road. In Kohima itself, the Japanese take the key defensive points known as the F.S.D. and Kuki Piquet after an intense overnight artillery bombardment.

APRIL 9

LAND WAR, *BURMA*
The Chindits in northern Burma receive glider-borne reinforcements.

APRIL 12

LAND WAR, *ADMIRALTY ISLANDS*
Pak Island is taken by US troops.

APRIL 13

LAND WAR, *INDIA*
The Japanese start to suffer serious setbacks in the U-Go offensive. Allied troops have today pushed the Japanese off Nung-shigum Hill on the Imphal plain, allowing them to intensify attacks on the

Japanese 15th Division. In Kohima, Japanese forces push into the centre of the settlement, throwing themselves at positions reaching from GPT Ridge in the south to the "Tennis Court" in the north around the district commissioner's residence. A tenacious defence by

▼ *A column of troops from the Japanese Fifteenth Army makes its way towards northeast India. By early July 1944, this 100,000-man force had suffered very heavy losses.*

APRIL 18

artillery fire down on the Japanese around Kohima.

APRIL 18

LAND WAR, *BURMA*
The Chindits finally occupy the Japanese supply base at Indaw. The occupation cuts a vital Japanese rail link between Myitkyina and southern Burma.

LAND WAR, *INDIA*
The beleaguered Allied garrison at Kohima is finally relieved by the 5th Brigade of XXXIII Corps. The fighting does not abate, however. Both the Japanese and the British are attempting encirclement and flanking manoeuvres against each other, and severe battles are raging in the hilly and jungle-covered terrain surrounding Kohima.

APRIL 19

SEA WAR, *DUTCH EAST INDIES*
An Allied naval force commanded by Admiral J.F. Somerville of the Royal Navy, and including the US carrier *Saratoga* and the British carrier HMS *Illustrious*, bombs and shells enemy positions around Sabang, Sumatra, as a diversion from imminent US operations in New Guinea.

APRIL 21–22

LAND WAR, *NEW GUINEA*
The US extends its operations by making major landings on the northern coastline of New Guinea. On the 21st/22nd, a US naval Task Force under Vice-Admiral M.A. Mitscher delivers a massive preliminary bombardment against Japanese positions at Sarmi, Sawar, Wadke Island and Hollandia before US Army troops are landed at Aitape, Tanahmerah Bay and Hollandia. The attack comes as Allied troops finalize their hold over the Huon Peninsula farther to the south. The Japanese on New Guinea are increasingly running out of space to retreat or evacuate.

◀ *A Gurkha fighting with the Fourteenth Army opens fire against a Japanese position with his Thompson submachine gun. This is the M1928 model, with a 30-round magazine.*

APRIL 17

STRATEGY, *JAPAN*
Japan attempts to reinvigorate its strategic policy towards China. Although already over-stretched in the Pacific and Burma, the Japanese Army is committed to a major offensive in China – Ichi-Go – which has the objective of occupying southern China, thus providing open land routes to Japanese forces in Malaya and Thailand, while also crushing US air bases in Honan and Kwangsi provinces.

APRIL 22

LAND WAR, *MARSHALL ISLANDS*
The US brings the Marshall Islands under full control by occupying the island of Ungelap. The capture of the Marshall Islands enables US forces in the central Pacific to begin their swing northwards up through the Mariana Islands towards the Japanese homeland.

APRIL 24

STRATEGY, *US*
Based on the fanaticism of Japanese resistance throughout the Pacific so far, Allied war leaders agree that the Japanese homeland will need to be invaded and occupied to secure Japan's final surrender.

APRIL 24–26

LAND WAR, *NEW GUINEA*
Australian soldiers of the 15th Brigade advance northwards out of the Huon Peninsula and take Madang and Alexishafen.

◄ *Japanese troops, either of the 15th or 31st Divisions, wait to cross a river in Burma as part of the U-Go offensive.*

downpours of rain from the 27th complicate movement. In central Kohima, a stubborn Allied resistance around features such as Garrison Hill is devastating Japanese forces, and on the 27th the British retake the important road junction around the district commissioner's bungalow. The Japanese and British settle into entrenched positions less than 22m (72ft) apart around the Tennis Court, and begin an horrific two-week, close-quarter battle.

APRIL 29–30

SEA/AIR WAR, *CAROLINE ISLANDS*
The Japanese base at Truk is bombed by aircraft from 12 US carriers, destroying ships, oil stores, ammunition dumps and 93 Japanese aircraft.

MAY 1

SEA/AIR WAR, *CAROLINE ISLANDS*
A large US battleship and carrier group bombards Ponape Island.

▲ *Admiral Soemu Toyoda, who in early May became Commander-in-Chief of the Japanese Combined Fleet. In 1945, Toyoda favoured continuing the war despite the dropping of atomic bombs on Japan.*

APRIL 26–27

LAND WAR, *INDIA*
The Allied XXXIII Corps begins a major pincer action to take Kohima. From the north, the 5th Brigade begins attacking the Japanese right flank; from the south, the 4th Brigade begins to hook upwards towards GPT Ridge. Torrential

▼ *Chindits about to board a C-47 transport aircraft at one of their strongholds in Burma, probably Broadway.*

MAY 4

LAND WAR, *MARSHALL ISLANDS*
A US naval base and naval air facility is established on Majuro Atoll, providing another logistics centre for US operations in the central Pacific. Just six days

▼ *A US air raid on the Japanese base at Rabaul. By mid-May it was effectively isolated. It would be left "to wither on the vine" until the end of the war.*

later, another US naval base is opened on Eniwetok. Five days later, naval air bases are established at Ebeye and Roi-namur, Kwajalein Atoll. The air bases are used for the next few weeks to hit remaining Japanese installations in the Marshalls.

MAY 4–13

LAND WAR, *INDIA*
The British 4th Brigade retakes GPT Ridge to the south of Kohima. On May

▲ *A US Coast Guard LST (Landing Ship, Tank), loaded with supplies and part of a large flotilla, makes its way to New Guinea. Note the anti-aircraft guns.*

4–7, Allied troops of the 6th and 33rd Brigades attacking Japanese positions between Jail Hill and the Tennis Court experience less success, and are beaten off with heavy casualties. A second attempt on 11–13th finally ejects the Japanese from these positions.

MAY 5

POLITICS, *JAPAN*
Following the death of Admiral Koga, the C-in-C of the Japanese Combined Fleet, on March 31, Admiral Soemu Toyoda is sworn in as his replacement.
LAND WAR, *INDIA*
The British Fourteenth Army begins extensive counterattacks in the Imphal area. Throughout April and into early May, IV Corps has been defending the long perimeter around Imphal, with fighting particularly heavy around the Shenan Saddle, Torbung and Mapao Ridge. Both sides are increasingly exhausted and are running out of basic foodstuffs.

MAY 6

LAND WAR, *BURMA*
Chinese troops are now fighting the Japanese at Ritpong, only 48km (30 miles) from Myitkyina.

eating grass and roots, he acts according to his humanity.

MAY 17

LAND WAR, *NORTHERN BURMA*
A combined force of Chindits, US soldiers of the 5307th Regiment and Chinese troops of the 30th and 38th Divisions attempt to take Myitkyina after their advance through Burma of more than 241km (150 miles). The attack is blunted against strong Japanese defences on the outskirts.

MAY 17

LAND WAR, *NEW GUINEA*
More US Army troops (41st and 6th Divisions) are landed on northern New Guinea, this time in the Wadke-Toem area, 320km (200 miles) west of Hollandia.

AIR WAR, *DUTCH EAST INDIES*
Carrier aircraft of the British Eastern Fleet destroy enemy oil installations at Surabaya and also sink 10 Japanese naval vessels.

MAY 18

LAND WAR, *ADMIRALTY ISLANDS*
Remaining Japanese resistance in the Admiralties is finally extinguished, leaving the fortified Japanese bases at Kavieng (New Ireland) and Rabaul

MAY 7

LAND WAR, *INDIA*
Fourteenth Army counterattacks around Imphal lose force and peter out in the face of ferocious Japanese resistance.

MAY 11

STRATEGY, *MARIANA ISLANDS*
Vice-Admiral Jisaburo Ozawa takes charge of the Japanese naval defence of the Mariana Islands. The defensive operation is codenamed A-Go.

▼ *Chinese troops, kitted out in American uniforms and shouldering US rifles, march down a road in northern Burma on their way to engage Japanese forces. A US P-40 fighter flies overhead.*

▲ *US troops come ashore on New Guinea as part of the American build-up on the island. The Japanese fought a tenacious rearguard campaign throughout 1944.*

MAY 15–31

LAND WAR, *INDIA*
Just south of Naga village, the 33rd Brigade makes repeated attempts to capture Hunter's Hill and Gun Spur. All attacks are initially repulsed. However, the Japanese are steadily pushed back from Kohima during subsequent days; and on May 31, Lieutenant-General Sato Kotoku orders his 31st Division to withdraw. The withdrawal is against official orders but, having lost around 6000 men, and with the survivors reduced to

▲ *Gurkhas and members of the West Yorkshire Regiment advance against Japanese troops at Kohima. The tank at left is an M3 Grant.*

(New Britain) entirely surrounded by Allied forces. They will remain this way until the end of the war, escaping invasion owing to the US policy of avoiding Japanese strongholds if they can be bypassed and isolated instead. The Japanese have lost 3280 men killed, while the US Admiralties campaign results in 326 dead and 1189 wounded.

MAY 17–18

LAND WAR, *BURMA*
US and Chinese troops battle hard to take Myitkyina. On the 17th, the Chinese 150th Regiment/50th Division captures Myitkyina airstrip, with the railway station falling the next day. However, severe exhaustion among Allied troops, particularly the US Marauders, means they make limited progress elsewhere and they dig in and wait for the Chinese 38th Division to arrive.

MAY 19

POLITICS, *US*
James Forrestal is appointed Secretary of the Navy, having been under-secretary since June 1940 under James Knox. Forrestal will prove himself a tough and capable naval administrator, and even experience combat by landing under fire on Iwo Jima when visiting US forces in April 1945.

MAY 19–20

SEA/AIR WAR, *MARCUS ISLAND*
US carrier aircraft conduct a two-day bombardment of Marcus Island.

MAY 28

LAND WAR, *NEW GUINEA*
Men of the US 158th, 162nd and 186th Infantry Regiments land on Biak off northwestern New Guinea. Although the landing is unopposed, the US advance towards an airstrip near Mokmer turns into a ferocious firefight after Japanese troops spring a huge machine-gun, artillery and mortar ambush from cliff-side positions.

▼ *Troops of the 2nd Battalion, 6th Marine Regiment, on the outskirts of Garapan on the island of Saipan.*

JUNE 6

AIR WAR, *NEW GUINEA*
Two US light cruisers are damaged after a Japanese bombing attack off Biak.

JUNE 7

LAND WAR, *NEW GUINEA*
The Japanese Mokmer airfield on Biak, off the coast of New Guinea, is secured by US troops.

JUNE 8

SEA WAR, *NEW GUINEA*
Five Japanese destroyers are intercepted and turned back by an Allied naval force as they attempt a supply run to beleaguered Japanese troops on Biak Island. The destroyer *Harusame* is sunk.

JUNE 9

SEA WAR, *PACIFIC*
Two Japanese destroyers are sunk by US submarines off the Bonin Islands and in the Celebes Sea. Although a good day of hunting, such sinkings are now unexceptional as US submarines inflict a grievous toll on Japanese merchant and military shipping.

JUNE 12

POLITICS, *CHINA*
In a dramatic political reversal, the Chinese Communist leader Mao Tse Tung makes a public announcement of his support for Chiang Kai-

▲ *A Japanese Type 96 light tank lies abandoned near Mokmer airstrip, on Biak Island, following a firefight with US forces which landed on the island.*

shek's Nationalist forces. However, such declarations have been made before, and the Communists still jealously guard their own territorial areas in northern China.

JUNE 12–14

AIR/SEA WAR, *MARIANA ISLANDS*
US Task Force 58 begins a huge three-day bombardment of Japanese positions on Saipan and Tinian, while US aircraft add their own firepower and damage or destroy around 200 Japanese aircraft. The battleship USS *California* and the destroyer USS *Braine* are damaged by Japanese coastal guns on the Marianas.

JUNE 14

LAND WAR, *NEW GUINEA*
General Douglas MacArthur replaces the commander of US forces on

MAY 29

SEA WAR, *NEW IRELAND*
US destroyers bombard the northern coastline of New Ireland. However, there will be no invasion – New Ireland will be bypassed in favour of Emirau Island and Hollandia.

LAND WAR, *NEW GUINEA*
US and Japanese tanks engage each other on Biak Island off the coast of New Guinea. The action, the first tank battle in the Pacific theatre, results in a Japanese defeat.

JUNE 1–3

LAND WAR, *INDIA*
The Japanese 31st Division at Kohima begins to withdraw, signalling the final end of the U-Go offensive into India. The collapse begins on June 1 when the 7th Indian Division overruns Japanese positions in Naga village before the 5th Brigade outflanks the Japanese around Aradura Spur on June 3. Although the Japanese have been militarily defeated, lack of supplies is also a major catalyst for the withdrawal.

▶ *The 16in guns of USS Iowa open fire against Japanese defences on Tinian. Her main armament was nine 16in guns.*

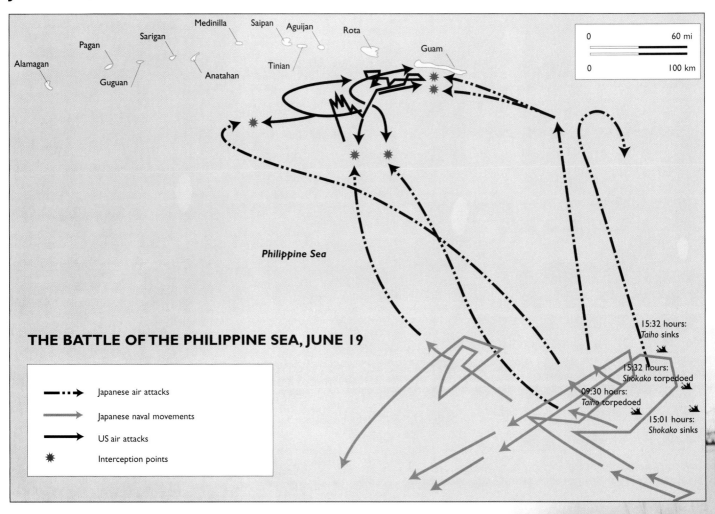

Medinilla Saipan Aguijan Rota
Pagan   Sarigan   Guam
Alamagan   Tinian
        Guguan   Anatahan

0   60 mi
0   100 km

Philippine Sea

THE BATTLE OF THE PHILIPPINE SEA, JUNE 19

15:32 hours:
Taiho sinks
15:32 hours:
Shokako torpedoed
09:30 hours:
Taiho torpedoed
15:01 hours:
Shokako sinks

- - ● →   Japanese air attacks

──────→   Japanese naval movements

──────→   US air attacks

✳   Interception points

▲ At the Battle of the Philippine Sea,
Ozawa had nine carriers and 473 aircraft.
The US fleet under Mitscher had 15
carriers and 902 aircraft.

Biak with Lieutenant-General Eichel-
berger. The change of command galva-
nizes the Biak offensive, which has
ground to a halt against vicious Japanese resistance in the caves and hills of
the island.

JUNE 15

LAND WAR, *MARIANA ISLANDS*
The US invasion of the Mariana Islands
– Operation Forager – begins with
landings on Saipan. While US reserve
regiments make a feint against Mucho
Point about halfway down the west
coast of Saipan, the US 2nd Marine
Division and 4th Marine Division put
ashore farther down the coast around
Charan Kanoa on eight individual
beaches. They meet heavy Japanese
fire, suffering 4000 casualties in the
first 48 hours, but manage to establish
beachheads. However, the bulk of
Lieutenant-General Saito Yoshitsugo's
32,000-strong garrison has been

relatively untouched by the US preliminary bombardment.
AIR WAR, *PACIFIC*
US carrier aircraft bombard Japanese
positions on Iwo Jima in the Volcano
Islands and Chichi Jima and Haha Jima
in the Bonin Islands. Iwo Jima is also
bombed the next day.
AIR WAR, *CHINA*
Industrial facilities on the
Japanese mainland at Yahata are

▼ Ships of the US Fifth Fleet
in the Philippine Sea in June.
These are some of the seven
battleships that Mitscher had
for the battle, plus 21 cruisers
and 69 destroyers.

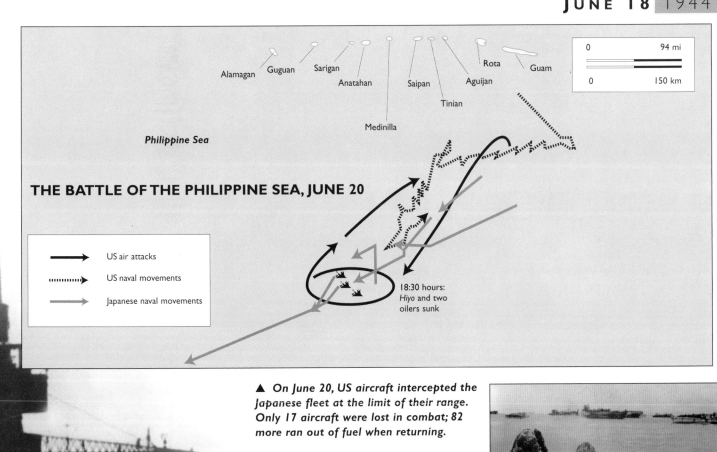

THE BATTLE OF THE PHILIPPINE SEA, JUNE 20

Alamagan Guguan Sarigan
Anatahan
Saipan
Tinian
Medinilla
Rota
Guam
Aguijan

Philippine Sea

0   94 mi
0   150 km

→ US air attacks

⇢ US naval movements

→ Japanese naval movements

18:30 hours:
Hiyo and two
oilers sunk

▲ *On June 20, US aircraft intercepted the Japanese fleet at the limit of their range. Only 17 aircraft were lost in combat; 82 more ran out of fuel when returning.*

bombed by a flight of 47 Boeing B-29 Superfortress bombers flying from bases in southern China.

JUNE 16

SEA WAR, *MARIANA ISLANDS*
As US troops fight ashore on Saipan, a force of US battleships, cruisers and destroyers under Rear-Admiral W.L. Ainsworth pounds Japanese coastal positions on Guam.

SEA WAR, *PHILIPPINE SEA*
Intelligence from US submarines indicates two large Japanese naval forces (First Mobile Fleet and a Southern Force) making a refuelling rendezvous east of the Philippines, before setting sail in the direction of the Mariana Islands. The combined force totals seven battleships, nine aircraft carriers (four of them light carriers), thirteen cruisers and twenty-eight destroyers. Its objective is to crush naval support of the Marianas landings. The full force of Mitscher's Task Force 58 begins redirecting itself to meet this threat.

▲ *Saipan was the first island conquered by the Americans that had a large number of Japanese civilians on it. Here, the inhabitants of a village are evacuated.*

JUNE 17–18

LAND WAR, *MARIANA ISLANDS*
Japanese resistance on Saipan is so heavy that the reserve 27th Infantry Division is landed to assist Marine operations. On the 18th, Aslito airfield in the south of the island is captured, and the US Marines begin to move northwards.

JUNE 18

SEA WAR, *PHILIPPINE SEA*
All US task groups rendezvous around 320km (200 miles) east of Saipan and

JUNE 19

▶ *Curtiss Helldivers on their way to attack Japanese ships during the Battle of the Philippine Sea.*

sail out to face the Japanese naval force heading its way. The Japanese are heavily outnumbered by US Task Force 58, which includes seven battleships, fourteen carriers (seven heavy), twenty-one cruisers and sixty-nine destroyers. The scene is set for the Battle of the Philippine Sea.

LAND WAR, *CHINA*
The Japanese offensive to take western and southern China makes good progress, with the Japanese Eleventh Army taking the cities of Chuchow and Changsa.

JUNE 19

SEA WAR, *PHILIPPINE SEA*
The Battle of the Philippine Sea. Japanese carriers launch their first air strikes against US forces at 08:30 hours, but these are intercepted by US aircraft and more than 200 Japanese planes are shot down. US submarines also begin to attack the Japanese. At 09:05 hours, the carrier *Taiho* is torpedoed by the USS *Albacore*, and the *Shokaku* is torpedoed at 12:20 hours. Both carriers sink by 16:30 hours. At 14:00 hours, surviving Japanese carriers launch a second strike, which goes off course towards Guam and is once again slaughtered by US fighters – more than 100 aircraft are destroyed. By 16:00 hours, the Japan-

ese fleet is withdrawing, but is attacked constantly by US aircraft. The first day of the battle is over. As well as losing two carriers, the Japanese have lost 346 aircraft in what US pilots subsequently dub "The Great Marianas Turkey Shoot".

◀ *A Japanese aircraft in flames, probably a Yukosuka P1Y1, passes over a US escort carrier during the invasion of Saipan.*

▲ *A Japanese aircraft plunges into the sea off Saipan on June 18. The ship in the foreground is the aircraft carrier USS Kitkun Bay, which had a complement of 18 fighters and 12 torpedo-bombers.*

JUNE 20

SEA WAR, *PHILIPPINE SEA*

US Task Force 58 continues its pursuit of Japanese forces retreating through the Philippine Sea. At 16:24 hours, a major US air strike (210 aircraft) is launched, which begins its attack at 18:44 hours at extreme range. The Japanese carrier *Hiyo* is hit by two air-launched torpedoes and sinks, and bombs damage the carriers *Zuikaku* and *Chiyoda*. Two oil tankers are also sunk. The US suffers seven ships damaged. However, 80 US carrier aircraft are destroyed when attempting night landings or from getting lost and having to ditch at sea. The Battle of the Philippine Sea is a major victory for the US; for the Japanese, a hideous defeat marking the decline of its navy.

JUNE 22

LAND WAR, *INDIA*

As the Japanese U-Go offensive unravels in India, the British 2nd Division from Kohima and the 5th Indian Division from the IV Corps area around Imphal finally meet up on the Imphal–Kohima road at Milestone 107. In total, the Japanese siege at Imphal lasted 88 days.

JUNE 26

LAND WAR, *BURMA*

The town of Mogaung falls to a combined force of the 77th LRP Brigade

STRATEGY AND TACTICS

AMPHIBIOUS WARFARE IN THE PACIFIC

Although naval infantry, such as the British Royal Marines and the US Marines, had elementary amphibious skills at the beginning of World War II, it was the Japanese who truly pioneered amphibious tactics. From experience in China in the late 1930s, and from their opening campaigns of World War II, the Japanese developed a systematic doctrine for amphibious campaigns, including the establishment of naval and air superiority in the area of landing; detailed intelligence concerning landing sites and enemy defences; and systematic disembarkation of troops, ammunition and supplies. They were also capable of night-time amphibious landings, with soldiers and equipment daubed in luminous paint to aid identification.

Yet, despite Japanese capabilities, the undeniable master of amphibious warfare in World War II was the US. American amphibious landings worked in three parts. An amphibious force was responsible for landing troops on the beaches and maintaining the flow of relevant logistics. Preparatory and support bombardments were provided by a force of warships surrounding the landing zone; farther out at sea, fleet carriers and other capital ships provided air and sea cover for the landing operations – and also interdicted Japanese reinforcement convoys.

By late 1944, the US had made amphibious landings a fine art, having learnt painful lessons about issues such as beach reconnaissance and the effectiveness of naval bombardments at Tarawa and Saipan. General MacArthur employed amphibious warfare nimbly at a tactical level, using simultaneous multiple landings to trap Japanese troops (see New Guinea, April 1944; and Leyte, October 1944) or bypassing heavily defended Japanese positions by leapfrogging down a coastline. The Japanese learnt equally painful lessons about US amphibious superiority, and at Okinawa in April 1945 they did not make a costly defence of the beaches but withdrew into the interior where they inflicted massive casualties on the US. The lesson came too late, however, and US amphibious tactics took the Allies to the very doorstep of the Japanese homelands.

US Marines in an LVT2 Water Buffalo amphibious vehicle off Tinian.

and the Chinese 38th Division. These forces then turn eastwards to make the 48km (30-mile) drive towards Myitkyina, which US and Chinese forces are already laying siege to.

LAND WAR, *CHINA*

Japanese forces capture Hengyang airfield in southern China, having cut through the Chinese Tenth Army with some ease (Chinese forces were generally second rate). The US needs to hold on to its Chinese air bases for planned B-29 Superfortress air strikes against targets in the Japanese homeland.

JUNE 28

LAND WAR, *MARIANA ISLANDS*

US troops reach Nafutan Point, Saipan's southeastern tip. It has taken them nearly two weeks to cover 6km (4 miles).

JULY 1–31

LAND WAR, *BURMA*

The British Fourteenth Army, capitalizing on its victories at Imphal and Kohima, pushes the Japanese Fifteenth Army back into Burma across the Kabaw Valley. The Japanese make command

JULY 1

▶ *A US Marine peers into a cave in search of Japanese defenders on Saipan. Note the M1911 semi-automatic pistol in his hand – ideal for close-range work.*

changes, with General Hoyotaro Kimura becoming commander of the Burma Area Army, and leadership of the Fifteenth Army passing to Lieutenant-General Shihachi Katamura. Tactically, the Japanese hope that the Allies will over-extend themselves during their advance, and leave themselves open to flanking counterattacks.

JULY 1

LAND WAR, *MARIANA ISLANDS*
The US 2nd and 4th Marine Divisions and the 27th Infantry Division advance up Saipan against heavy Japanese resistance, pushing forward 0.6km (1 mile) in some sectors and bringing right flank troops to within 9km (5.5 miles) of the northern tip of the island. On the left flank of the advance, US troops have seized the heights overlooking Tanapag harbour.

JULY 2

LAND WAR, *DUTCH EAST INDIES*
US troops are landed at Noemfoor Island, off the coast of New Guinea.
AIR WAR, *IWO JIMA*
US carrier aircraft attack Japanese forces on Iwo Jima, shooting down 16

▼ *Dead Japanese litter a beach near Tanapag, Saipan, following a disastrous counterattack on July 9. Thereafter Japanese resistance collapsed.*

Japanese aircraft and destroying 29 on the ground.

JULY 4

AIR WAR, *BONIN ISLANDS/IWO JIMA*
US carrier-based aircraft have a good day hunting Japanese shipping around the Bonin Islands and Iwo Jima. Backed

by a bombardment from US cruisers and destroyers, they help sink four destroyers and several transport vessels.

JULY 7

LAND WAR, *MARIANA ISLANDS*
Having been squeezed into the northern tip of Saipan, the remaining Japanese

forces mount a large counterattack around Makunsha. The attack is repulsed (an estimated 1500 dead) by the massive firepower of the 4th Marine Division and the 27th Infantry Division, despite the Japanese troops breaking through the US lines at points. Yesterday, the Japanese commanders of the Saipan defence, General Yoshitsugo Saito and Admiral Chichi Nagumo, committed suicide.

SEA WAR, *PACIFIC/SOUTH CHINA SEA*

US submarines sink two Japanese destroyers, one around the Kurile Islands and the other in the South China Sea.

JULY 8

AIR WAR, *JAPAN*

Yahata iron and steel works and several

▼ *US troops of the 503rd Parachute Infantry Regiment land on Kamiri airstrip, Noemfoor Island, on July 2. The island was secured by the end of August 1944.*

other key military industrial targets are hit by the second B-29 raid in three weeks, the US bombers utilizing air bases in China.

JULY 9

LAND WAR, *MARIANA ISLANDS*

Japanese resistance eventually collapses on Saipan. The final death toll is high on both sides: 3126 US soldiers killed and 27,000 Japanese (including 8000 suicides), horrific casualty figures for an island only 16km (10 miles) long. The next objective for the 2nd and 4th Marine Divisions is Tinian.

JULY 11

POLITICS, *US*

President Franklin D. Roosevelt states his intention to run for an unprecedented fourth term as president.

JULY 14

LAND/SEA WAR, *NEW GUINEA*

Warships bombard Japanese positions around Aitape, providing aid to Allied troops advancing along New Guinea's northern coastline. Heavy fighting, including a large Japanese counterattack on the Wewak River, has slowed the advance.

JULY 18

POLITICS, *JAPAN*

General Hideki Tojo, the Japanese prime minister and chief of staff,

▼ *Truck-mounted US Marine rocket launchers on Saipan. Rocket-launcher units were usually deployed just behind frontline troops on the battlefield.*

▲ *US Marines use a flamethrower to clear a cave on Saipan. Note how the soldier operating the flamethrower has turned his face away from the heat.*

resigns along with the whole of his cabinet. A group of former premiers engineered the resignation by asking the emperor to form a new government. The move marks increasing desperation among Japanese politicians as they face defeat by the US. General Kuniaki Koiso and Admiral Mitsumasa Yonai will form the new cabinet, and separate the commands of the army that Tojo had previously held in one office.

STRATEGY AND TACTICS

THE STRATEGIC DEBATE

In July 1944, US military leaders, the joint chiefs of staff and the US president met to debate strategic options for complete victory in the Pacific. Those present divided themselves roughly into two camps. General MacArthur advocated the Philippines as the principal objective following the campaign in New Guinea, whereas Admiral King (chief of the US Navy) wanted to bypass the Philippines and cut straight to the island of Formosa, south of the Japanese mainland. By taking Formosa, King contended, Japan would be isolated from its resources in the Dutch East Indies. Also, Formosa would be an excellent jumping-off point in the final invasion of Japan, and would avoid any wasteful slaughter in the Philippine jungles. MacArthur's plan had a strong ethical dimension to it; he believed that the US was under a "moral obligation" to return to the Philippines and liberate its inhabitants. Militarily, he argued that it would not be advisable to leave a large Japanese presence in the rear for a strike towards Formosa.

The other key figure in the debate was Admiral Halsey. He wanted to develop the central Pacific campaign by capturing Okinawa in the Ryukyu chain, part of Japanese territory itself, and use this as the launch pad for the invasion of the mainland.

The momentum was towards MacArthur and Halsey's plan, and the president and the joint chiefs of staff gave their assent. Formosa would be bypassed.

JULY 19

SEA/AIR WAR, _MARIANA ISLANDS_
US Navy ships and aircraft begin their pre-landing bombardment of Guam, focusing on the Asan and Agat beaches.

JULY 21

LAND WAR, _MARIANA ISLANDS_
The US 3rd Marine Division, 1st Marine Brigade and 77th Army Division are landed on the western coast of Guam, before beginning a slow advance northwards.

JULY 24–25

LAND WAR, _MARIANA ISLANDS_
The US 4th Marine Division lands on northern Tinian while the 2nd Marine Division makes a feint attack off the southern coast around Sunhanon

▼ _US Marines advance north on the island of Guam. The vehicle on the left is an M4 Sherman medium tank._

▲ _The Japanese cabinet that resigned on July 18 in response to a group of former premiers asking the emperor to form a new government. Tojo is second from left._

harbour. Japanese resistance is typically ferocious; on the 25th, the 2nd Marine Division moves up the coastline to support the 4th Marines' action.

JULY 25–29

LAND WAR, _MARIANA ISLANDS_
Japanese forces on Guam launch a massive counterattack against the US 3rd Marine Division, but suffer appallingly with nearly 20,000 dead (the US loses 1744 men). On the 29th, the Orote Peninsula, which contains Guam's main airfield at the southern end of the US advance, is occupied.

JULY 26–31

STRATEGY, _US_
Top military chiefs, including General

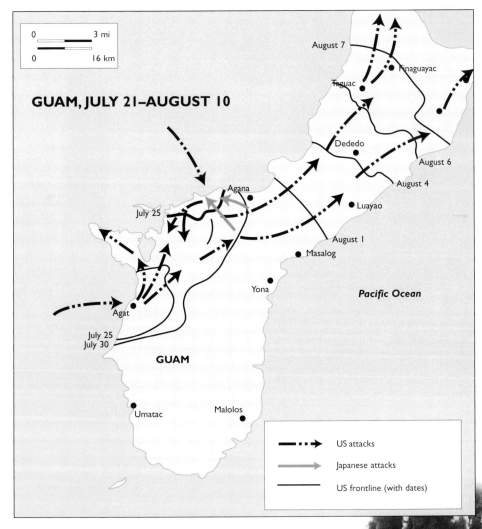

GUAM, JULY 21–AUGUST 10

August 7

Finaguayac

Taguac

Dededed

August 6

August 4

Agana

July 25

Luayao

August 1

Masalog

Yona

Pacific Ocean

Agat

July 25
July 30

GUAM

Umatac

Malolos

	US attacks
	Japanese attacks
	US frontline (with dates)

◄ *The conquest of Guam cost the Americans 1744 dead. Most of the Japanese garrison was wiped out, though some held out in the jungle until 1972.*

aviators with an air base suitable for long-range bombing missions against the Japanese homeland.

LAND WAR, *MARIANA ISLANDS*
US troops maintain a strong advance into Guam, occupying the towns of Utana, Pado, Pulan and Matte while US aircraft soften up Japanese resistance in the north of the island. Fighting is heavy, however, and to this date the US has already suffered 1022 dead and 4926 wounded. By August 2, half the island is in US possession.

AUGUST 3

LAND WAR, *BURMA*
The Japanese withdraw from Myitkyi-na, allowing British, US and Chinese forces to occupy the town, which sits at the head of a vital rail link running down into southern Burma. The capture of the town after an 11-week blockade is a vindication of General Stilwell and General Wingate's views on long-range penetration operations, although the two men had a frequently difficult relationship.

AUGUST 3–4

SEA WAR, *PACIFIC*
Strikes by US carrier aircraft and warships around the Bonin and Volcano Islands inflict heavy punishment on Japanese shipping. In a two-day onslaught, at least five destroyers, one cruiser, five cargo vessels and twelve other vessels are sunk.

AUGUST 5

LAND WAR, *MARIANA ISLANDS*
Fighting on Guam intensifies as US Marines and infantry push about 5km (3 miles) up the island against fanatical Japanese resistance.

MacArthur, Admiral King, Admiral Nimitz and Admiral Halsey, debate future military strategy for the Pacific war during a conference at Pearl Harbor. President Roosevelt is also present, and sides with MacArthur and Halsey, who argue that the Philippines should be taken before assaulting the Japanese homeland.

AUGUST 1

LAND WAR, *MARIANA ISLANDS*
Final Japanese resistance on Tinian crumbles after a well-executed but difficult US campaign, during which 9000 Japanese have been killed. Such was the excellence of the operation that Lieutenant-General Holland Smith later classes it as the finest amphibious operation of the Pacific war. Tinian provides US

▶ *A Japanese ammunition dump explodes on Tinian after being hit by a US bomb. US Marines have left their foxholes to watch the display.*

AUGUST 8

By this point in the fighting, the Japanese have lost more than 8100 men. Some 22,000 civilians are sheltering behind US lines.

AUSTRALIA, POWS
Japanese prisoners of war attempt a mass breakout from the Coworra POW camp, Sydney. Three

▼ *Chinese-crewed Stuart light tanks of a composite Chinese-American reconnaissance force move down a road in Burma in the aftermath of the Japanese withdrawal from Myitkyina.*

Australian guards are killed and 334 Japanese manage to escape, but Australian machine-gun fire kills 234 inmates and wounds 108 others.

AUGUST 8

SEA WAR, *PHILIPPINES*
The Japanese escort carrier *Oraka* is sunk by the submarine USS *Rasher* off the coast of northwest Luzon.

AUGUST 10

LAND WAR, *MARIANA ISLANDS*
Significant Japanese resistance on Guam collapses. Pockets of Japan-

▲ *Two US B-24 Liberators on their way to bomb Haha Jima in the Bonin Islands. The B-24 could carry up to 3629kg (8000lb) of bombs up to a range of over 3200km (2000 miles).*

ese soldiers continue the fight in isolation, one determined individual surrendering only in 1972. More than 10,000 Japanese soldiers have been killed compared with 1744 US troops. The occupation of Guam brings the Marianas campaign to a close. Now the island will be transformed into a bomber base for an offensive against the Japanese homeland by B-29 Superfortresses.

AUGUST 17–20

LAND WAR, *NEW GUINEA*
The US crushes resistance on Noemfoor and Biak Islands off the coast of New Guinea. While US paratroopers take over Noemfoor Island, other US troops make an amphibious landing at Wardo Bay on Biak to overcome final Japanese resistance. The Biak engagement alone has cost the Japanese Army 4700 dead.

AUGUST 22–24

SEA WAR, *PHILIPPINES*
US Marines prosecute a hard campaign against Japanese shipping around the Philippines. On the 22nd, Japan loses three frigates to US torpedoes with the destroyer *Asakaze* being sunk by the USS *Haddo* the next day. Retaliation comes on the 24th when the USS

▶ *Mopping up on Tinian. A US 75mm Pack Howitzer M8, lashed to rocks and crewed by Marines, opens fire on a cave containing Japanese soldiers.*

Harder is sunk off the coast of Luzon by Japanese depth charges.

AUGUST 27

LAND WAR, *BURMA*

Having undertaken several months of exhausting operations in northern Burma, the final groups of Chindits are evacuated to India.

AUGUST 31

AIR WAR, *BONIN/VOLCANO ISLANDS*

US carrier aircraft begin an intensive three-day bombing campaign against the Bonin and Volcano Islands. Japanese positions on these islands will suffer months of relentless bombardment.

SEPTEMBER 1

LAND WAR, *PHILIPPINES*

The US submarine *Narwhal* lands men and supplies on the eastern coast of Luzon in the Philippines, beginning the build-up of troops and logistics ready for the main Philippines offensive.

AIR WAR, *BONIN/VOLCANO ISLANDS*

The Japanese suffer heavy losses of material during the US navy's latest bombing offensive against the Bonin and Volcano Islands. A US Navy communiqué lists the damage as including around 50 Japanese aircraft destroyed either on the ground or in air combat; around 15 ships sunk; and extensive damage to shore installations, hangers and ammunition and fuel dumps.

SEPTEMBER 2

SEA WAR, *WAKE ISLAND*

A US naval task group consisting of one aircraft carrier, three cruisers and three destroyers bombards Japanese positions on Wake Island. The island is one of the most isolated outposts of the

▼ *Two M4 Shermans burn after being hit by Japanese anti-tank rounds on Guam. These are M4A1 versions of the Sherman, armed with a 75mm main gun and three machine guns.*

DECISIVE WEAPONS

THE US TORPEDO SCANDAL

For well over a year, the US Navy's submarine campaign against Japanese shipping in the Pacific was dogged by problems with its primary armament, the Mark XIV torpedo. There were two main problems: the depth-control mechanism of the torpedo was malfunctioning and directed the torpedo too far beneath its target (it ran at about 3–4m/10–12ft below set depth). Also, the torpedoes were equipped with the Mk VI magnetic influence exploder mechanism, an unreliable proximity detonator designed to explode the torpedo underneath a ship rather than on contact. The Germans had already abandoned magnetic detonators, finding that they were affected by magnetic variations at different longitudes and latitudes. US submarines would engage Japanese ships with spreads of four or five torpedoes at close range in good conditions, and none would explode despite being on target. No decision was taken until July 24, 1943, when Admiral Lockwood, a severe critic of the Mk XIV torpedo, finally ordered the deactivation of the Mk VI magnetic detonator and switched to contact detonators.

Unfortunately, problems continued. US submarines began reporting that, although the torpedoes were now striking the targets, many were

A US Tench class submarine on patrol in the Pacific.

failing to detonate. In a landmark incident, the submarine USS *Tinosa* fired 14 torpedoes at the Japanese tanker *Tonan Maru 3*, hitting the ship with at least half of them, none of which exploded. Subsequent tests found the detonator mechanism had a 70 percent failure rate if the torpedo struck at a 90-degree angle. Only when this problem was resolved in mid-1943 did US torpedoes become effective weapons.

Japanese Empire, and will be bypassed by the main US advance across the Pacific towards the Philippines and the Ryukyu Islands.

SEPTEMBER 6-8

AIR WAR, *CAROLINE ISLANDS*
A massive naval force, including 16 aircraft carriers and numerous cruisers and destroyers, attacks the Caroline Islands. Targets on Yap, Ulithi and the Palau Islands are struck. Although most of the Carolines are bypassed, the US hopes to establish a naval anchorage on Ulithi Atoll.

SEPTEMBER 8-11

AIR WAR, *PHILIPPINES*
US carrier aircraft from Vice-Admiral Mitscher's fast carrier task force make a three-day bombing attack against Japanese industrial, naval and aviation targets around Mindanao. Airfields at Del Monte, Valencia, Cagayan, Buayan and Davao are

targeted; and, on the first day of the attack, 60 Japanese aircraft are destroyed.

SEPTEMBER 11-16

POLITICS, *ALLIES*
US President Roosevelt and British Prime Minister Churchill meet together for their eighth war summit, known as the Octagon Conference. Although much of the discussion centres on the European theatre, the two leaders also establish grounds for Anglo-American cooperation in the production of the atomic bomb after the war. They also agree that the atomic bomb may be used operationally against Japan, following a warning.

SEPTEMBER 15

LAND WAR, *PALAU ISLANDS*
The 1st Marine Division under Major-General W.H. Rupertus is landed at

▶ *A US destroyer squadron in the Solomons. By mid-1944, US submarines and surface combatants were inflicting major losses on Japanese merchant shipping.*

Peleliu in the Palau Islands, as the US begins its operation to take the most westerly point in the Carolines. For the central Pacific forces, the Palau Islands are the last major island land mass before the Philippines. Taking the islands will provide a jumping-off point for landings on the east coast of the Philippines, as well as giving vital air bases to support Philippine operations. By nightfall on the 15th, the Marines have consolidated the beachhead and captured the airfield at the southern end of the island.

LAND WAR, *DUTCH EAST INDIES*
US troops are landed at Morotai in the eastern territories of the Dutch East Indies. Resistance is light, although the island is strategically important as it sits astride the entrance to the Celebes Sea, off the southern coast of the Philippines, and is a useful starting point for further operations into the Dutch East Indies.

▶ As well as American warships and submarines, Japanese shipping also had to contend with US air attacks. Here, a B-25 Mitchell strafes a Japanese warship.

SEPTEMBER 16

SEA WAR, *SOUTH CHINA SEA*
The Japanese escort carrier *Unyo* is sunk in the South China Sea by the submarine USS *Barb*. Although the US surface fleet has no presence in the South China Sea, US submarines are effectively interdicting Japanese supply convoys running between the Dutch East Indies and Japanese forces in Southeast Asia.

LAND WAR, *CAROLINE ISLANDS*
US Army troops of the 81st Infantry Division go ashore on Angaur Island, the southernmost of the Palau Islands. They establish a beachhead and advance inland against light resistance.

SEPTEMBER 17

LAND WAR, *CAROLINE ISLANDS*
US Marines advancing up Peleliu experience heavy opposition. Japanese forces lay down withering fire from mortars and artillery. Many of these weapons are subsequently destroyed by accurate aerial close-support strikes and naval counter-battery fire. US progress is steady, with the Marines capturing Asias and killing, to date, nearly 6000 Japanese soldiers.

SEPTEMBER 19

SEA WAR, *PACIFIC*
A typical US Navy communiqué (No 554) from this period reports 29 enemy cargo vessels sunk on this date.

LAND WAR, *CAROLINE ISLANDS*
US Marines capture Ngardololok and flush out most Japanese resistance on the eastern coast of Peleliu. They also take Peleliu airfield, capturing 77 fighter aircraft, 36 bombers and 4 transport planes, although most are badly damaged. However, the Japanese are deeply embedded in fortified positions and are well armed, and the advance is painfully slow. US estimates now put the Japanese death toll on Peleliu at 8792. On Angaur Island, most organized Japanese resistance has now collapsed, with 600 Japanese killed.

SEPTEMBER 20–24

AIR WAR, *PHILIPPINES*
Japanese aviators suffer terribly during a massive US air raid against Japanese ships and installations at Manila Bay, Subic Bay, Clark Field, Nichols Field and Cavite Naval Base. The US reports (on

the 24th) 169 Japanese aircraft shot down in aerial combat, and a further 188 destroyed on the ground. In addition, more than 50 Japanese transport and cargo vessels are sunk and a further 46 damaged.

SEPTEMBER 23

LAND WAR, *CAROLINE ISLANDS*
US Army troops are landed at Ulithi Atoll in the Carolines as part of the first stage of converting the atoll into a US naval base. The island was abandoned by the Japanese in August.

SEPTEMBER 29

SEA WAR, *PHILIPPINES*
The submarine USS *Narwhal*, always active in the waters of the Philippine Islands, picks up 81 Allied prisoners of war following the sinking of the Japanese vessel *Shinyo Maru*. More than 2000 Allied prisoners went down on the ship.

SEPTEMBER 30

LAND WAR, *PALAU ISLANDS*
Peleliu falls under US control, the US 1st Marine Division having fought metre by metre into the northernmost extremities of the island. Casualties have been appalling on both sides.
Almost all of the 10,600 Japanese soldiers, commanded by Colonel Nakasawa Kunio, have been killed, although 150 become POWs. The Marines have lost 1252 killed and 5274 wounded, a high toll for an island only 18km (11 miles) square. However, intense fighting continues in several pockets around the island, particularly on the aptly named "Bloody Nose Ridge" where Japanese survivors refuse to surrender.

▼ *The US invasion of Peleliu. To the left can be seen small amphibious vessels carrying US Marines, while in the centre the battleship USS* Pennsylvania *shells enemy positions.*

▲ *The US 1st Marine Division heads for Peleliu. The plan was to land on the western beaches, three regiments abreast.*

OCTOBER 2

STRATEGY, *BURMA*
Lord Louis Mountbatten, the supreme commander of SEAC, gives orders for an Allied offensive in Burma against Mandalay. Mountbatten has maintained pressure on the Japanese Fifteenth Army after its defeat in the Imphal offensive by ordering the campaign to continue during the monsoon season.

OCTOBER 4

LAND WAR, *PALAU ISLANDS*
US Marines and infantry battle to remove the final pockets of Japanese resistance in the Palau Islands. Although the islands were effectively secured in late September, the mopping-up operations have been costly. Between September 25 and October 5, 336 US soldiers have been killed and 1707 wounded. The Japanese death toll on Peleliu and Angaur has been put at 2755 in the same period.

OCTOBER 6

POLITICS, *CHINA*
General Joseph Stilwell is removed from his post as chief of staff to the

▲ *Two Sherman tanks assist the Marine advance on Peleliu. Taking the island cost 6526 US casualties, including 1252 killed.*

Chinese Nationalist leader Chiang Kai-shek. Relations between the two men had been frequently difficult, and suggestions by President Roosevelt that Stilwell take charge of all Chinese forces in the war were received badly by Chiang. Stilwell maintains control over Chinese troops in Burma and southern Yunnan Province.

OCTOBER 9

AIR WAR, *RYUKYU ISLANDS*
US carrier aircraft take the war close to the Japanese mainland in a major air attack against naval and shore in-

stallations in the Ryukyu Islands. In an attack that achieves complete surprise, 75 Japanese aircraft are destroyed on the ground and 14 shot down. Thirty-eight ships are either sunk or damaged.

STRATEGY, *PACIFIC*

Admiral Nimitz informs Lieutenant-General Holland M. Smith, the US Marine Corps commander in the Pacific, that his next target will be the island of Iwo Jima. Meanwhile, US forces in the Philippines move into the Lingayen Gulf.

SEA WAR, *PACIFIC*

US Navy surface vessels conduct a 15-hour bombardment of enemy shore installations on Marcus Island. The attack is the first surface ship bombardment directed at the island, which offers the

▶ *The reason for the US assault to capture Peleliu – the island's airstrip. The craters were caused by US naval gunfire.*

US a forward base in the western Pacific less than 1600km (1000 miles) from the Japanese mainland.

OCTOBER 10

LAND WAR, *PALAU ISLANDS*

The 1st Marine Division steadily flushes out Japanese defenders from Bloody Nose Ridge. Many of the Japanese are killed today when US fire detonates an ammunition dump held within the ridge's cave system.

AIR WAR, *NORTH BORNEO*

The oil refineries at Balikpapen are devastated by a US raid by B-24 bombers. Oil is one of Japan's most

threatened raw materials. Prior to the war it imported nearly 80 percent of its oil supplies, around 60 percent of that coming from the US. The Balikpapen refinery alone produces 40 percent of Japan's oil imports at this stage of the war.

OCTOBER 10–15

AIR WAR, *FORMOSA*

The US continues to demonstrate its air superiority in a massive five-day air campaign against the island of Formosa. During one action on the 13th, 124 Japanese fighters are shot down in a massive aerial dogfight. More than 95 further aircraft are destroyed on the ground. US losses are 22 aircraft. The total Japanese losses in the Formosa-Ryukyus-Luzon area at the end of the five days are 350 aircraft destroyed on the ground and 596 shot down. In addition, more than 70 Japanese cargo, oiler and escort ships are sunk.

◀ *Marines on the beach at Peleliu. It soon became apparent that the naval bombardment had not eliminated the enemy's heavy weapons positions.*

OCTOBER 15

AIR WAR, *MANILA BAY*
The Japanese attempt to break the US build-up against the Philippines. A large air strike is launched against a carrier task force in Manila Bay, but does insignificant damage while losing 30 aircraft to US fighters and anti-aircraft fire.

▼ **General Walter Krueger, the commander of the US Sixth Army.**

▲ *A Curtiss Helldiver, its arrestor hook down prior to a carrier landing, returns from a bombing mission against the island of Formosa in October.*

OCTOBER 20

LAND WAR, *PHILIPPINES*
The US invasion of the Philippines begins in earnest with X and XXIV Corps of the US Sixth Army under General Krueger. Troops go ashore along a 40km (25-mile) stretch of east Leyte coastline between Dulag and Tacloban, and initially experience only light opposition by soldiers of the Japanese Thirty-Fifth Army that occupies Leyte. On a strategic level, the landing at

Leyte threatens to split Japan's Philippine garrison in half, isolating Japanese forces on Mindanao in the south from those occupying Luzon.

OCTOBER 21

LAND WAR, *PALAU ISLANDS*
Final Japanese resistance on Angaur collapses, with 1300 Japanese military

▼ *The Japanese airfield at Karenko, Formosa, is hit by US bombs. This was one of the targets in a five-day campaign that destroyed 946 Japanese aircraft.*

KEY PERSONALITIES

LORD LOUIS MOUNTBATTEN

Lord Louis Mountbatten (1900–79) was appointed C-in-C SEAC in August 1943 during the Quebec Conference, at the same time being promoted to admiral (the youngest in the history of the Royal Navy). Mountbatten was known for his vanity and desire for power, which at times led to poor military judgement. Other military leaders frequently overrode his operational decisions in the Far East, but he certainly made significant improvements to British campaigning in Burma. The three cornerstones of his Burma policy were morale, monsoon and malaria. He raised Allied morale in Burma mainly through capitalizing on the victories at Imphal and Kohima, promoting the idea that Japanese invincibility was a myth. "Monsoon" refers to his policy of maintaining the Allied campaign through the five-month monsoon season to enforce the Japanese collapse. As a corollary, he created the Medical Advisory Division to tackle tropical diseases such as malaria, which cost the Allies 120 men for every single battle casualty. By 1945, only 13 percent of Allied casualties were illness related.

Such policies aided the British victory in Burma, and Mountbatten had further distinguishing moments in the Pacific war. He knew

about the planned use of the atomic bomb in 1945, and received the surrender of more than 600,000 Japanese troops at Singapore on September 12, 1945. When taking the Japanese surrender, he insisted on Japanese officers giving up their swords to induce loss of face.

dead on the small island. US losses are 264 fatalities.

LAND WAR, *PHILIPPINES*

Japanese resistance to the Leyte landings starts to thicken with an intensive Japanese counterattack. It is beaten off with 600 Japanese killed, but 21,500 Japanese soldiers remain on Leyte, most of them taking up positions inland. In total, there are 225,000 Japanese soldiers in the Philippines under the command of General Yamashita.

OCTOBER 22

SEA WAR, *LEYTE GULF*

The whole Japanese Combined Fleet sets sail in "Operation Sho", an attempt to crush the Allied landings in the southern Philippines. The operation is divided into two strikes approaching from opposite directions. From the west, sailing from British North Borneo, is the First Striking Force under Vice-Admiral Kurita. This itself is split into two parts. Kurita's own unit (known to the US as "Centre Force") consists of five battleships, twelve cruisers and fifteen destroyers, and is sailing to the northeast where it intends to move through the Subuyan Sea and attack the US Seventh Fleet from the north. At the same time, a second group ("Southern Force") under Vice-Admiral Nishimura and Vice-Admiral Shima, consisting of two battleships, four cruisers and eight destroyers, intends to attack the Leyte landings from the south through the Surigao Strait.

As these two forces sail from Borneo, approaching the Philippines from the north is the Carrier Decoy Force under Ozawa, featuring four carriers, two battleships, four cruisers and eight destroyers. Its mission is to draw the US Third Fleet away from Leyte so

◀ *US troops land at Tacloban in the Philippines. The US amphibious force for the invasion was very large, comprising 738 ships of the US Navy's Third Fleet.*

▲ A deck hand rushes to release the arrestor hook of a Grumman Avenger that has just landed on a US aircraft carrier at the Battle of Leyte Gulf.

that Kurita's vessels can destroy the American landings.

The scene is set for the Battle of Leyte Gulf. The name "Sho" given to the Japanese operation means "victory", a testimony to the importance of the action for the battle-scarred Japanese Imperial Navy.

▼ The 14in guns of the USS Pennsylvania open fire against enemy positions at Leyte Gulf. During the naval battle the ship fired a total of 866 14in rounds.

OCTOBER 23

SEA WAR, *LEYTE GULF*
Operation Sho suffers its first casualties and loses the element of surprise. Two US submarines off Palawan Island spot the ships of Kurita's First Striking Force and sink the cruisers *Atago* and *Maya*. The Japanese positions are reported to the US carrier units of Task Force 38, US Third Fleet, which set sail to intercept Japanese vessels in the Sibuyan Sea.

OCTOBER 24

SEA WAR, *LEYTE GULF*
The Battle of Leyte Gulf begins in earnest. Vice-Admiral Mitscher's carrier aircraft launch a massive air assault on Kurita's Centre Force and Nishimura/Shima's Southern Force, while Japanese aircraft reply with their own strikes against US shipping around the Philippines. The US suffers numerous ships damaged, including the light carrier USS *Princeton* (she later sinks

▲ The Japanese battleship **Nagato** (foreground) and a cruiser under air attack at Leyte Gulf. **Nagato** survived the battle, and indeed the war.

following magazine fires), the light cruiser USS *Birmingham* and five destroyers. Japanese losses, however, are more severe. The massive battleship *Musashi* – the largest warship ever built, and sister ship of the mighty *Yamato* – is bombed and torpedoed to the bottom of the ocean, although it takes 19 torpedoes and 17 bombs to do so. Other losses include the destroyer *Wakaba*. Towards the end of the day, Kurita's Centre Force turns northwards as if retreating, but later switches back and heads for the San Bernardino Strait, north of Leyte.

OCTOBER 24–25

SEA WAR, *LEYTE GULF*
The Japanese Southern Force is engaged in the night by the warships of Task Group 77. A

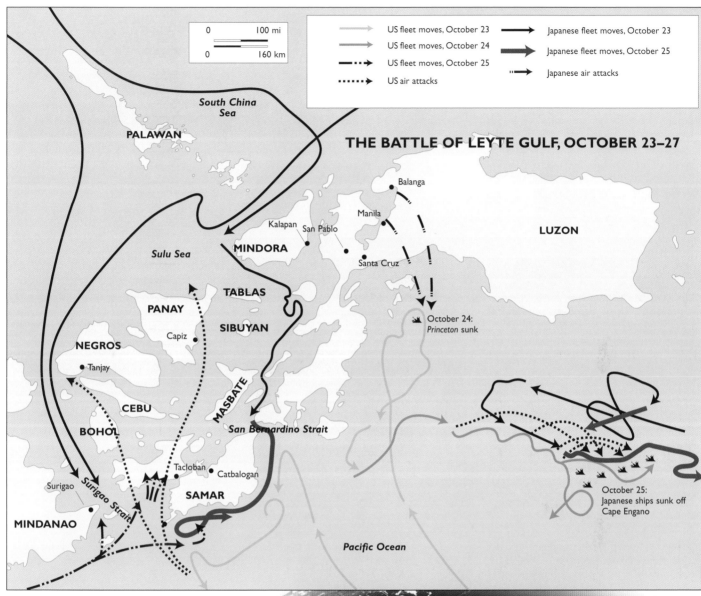

THE BATTLE OF LEYTE GULF, OCTOBER 23–27

Map legend:
- US fleet moves, October 23
- US fleet moves, October 24
- US fleet moves, October 25
- US air attacks
- Japanese fleet moves, October 23
- Japanese fleet moves, October 25
- Japanese air attacks

South China Sea

PALAWAN

Balanga

Sulu Sea

Kalapan • San Pablo • Manila

MINDORA

Santa Cruz

LUZON

October 24: *Princeton* sunk

TABLAS

PANAY

SIBUYAN

Capiz •

NEGROS

• Tanjay

MASBATE

CEBU

San Bernardino Strait

BOHOL

Tacloban • Catbalogan

Surigao • Surigao Strait

SAMAR

MINDANAO

October 25: Japanese ships sunk off Cape Engano

Pacific Ocean

▲ The Battle of Leyte Gulf was the last great naval engagement of the Pacific war, and signalled the end of the Japanese Navy's effectiveness.

masterful torpedo run by US destroyers in the early hours of the 25th, followed by a huge gun barrage from cruisers and battleships, devastates Nishimura's entire force (two battleships, one heavy cruiser and four destroyers) in less than two hours, only one destroyer surviving. Shima's unit suffers two cruisers sunk and a battleship damaged, and begins to retreat.

OCTOBER 25

SEA WAR, *LEYTE GULF*

US Task Force 38 heads northwards to intercept Ozawa's carrier force, believing the Japanese Centre and Southern Forces to be in retreat. However,

▶ The Japanese carrier **Zuiho** under attack during the battle off Cape Engano on October 25.

OCTOBER 26

Kurita's Centre Force has turned back and attacks a US escort carrier group known as TG 77.4.3. "Taffy 3", under Rear-Admiral Sprague, is heavily out-numbered and outgunned by the Japanese force, which includes four battleships. Despite suffering severe damage, including three destroyers and two escort carriers sunk (the USS *St Lo* is sunk later that day by a suicide air-craft in a kamikaze strike), most of TG 77.4.3 manages to escape. Carrier aircraft sink the Japanese cruisers *Kumano*, *Chokai* and *Chikuma*. Kurita withdraws, believing he is engaging the bulk of Task Force 38 – which is actually heading north.

Task Force 38 finds and engages Ozawa's Carrier Decoy Force with overwhelming airpower around first light on the morning of the 25th. The Japanese carriers are chronically de-pleted of aircraft, and in a day of relent-less bombardment all four carriers are sunk (*Zuikaku*, *Zuiho*, *Chitose* and *Chiyoda*) plus five other warships.

OCTOBER 26
SEA WAR, *LEYTE GULF*
The Battle of Leyte Gulf ends in a mas-sive US victory. Several more Japanese cruisers and destroyers are sunk today by pursuing US aircraft. The final tally of Japanese shipping sunk is four air-craft carriers, three battleships, ten cruisers, eleven destroyers and one submarine, with most other Japanese ships severely damaged. In addition, 10,000 sailors and 500 aircraft are also lost. The Battle of Leyte Gulf marks the undeniable collapse of Japanese naval power in the Pacific. From this point on, the suicide air strikes that had their inauguration over Leyte Gulf become an increasing feature of a desperate Japanese military that can no longer oppose the mighty US Navy.

OCTOBER 31
AIR WAR, *PACIFIC*
US Navy communiqué No 170 makes an assessment of Japanese air losses be-tween August 30, 1944 and today's date. The report is compiled by the Third and Seventh Carrier Fleets. Be-tween the two dates, the US lost 300 aircraft, but the Japanese suffered a cat-astrophic 2594 aircraft losses – 1462 shot down and 1132 destroyed on the ground. Even allowing for some pilot exaggeration, it is clear that the Japan-ese Air Force is utterly outclassed and outnumbered in the Pacific war.

STRATEGY AND TACTICS

AERIAL KAMIKAZE ATTACKS
On October 19, 1944, Vice-Admiral Onishi Takijino ordered the formation of a kamikaze force to intercept Allied shipping around the Philippines, officially termed Tokubetsu Koge-ki Tai (Special Attack Group). The term kamikaze literally means "divine wind", refer-ring to the typhoons that destroyed Kublai Khan's fleets in 1274 and 1281, saving Japan from a Mongol invasion. Kamikaze pilots were all volunteers, usually very young, who were given the most rudimentary flying training and piloted old or battle-repaired aircraft, usually with only enough fuel to reach their attack destination. Fed on a

Bushido ideology of death being preferable to defeat, they accepted that to return from a kamikaze mission invited disgrace.

The kamikaze pilots inflicted a horrifying experience on the sailors and soldiers of the US Pacific Fleet. Although hundreds of suicide aircraft were shot down before reaching their targets (the pilots did not have experience of air combat, and could not fly low beneath US radar), thousands still got through. The first mass attack of 55 kamikaze aircraft came on October 23–26, 1944, around Leyte, sinking five ships (in-cluding the carrier USS *St Lo*) and damaging 40 others, 23 severely. In April 1945, the kamikaze attacks reached a frenzied pitch off Okinawa. Around 1900 suicide aircraft attacked in "kikusui" (floating chrysanthe-mum) waves of up to 320 planes at a time. Thirty-six US ships were sunk, and three hundred and sixty-eight damaged. In total, Japan lost 5000 pilots in suicide actions dur-ing the war.

◀ *A group of kamikaze pilots are given a ceremonial cup of sake prior to their one-way mission.*

NOVEMBER 1
AIR WAR, *US*
As an indicator of Japanese despera-tion, 9000 balloons carrying explo-sive charges are released from the Japanese mainland by army forces. The balloons are meant to cross the Pacific Ocean on prevailing winds and detonate in the US. Few balloons make the journey successfully.
AIR WAR, *LEYTE GULF*
Kamikaze attacks intensify around Leyte Gulf. Today, the destroyer USS *Abner Road* is sunk and the destroyers USS *Anderson*, USS *Claxton* and USS *Ammen* are badly damaged by suicide attacks. Dive-bombers dam-age two other destroyers.

NOVEMBER 2
LAND WAR, *PALAU ISLANDS*
Japanese troops are still holding out on Mount Umurbrogol, causing heavy casualties among US forces.

▶ *Fulfiling a pledge he made nearly three years earlier, General Douglas MacArthur (second from left) returns to the Philippines on October 20, 1944.*

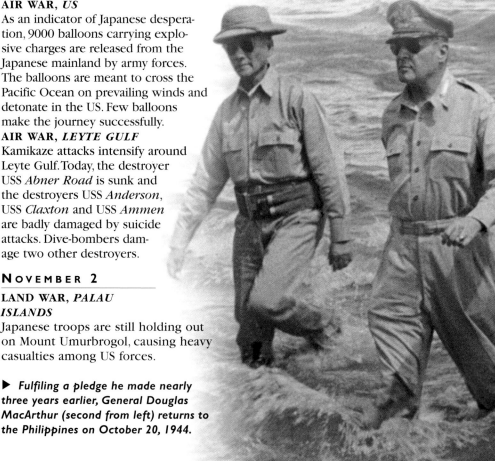

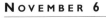

◄ *The escort carrier USS* St Lo *after being hit by a kamikaze attack on October 25 at Leyte. She later sunk.*

NOVEMBER 3

POLITICS, *PACIFIC*

Admiral Nimitz announces that Rear-Admiral Walden L. Ainsworth is now Commander, Cruisers, and Commander, Destroyers, Pacific Fleet. As a veteran of every major naval action in the south Pacific area since December 1942, Ainsworth replaces Rear-Admiral James L. Kauffman.

NOVEMBER 5

AIR WAR, *SINGAPORE*

Fifty-three B-29 bombers from the Twentieth US Army Air Force make a round trip of 5950km (3700 miles) from Calcutta to bomb coastal installations around Singapore and the Pangkalan Brandon oil refinery on the island of Sumatra.

NOVEMBER 2–3

AIR WAR, *PACIFIC*

The Japanese attempt to reduce enemy airpower by attacking US airstrips at Tacloban, Leyte, and at Saipan and Tinian in the Mariana Islands. The attacks are extremely costly for the Japanese, many of the aircraft being brought down by accurate anti-aircraft fire.

NOVEMBER 6

AIR WAR, *LUZON*

US Hellcat fighters, Avenger torpedo planes and Helldiver dive-bombers attack Japanese airfields and shipping installations throughout southern Luzon. A heavy dogfight results after 80 Japanese fighters intercept the US force over

KEY PERSONALITIES

ADMIRAL HALSEY

Admiral William Frederick Halsey (1882–1959), an expert in the use of destroyers in the early 1930s, was attracted to the new technology and theory surrounding naval airpower during the prewar years. Indeed in 1935, at the age of 52, he qualified as a pilot. He became one of the US Navy's most talented air power commanders, and was in command of the US Pacific Fleet's airpower when war broke out. In the difficult early months of the war, his aggressive counterstrikes, including the Doolittle Raid on April 18, 1942, led the press to nickname him "Bull" Halsey. Though he missed the Battle of Midway through ill health, he was given tactical command in the south Pacific in 1943, specifically to give more belligerence to the efforts of the naval leadership. As much as his bravery and belligerence was appreciated by the common soldier, his aggressive tendencies occasionally led him to run dangerous risks – most notably at the Battle of Leyte Gulf. His penchant for attacking the Japanese whenever possible caused him to fall for the Japanese attempt to lure him away from protecting MacArthur's men landing on Leyte. Had it not have been for mistakes on the Japanese side, then total disaster could have befallen the US forces because of his actions. Nonetheless, he alternated command of the Pacific Fleet with Admiral Spruance until the end of the war.

▲ *A Japanese merchant ship carrying ammunition explodes following a direct hit on its cargo from a US dive-bomber.*

Clark Field. Fifty-eight of the Japanese aircraft are shot down in the incident, and twenty-five more later that day. More than 100 Japanese aircraft are destroyed on the ground; by November 7, that figure has risen to 327. One heavy cruiser is left sinking in Manila harbour, and ten other ships are either sunk or damaged.

November 7

ESPIONAGE, *TOKYO*
The Soviet spy Richard Sorge is executed in Tokyo, having been held in prison for three years.

LAND WAR, *NORTHERN BURMA*
The Chinese 22nd Division crosses the Irrawaddy River near Shwegu. The 22nd Division is part of a major thrust by Allied units to encircle the Japanese Thirty-Third Army in its positions between Lashio and Mogok. Although the advance has been hampered by politics (General Stilwell having lost his position as Chiang Kai-shek's chief of staff and Commander of the Northern Area Combat Command), it is steadily making progress.

November 7–8

LAND WAR, *PALAU ISLANDS*
A Japanese force of around 200 men land on Ngeregong Island, northeast of Peleliu in the Palau Group. Although the island was previously occupied by a small unit of US Marines, it is now deserted. However, the US responds vigorously, imposing a naval blockade on the Denges Passage – the sea route taken by the Japanese to the island – before pounding the island with naval and aerial attacks.

◄ *When the Japanese tried to supply their troops fighting on Letye, the convoy was intercepted at Ormoc Bay. Here, a B-25 attacks a destroyer in the bay.*

down the Kabaw Valley out on to the western side of the Pondaung Range. Its objective is to reach Pakokku to the southwest of Mandalay, cutting off forces of the Japanese Fifteenth Army as Britain's XXXIII Corps drives down on Mandalay from the north.

NOVEMBER 10

AIR WAR, *PHILIPPINES*
The Japanese attempt to run a 10-ship supply convoy through to Japanese troops on Leyte, but it is intercepted by US Third Fleet carrier aircraft just outside Ormoc Bay. The convoy is massacred, with nine of the ships (four transports and five destroyers) being sunk and the remaining destroyer badly damaged. Thirteen of the twenty Japanese aircraft providing air cover for the convoy are shot down.

LAND WAR, *CHINA*
The Japanese offensive into southern China makes further progress, capturing the US air bases at Kweilin and Liuchow in Kwangsi Province.

NOVEMBER 11

SEA WAR, *JAPAN*
The Japanese launch the aircraft carrier *Shinano*, a 69,148-tonne (68,059-ton)

vessel that is supposedly bomb-proof owing to a steel and concrete construction. She is not torpedo-proof, however, and on November 29 she is sunk by the submarine USS *Archerfish*.

NOVEMBER 12

AIR WAR, *MANILA BAY*
US carrier aircraft damage one light cruiser and two destroyers in air raids over Manila Bay. The destroyers are devastated in massive magazine explosions caused by accurate bomb and torpedo hits.

▼ *The Japanese provided air cover for supply convoys to Leyte, but the aircraft were shot out of the skies. The last moments of this Zero were caught on film.*

NOVEMBER 8

LAND WAR, *BURMA*
Troops of the 7th and 17th Indian Divisions take Fort White, an important point on the Imphal–Kalemyo road near Tiddim. The British IV Corps is pushing directly south of Imphal

◄ *Men of the 7th Indian Division advancing to Fort White, northern Burma, which they captured on November 8. The fort was originally a British outpost.*

KEY MOMENTS

RICHARD SORGE AND THE TOKYO SPY RING

Richard Sorge (1895–1944) was one of the most influential spies of the war. Although born in Baku, Azerbaijan, in 1895, Sorge was raised in Germany where he became active in his youth in the Communist Party. He fled to Moscow in 1920 following German anti-communist activities, and there was recruited into Soviet intelligence. He returned to Germany in 1921, and worked his way up through civil service positions. In the 1930s, he received postings to China, then went to Japan to work as a newspaper correspondent and later as press attaché to the German Embassy. It was from there that Sorge did the bulk of his spying work, and he recruited a network of individuals (code-named "Ramsay") to gather his intelligence from many sources. One of them, Ozaki Hotsumi, was a senior adviser to the Japanese prime minister.

During World War II, Sorge provided some valuable intelligence to the Soviets, including the date of the German invasion of Russia, although Stalin ignored this intelligence, and that Japan would not attack the USSR in Siberia in 1941. Regarding the Pacific theatre, Sorge discovered that Japan was planning to attack the US and Allied interests in Southeast Asia and the Pacific. The last message sent read: "Japanese carrier force attacking United States Navy at Pearl Harbor, probably dawn, November 6".

In September 1941, Japanese intelligence officers started to unravel the Tokyo spy ring following routine operations – on October 18, Sorge was finally arrested. He was tortured for six days before confessing. The next three years were spent in prison, during which time he had to write a 50,000-word report detailing his espionage activities. On November 7, 1944, in Sugamo prison, he was marched into the courtyard and hanged.

NOVEMBER 13

LAND WAR, *PALAU ISLANDS*
The last elements of Japanese resistance on Bloody Ridge are wiped out.

NOVEMBER 13-14

SEA WAR, *MANILA BAY*
The Japanese cruiser *Kiso* is sunk and five destroyers severely damaged during a raid on Manila Bay by US aircraft.

NOVEMBER 14

LAND WAR, PALAU ISLANDS
Troops of the 81st Infantry Division re-occupy Ngeregong. They meet no Japanese resistance, which has been crushed by air and naval actions.

NOVEMBER 17

SEA WAR, *PACIFIC*
The Japanese escort carrier *Shinyo* is sunk by the submarine USS *Spadefish* in the Yellow Sea. The first torpedo out of four hit the stern, instantly disabling the turbo-electric motors and stopping the carrier. The impact detonated the poorly protected fuel tanks and caused a tremendous explosion and fire. Other hits followed, and *Shinyo* becomes a blazing inferno, begins to list rapidly to starboard and settle aft. More than 700 of her crew of 900 are killed. At this stage of the Pacific campaign, the US submarine war has been boosted by increasing numbers of British submarines being

▲ USS Intrepid *under kamikaze attack off Luzon in late November. Two Japanese aircraft hit the aircraft carrier, forcing her to return to the US for repairs.*

deployed from the Atlantic and Mediterranean to the Pacific. An Admiralty statement on November 15 reveals that British submarines have sunk 69 Japanese vessels in five days.

NOVEMBER 19

LAND WAR, *BURMA*
The British Fourteenth Army under General William Slim begins a major operation to capitalize on the Japanese defeat at Imphal and Kohima, and hopefully clear the Japanese from Burma. "Operation Extended Capital" involves the British IV Corps around Sittaung and XXXIII Corps at Mawlaik making the push across the Chindwin River, recapturing Mandalay, Rangoon and Meiktila, and destroying General Shihachi Kata-

mura's Japanese Fifteenth Army in the process. Initial objectives include the Japanese airfields at Yeu and Shwebo, the capture of which will help efficient re-supply by air. To the north of British operations, Chinese and US troops formerly under the command of General Stilwell are pushing down towards Indaw.

NOVEMBER 21

SEA WAR, *WESTERN PACIFIC*
The Japanese battleship *Kongo* is sunk by the submarine USS *Sealion* in the

▼ A crowd of engineers and ground crew personnel watch a US B-29 Superfortress take off from the airstrip on Saipan to begin the first B-29 mission against Tokyo.

▲ *A British IV Corps 25-pounder in action against Japanese forces in Pinwe, Burma. The town was a railway centre and was doggedly defended by the Japanese.*

Formosa Strait. *Kongo* was actually built in England as a battlecruiser, and delivered to the Japanese in 1913. The ship was modernized in 1936–37 to gain battleship status.

NOVEMBER 24

STRATEGIC BOMBING, *TOKYO*
The USAAF launches its first long-range bombing mission on Tokyo using 111 B-29 Superfortress bombers. However, only 24 manage to drop their bombs on target.

NOVEMBER 25

KAMIKAZE, *PHILIPPINES*
Around Luzon, Japanese kamikaze aircraft severely damage four US aircraft carriers: USS *Essex*, USS *Intrepid*, USS *Hancock* and USS *Cabot*. However, Japanese shipping also has a bad day, with the heavy cruiser *Kumano* and the cruiser *Yasoshima* being sunk by US carrier aircraft.

NOVEMBER 29

AIR WAR, *IWO JIMA*
US B-24 Liberator and B-25 Mitchell bombers continue the softening up of Iwo Jima, concentrating their attacks against airfields.

NOVEMBER 30

LAND WAR, *CHINA*
As the Japanese offensive in southern China gains ground, Chiang Kai-shek

▲ *Japanese shipping under attack from US carrier aircraft in Manila Bay at the end of November.*

withdraws his 22nd and 38th Divisions from Burma and re-deploys them around Kunming.

DECEMBER 4

LAND WAR, *BURMA*
The British Fourteenth Army establishes three bridgeheads on the Chindwin River as part of Operation Extended Capital. From here, XXXIII Corps will drive southeast towards Schewbo and

Mandalay in a two-pronged attack; while, in the south, IV Corps will push down the Kabbaw Valley aiming towards Tilin and Pakokku, roughly 160km (100 miles) southwest of Mandalay itself. In the far north, the 19th Indian Division begins a decoy offensive out from Sittaung towards Indaw.

DECEMBER 6

AIR WAR, *MARIANA ISLANDS*

A US B-29 Superfortress is destroyed and two others damaged during an early morning air raid by ten Japanese Betty bombers. Six of the attackers are shot down by anti-aircraft fire.

DECEMBER 8

AIR WAR, *IWO JIMA*

The US Air Force begins one of the most intensive aerial campaigns of World War II, a 72-day bombardment of Iwo Jima by B-24 and B-25 bombers. The bombardment is preparation for the US invasion of Iwo Jima sched-

▶ *The one bright spot for Tokyo in late 1944 was southern China, where its offensive made good progress. Here, a Japanese river boat searches for the enemy.*

▲ *Admiral Nimitz (left) was made Commander-in-Chief of the US Pacific Fleet and Pacific Ocean Areas at the end of 1944. On his left is Admiral Spruance.*

uled for mid-February 1945, although the island has already sustained heavy air attacks against its shipping and shore installations.

LOGISTICS, *PACIFIC*

The commander of the US Third Fleet, Admiral William F. Halsey, proudly announces the achievements of US oiling vessels in maintaining US Navy and air operations in the Pacific. During September and October 1944, oilers had supplied the carrier task force with more than one hundred million gallons of fuel, enough to run every car in every major US city for an entire year.

DECEMBER 10

LAND WAR, *PHILIPPINES*

US troops on Leyte take the main Japanese supply base at Ormoc on the west coast of the island, the US 7th and 77th Divisions having made an amphibious landing in the area three days earlier. The US action on Leyte has followed three broad lines of advance:

▲ *A US destroyer opens fire during the invasion of Mindoro. Naval support for the invasion included six escort carriers, three battleships and six cruisers.*

through the north of Leyte up the Leyte Valley; across the centre towards Ormoc then northwest up the Ormoc Valley; and directly southwards following the coastlines. Fighting is heavy, but the US soldiers are making steady progress. The plight of Suzuki's Thirty-Fifth Army on Leyte is desperate, especially now the fall of Ormoc has cut his troops off from naval resupply.

LAND WAR, *CHINA*
The Ichi-Go offensive brings the Japanese victories not experienced elsewhere in the Far East. Throughout November, Japanese forces have occupied southern China up to the borders of French Indochina. Today, the advancing armies meet up with Japan's Indochinese garrison forces, thus providing a new supply route for the offensive through the Indochina to China rail link, which stretches across the entire length of China up into Mongolia.

DECEMBER 13

SEA WAR, *PHILIPPINES*
US shipping around the Philippines suffers increased suicide attacks. Today, the cruiser USS *Nashville* and the destroyer USS *Haraden* are both damaged by kamikaze aircraft.

DECEMBER 15

LAND WAR, *BURMA*
British troops in the north of Operation Extended Capital meet up with General Stilwell's Chinese and US

▲ *The crew of a US Navy Patrol Craft Escort vessel scans the sky for enemy aircraft following a kamikaze attack on the ship behind. Mindoro, December 15.*

forces at Banmauk, having captured Bhamo. This combined group now focuses directly southwards towards Shwebo and Mandalay, and begins an

DECEMBER 16

▶ *A line of B-29s waits to take off. The first high-altitude daylight raids on Tokyo were not a success. B-29s bombing at night at low level were more effective.*

advance down the Myitkyina–Mandalay railway and the Irrawaddy River.

LAND WAR, *PHILIPPINES*
The US invasion of the Philippines spreads as the US 24th Division is landed on the island of Mindoro, just off the southwest coast of Luzon. Japanese resistance amounts to little, the Mindoro garrison numbering just 100 men. Mindoro features four abandoned airfields that will enable the Allies to extend fighter air cover to the Lingayen Gulf and Manila Bay.

AIR WAR, *PHILIPPINES*
US carrier aircraft destroy 225 Japanese aircraft on and over Luzon in three separate attacks. Japanese aircraft production has increased dramatically during 1944. In 1943, Japan produced 7147 fighters and 4189 bombers. By the end of 1944, that figure has risen to 13,811 fighters and 5100 bombers. The signifi-

cant increase in fighter, rather than bomber, production indicates that air defence rather than offensive air action is the Japanese priority. However, the US is now destroying Japanese aircraft faster than they can be built.

DECEMBER 16

POLITICS, *PACIFIC*
Douglas MacArthur is promoted to the rank of five-star general in recognition of his handling of the US campaign in the south Pacific.

AIR WAR, *SUMATRA*
British carrier aircraft bombard Japanese oil installations at Belawan-Deli.

DECEMBER 18

SEA WAR, *PHILIPPINES*
The US Navy suffers heavy losses in shipping and manpower after a typhoon hits the seas off the Philippines. The destroyers USS *Hull*, USS *Monghan* and USS *Spence* are sunk and 22 other ships damaged in the storm, while 150 aircraft are blown off

▼ *Troops of the Japanese Fourteenth Area Army in the Philippines, which was led by Lieutenant-General Tomoyuki Yamashita.*

▲ A British pontoon bridge across the River Chindwin, Burma, which Slim's Fourteenth Army had reached in November and had crossed by December.

▼ Troops of the British 36th Division in Burma. By the end of 1944 the division was across the Irrawaddy, and was mopping up enemy troops falling back to the River Shweli at Myitson.

the decks of carriers into the sea. More than 750 sailors drown.

DECEMBER 19

POLITICS, *US*
Admiral Nimitz, C-in-C of the US Pacific Fleet and Pacific Ocean Areas, is promoted to the rank of Fleet Admiral of the US Navy.

SEA WAR, *EAST CHINA SEA*
The submarine USS *Redfish* sinks the Japanese carrier *Unryu*.

DECEMBER 21–22

KAMIKAZE, *PHILIPPINES*
Two more US destroyers, USS *Foote* and USS *Bryant*, are damaged by Japanese kamikaze air raids off Mindoro.

DECEMBER 23

LAND WAR, *BURMA*
The 74th Brigade of the 25th Indian Division takes Donbaik on the approaches to Akyab Island. Meanwhile, the 81st and 82nd West African Divisions have advanced southeast to Muohaung, isolating Akyab from the bulk of the Japanese Twenty-Eighth Army.

DECEMBER 25

LAND WAR, *PHILIPPINES*
Organized Japanese resistance on Leyte finally crumbles, the Japanese having lost 70,000 men while the Americans suffered 15,584 casualties.

DECEMBER 26

SEA WAR, *PHILIPPINES*
A Japanese naval force bombards US positions on Mindoro. The US naval retaliation sinks the destroyer *Kiyoshimo*.

DECEMBER 27

SEA WAR, *PACIFIC*
US submarines report the sinking of 27 Japanese vessels throughout Pacific and Far Eastern waters. The Japanese ships sunk include an aircraft carrier, a cruiser and a destroyer. The balance are escort and cargo vessels.

1945

The last year of the Pacific war saw heavy fighting on all fronts. Though US war production far outstripped that of Japan, overwhelming superiority in ships, aircraft and tanks did not translate into easy victories. On Iwo Jima and Okinawa US forces suffered heavy losses, which boded ill for the invasion of Japan itself. The Americans thus dropped atomic bombs on Japan to hasten the end of the war.

▲ *Ships of the US fleet assembled off Luzon. Landing craft heading for shore can be seen in the bottom of the photograph.*

JANUARY 1

LAND WAR, *CAROLINE ISLANDS*
US Army forces are landed on Fais Island in the Carolines with the objective of capturing and destroying a Japanese radio station.

JANUARY 2–8

LAND WAR, *PHILIPPINES*
The US high command in the Philippines re-deploys the Sixth Army under General Krueger from Leyte to positions off Lingayen Gulf on Luzon.

▼ *A kamikaze aircraft dives towards the light cruiser USS* Columbia *during the Lingayen Gulf invasion on January 6, 1945. The ship was hit by two kamikaze aircraft and severely damaged.*

JANUARY 3

KAMIKAZE, *LUZON*
The US escort carrier USS *Ommaney Bay* is severely damaged by a Japanese suicide aircraft. It is later scuttled.

JANUARY 4

LAND WAR, *BURMA*
Akyab Island off the west coast of Burma, previously the objective of many failed Allied offensives, is taken by British troops in an unopposed amphibious landing. While the Allies in central Burma have been making progress towards Mandalay, XV Corps is pursuing "Operation Talon", driving farther down into the Arakan and aiming for the port of Rangoon.

AIR WAR, *DUTCH EAST INDIES*
British carrier aircraft strike Japanese-controlled oil refineries at Pankalan.

JANUARY 4–9

KAMIKAZE, *LUZON*
The Japanese open a relentless aerial kamikaze campaign against US shipping around Luzon. From January 5–9 alone, the US Navy suffers at least 30 hits on shipping by suicide aircraft. In total, more than 1000 Allied personnel are killed. The confusion and turmoil in the waters around Luzon is evident by the high number of collisions between US vessels reported.

JANUARY 2–3

AIR WAR, *RYUKYU ISLANDS*
A total of 111 Japanese aircraft are destroyed on and above Formosa and the Ryukyu Islands following an attack by carrier aircraft of the US Third Fleet. Another 220 aircraft are damaged.

▼ *British M4 Sherman medium tanks and infantry on the island of Akyab following their unopposed landing on January 4.*

▲ *Indian troops of XV Corps wade across to Akyab Island in early January. The British occupied the island two days after the Japanese had evacuated it.*

JANUARY 5

LAND WAR, *BURMA*
The British 2nd Division takes the vital airfields at Yeu and Shwebo to the northwest of Mandalay.

JANUARY 5

AIR/SEA WAR, *BONIN ISLANDS*
A combined US Force of cruisers, destroyers and carrier aircraft bombard shipping and installations on Chichi Jima and Haha Jima in the Bonin Islands.

JANUARY 9

LAND WAR, *PHILIPPINES*
At 09:30 hours, the US Sixth Army opens the campaign to take Luzon. It lands the 6th and 43rd Divisions of I Corps and the 337th and 40th Divisions of XIV Corps in Lingayen Gulf at positions between Lingayen and Damortis. Japanese resistance at the beachheads is light – General Yamashita of the Fourteenth Army has pulled his troops back from the beachhead to conserve them for later combat.

JANUARY 10

LAND WAR, *BURMA*
Troops of the 28th East African Brigade, part of the British IV Corps, advance towards Pakkoku, taking Gangaw in the Kabaw Valley.

▼ *The light cruiser USS Louisville under kamikaze attack off Luzon in early January. Despite being hit twice, she remained on station to support the invasion.*

JANUARY 11

LAND WAR, *BURMA*
The British 19th Division comes under heavy counterattack from the Japanese Thirty-Third Army as it attempts to cross the Irrawaddy River at Thabeikkyin and establish a bridgehead. Thabeikkyin is only 100km (60 miles) north of Mandalay, and fighting is extremely fierce – Japanese troops make mass assaults with fixed bayonets. But

▲ *Indian Punjabi troops of the British Fourteenth Army in action near Monywa, 96km (60 miles) from Mandalay.*

Honda's Thirty-Third Army has fallen into a trap. General Slim, predicting the Japanese countermeasures, has swung troops of the British IV Corps southwards towards Pakokku to prevent Japanese troops retreating south.

JANUARY 16

LAND WAR, *NORTHERN BURMA*
The Chinese New First Army captures Namkhkam, an important position that secures the Burma Road for Allied use.

JANUARY 18

LAND WAR, *PALAU ISLANDS*
Two Japanese commando raiding groups land on Peleliu in an attempt to destroy US aircraft on the ground. The groups are wiped out and thus are unable to complete their mission.

JANUARY 20

KAMIKAZE, *LUZON*
Japanese suicide aircraft attack US naval vessels in the Formosa-Ryukyu Islands area. The carriers USS *Ticon-*

▲ *US troops cross the River Shweli in Burma over a hastily constructed bamboo bridge in pursuit of Japanese forces.*

deroga and USS *Langley* are damaged, as is the destroyer USS *Maddox*. An accidental explosion damages another carrier, USS *Hancock*.

JANUARY 20

LAND WAR, *PHILIPPINES*
US XIV Corps troops push up to the outskirts of San Miguel. After an almost uncontested landing, US forces on the island of Luzon are now locked in heavy fighting against General Yamashita's 260,000 men, as they are now less than 160km (100 miles) from Manila itself.

JANUARY 12

AIR WAR, *INDOCHINA*
US carrier aircraft operating from the South China Sea bomb Japanese airfields, shore installations and shipping in French Indochina.

JANUARY 15

AIR WAR, *FORMOSA*
US carrier aircraft sink two Japanese destroyers in renewed attacks off Formosa.
LAND WAR, *PHILIPPINES*
US forces advance out of Lingayen Bay, today crossing the Agno River at points about 24km (15 miles) inland.

DECISIVE WEAPONS

THE BATTLESHIP *YAMATO*

The battleship *Yamato* and her sister ship *Musashi* were built for the Imperial Japanese Navy in the late 1930s and early 1940s under conditions of total secrecy, as the specifications of both vessels breached international treaty limits. Work on the *Yamato* began in November 1937, and she was completed in December 1941. Her combat specifications were impressive. Her main turrets carried nine 18in guns which had a maximum range of 48km (30 miles), and she was armed with forty anti-aircraft guns of various calibres. The *Yamato* also carried six float planes for reconnaissance duties. This 69,088-tonne (68,000-ton) vessel required 2500 officers and men to crew it; yet, with the rising supremacy of naval aviation and submarine warfare, she became an anachronism from the moment she was launched.

Yamato's combat experience bore this out. In early 1944, she was damaged by a submarine torpedo from the USS *Skate*, but she was later able to participate in the Battle of the Philippine Sea. During this action she fired her main armaments, but poor visibility and fast-moving US warships made her contribution negligible. She returned home for refitting, and the lessons of the Philippine Sea led to a substantial upgrad-

ing of anti-aircraft armaments. She would have a total of 145 25mm anti-aircraft guns for her final operation, a suicide mission against US invasion forces around Okinawa in April 1945. With enough fuel for only a one-way trip, *Yamato* was spotted by US aircraft well before she reached her destination. An attack by more than 400 US carrier aircraft led to more than 20 bomb and torpedo hits. At 14:20 hours on April 7, her magazine exploded, ripping the ship apart and sending her to the bottom of the Pacific. A total of 2475 crew went down with her.

DECISIVE WEAPONS

B-29 SUPERFORTRESS

The Boeing B-29 Superfortress is best known for its role in ending World War II. On August 6, 1945, the B-29 Enola Gay dropped the first operational atomic bomb on Hiroshima; three days later, another B-29, Bockscar, dropped the second on Nagasaki. The B-29 was designed as an extreme long-range "Hemisphere Defence Weapon". When it entered service in July 1943, this huge 10-crew bomber had a range of 6598km (4100 miles) and a bomb load of 9072kg (20,000lb). It was an advanced aircraft – the gun turrets dotted around the fuselage were controlled remotely by gunners sitting inside the fuselage who aimed the weapons via periscopes. The B-29 was ideal for the vast distances of the Pacific theatre. From March 1945, B-29s began operations from five bases in the Marianas Islands, causing devastation on the Japanese mainland. Attacking mostly at night (previously, the B-29s had mainly conducted high-level daylight raids), the B-29s scattered millions of incendiaries over Japanese cities – the wood and plaster construction of Japanese housing made the buildings intensely vulnerable to fire attacks. The first such fire attack on Tokyo caused 80,000 deaths, a similar death toll to that caused by the Hiroshima bomb. Some 3970 B-29s were produced during the war, and some went on to serve in the Korean conflict of 1950–53.

◀ *A Boeing B-29 returns to Iwo Jima after a raid on Japan. Note that one of its port engines has been disabled.*

SPECIFICATIONS

CREW: 10

POWERPLANT: four 1641kW (2200hp) Wright R-3350-57 radial piston engines

PERFORMANCE: maximum speed 576kmh (358mph); service ceiling 9696m (31,800ft); range 6598km (4100 miles)

DIMENSIONS: wingspan 43.36m (142.25ft); length 30.18m (99ft); height 9.01m (29.6ft)

ARMAMENTS: 10 x 12.5mm machine guns (four-gun nose turret, two-gun turrets under nose and under and over rear fuselage); tail gun turret featuring one 20mm cannon and two 12.5mm machine guns; internal bomb load of up to 9072kg (19,958lb)

JANUARY 21

LAND WAR, *BURMA*
The 71st Brigade, 26th Indian Division, makes an amphibious jump down the Arakan to Kyaukpyu on Ramree Island, putting further pressure on the Japanese forces retreating between the west coast

▼ *A US 81mm mortar shells Japanese positions north of Lashio in northern Burma in late January.*

of Burma and the Irrawaddy. Most of the Arakan coastline is now in Allied hands.

JANUARY 23

LAND WAR, *PHILIPPINES*
US XIV Corps troops push down into southern Luzon to take Clark Field, having advanced around 113km (70 miles). Clark Field will be essential during forthcoming US operations against Iwo Jima, and General MacArthur has been leaning heavily on US commanders to take the air base. I Corps troops

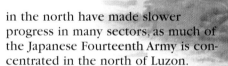

▶ *A flight of Chance Vought Corsair fighters. The Corsair was one of the best combat aircraft of World War II.*

in the north have made slower progress in many sectors, as much of the Japanese Fourteenth Army is concentrated in the north of Luzon.

JANUARY 26

LAND WAR, *BURMA*
The 7th and 17th Indian Divisions occupy Pauk, 48km (30 miles) from Pakokku. The 28th East African Brigade breaks away from Pauk and swings farther south towards Seikpyu on the Irrawaddy.

JANUARY 27

LAND WAR, *NORTHERN BURMA*
The Chinese New First Army and the Chinese Y Force meet around Mongyu, bringing together two separate lines of advance down through northern Burma. The forces now combine and drive down towards Lashio against the Japanese 56th Division. Farther west, the Chinese New Sixth Army has pushed out from Bhamo and is heading for Hsipaw, 65km (40 miles) to the southwest of Lashio.

JANUARY 28

LOGISTICS, *BURMA*
With Chinese troops having reopened the Ledo Road to Burma,

▶ *As US troops neared Manila, the city came under artillery and aerial bombardment. This bridge was demolished by the garrison to hinder enemy movements.*

the first truckloads of supplies reach China. The open flow of logistics will now help the Chinese to stem the Japanese Ichi-Go offensive into Chinese southern territories.

JANUARY 29–31

LAND WAR, *PHILIPPINES*
The US opens more fronts in the Luzon campaign by landing troops in positions around Manila Bay. XI Corps forces go ashore at San Antonio, just north of the Bataan Peninsula, on the 29th, and on the 31st the 11th Airborne Division is landed at Masugbu, south of Manila Bay, making up the southern thrust of a three-pronged assault against the Philippine capital, Manila.

FEBRUARY 1

TECHNOLOGY, AIR WAR
Chance Vought Corsair fighters make their first regular operational flight

from US Navy aircraft carriers. The Corsair will become the best carrier-launched aircraft of World War II, with its manoeuvrability, high maximum speed (671kmh/417mph) and six machine guns. The Corsair will achieve a kill ratio of eleven to one.

FEBRUARY 2

SEA WAR, *PACIFIC*
A US Navy communiqué announces that, since June 19, 1944, total Japanese shipping losses have amounted to more than 50 vessels a week. Japan's maritime assets are being decimated.

AIR WAR, *SINGAPORE*

A large force of US B-29s demolishes Singapore harbour and Japanese naval shipping moored there.

FEBRUARY 3

LAND WAR, *PHILIPPINES*

The battle for Manila begins. Japanese forces in the city are trapped between the 11th Airborne Division moving up from the south (the remainder of the 11th Airborne are parachuted into action today), XI Corps troops from the west, and units of XIV Corps from the north. The Japanese put up a ferocious defence, and the battle for the Philippines capital will go on for another month.

► The "Big Three" at Yalta (left to right): Winston Churchill, a sick Franklin D. Roosevelt and Joseph Stalin. The latter agreed to declare war on Japan.

FEBRUARY 4–11

POLITICS, *ALLIES*

British Prime Minister Churchill, US President Roosevelt and Russia's Joseph Stalin meet at Yalta in the Crimea for a six-day conference to discuss the politics of an Allied Europe as Germany faces certain defeat. Stalin also commits himself to declaring war on Japan

▲ US troops fighting on Luzon in January. The Japanese under General Tomoyuki Yamashita fought a skilful rearguard campaign in the face of superior forces.

within two months of Germany's final military defeat.

FEBRUARY 6

LAND WAR, *PHILIPPINES*

Some 510 Allied POWs, many taken captive by the Japanese in Bataan in 1942, are freed following a dramatic raid on a POW camp by US Rangers and Filipino insurgents. More than 200 Japanese guards are killed.

FEBRUARY 8

AIR WAR, *KURILE ISLANDS*

Ventura aircraft of the Fleet Air Arm make a rocket attack against radio and lighthouse in-

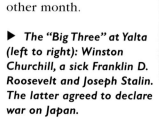

stallations at Kokutan Zaki, at the northern tip of Shimushu in the Kurile Islands.

FEBRUARY 9–12

SEA WAR, *PACIFIC*
The American submarine USS *Batfish* sinks three Japanese submarines in only four days.

▼ *The Japanese launched a large number of kamikaze attacks against the US invasion fleet off Iwo Jima. Here, the carrier Saratoga burns after one such attack.*

▲ *Soldiers of the US 5th Marine Division on the black volcanic sands of Iwo Jima. In the background is Mount Suribachi, which the Marines captured within three days.*

FEBRUARY 10

ALLIES, WAR CRIMES
The US Navy announces increased cooperation with the US Army in the gathering of evidence for the prosecution of war criminals. The US War Crimes office was established in the autumn of 1944 under the supervision of

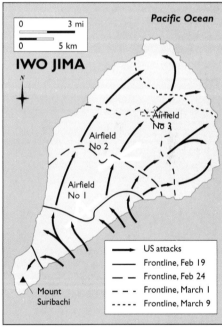

▲ *The US objective on Iwo Jima was to capture the island's three airfields to establish a forward air base for the planned Allied attack on the Japanese home islands.*

Major-General Myron C. Cramer, the Judge Advocate General of the Army.

FEBRUARY 11

AIR WAR, *PACIFIC*
Vice-Admiral George D. Murray, US Navy, Commander Air Forces, Pacific Fleet, releases figures that demonstrate US air superiority over the Pacific theatre.

147

Marine 4th and 5th Divisions go ashore in the southeast corner of the island, landed by US V Amphibious Corps. Offshore is the US 3rd Marine Division held in reserve. The first few minutes of the landings are relatively uncontested but, once the Japanese recover, the beaches turn into places of slaughter. Despite heavy casualties, US forces manage to land 30,000 Marines throughout the day and establish a solid beachhead about 450m (1476ft) in depth. By the end of the day, units of the 5th Marine Division have moved across the southern section of the island, cutting off Japanese forces on the 150m- (500ft-) high Mount Suribachi, while the bulk of the Marine forces work their way northwards up the island.

▲ A US Sherman tank crashes through the entrance to Fort Santiago in Manila. The battle for the city cost the lives of 16,000 Japanese troops and 100,000 Philippine civilians.

From June 11–October 30, 1944, Pacific Fleet carrier aircraft destroyed 2472 Japanese aircraft in aerial combat and lost 123 aircraft. The ratio of US kills to losses is about 20 to 1.

FEBRUARY 13

LAND WAR, *BURMA*
Units of the 7th and 17th India Divisions cross the Irrawaddy River south of Pakokku at Nyaungu.

LAND WAR, *PHILIPPINES*
American forces capture the Nicholls Field air base and the Cavite naval base in Manila, further closing their grip around the capital.

FEBRUARY 16–27

LAND WAR, *PHILIPPINES*
The fortress island of Corregidor is reoccupied by US troops following a paratroop landing by men of the 11th Airborne Division on the 16th, supported by amphibious forces crossing from the Bataan Peninsula.

FEBRUARY 16–17

AIR WAR, *TOKYO*
US Pacific Fleet carrier aircraft make a highly successful two-day attack on Tokyo. Taking advantage of bad weather to make an undetected approach, the aircraft subsequently shoot down 322 Japanese fighters and destroy a further 177 on the ground. US aviation losses are 49 aircraft. Shipping around Tokyo also suffers heavily, with one escort carrier, three destroyers and nine coastal vessels sunk and more than twenty other ships damaged. In terms of ground installations, the Ota aircraft factory and the Musashine Tama and Tachigawa engine plants are heavily bombed.

FEBRUARY 19

LAND WAR, *IWO JIMA*
The US invasion of Iwo Jima begins after the island, only 13 sq km (5 sq miles) of territory, has suffered 72 days of solid bombardment. The US

▶ In one of the most famous scenes of World War II, soldiers of the US 5th Marine Division raise the Stars and Stripes on Mount Suribachi, February 23, 1945.

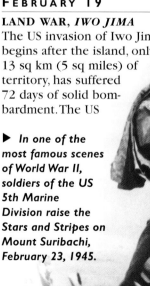

▲ *Gurkhas of the 19th Indian Division, nicknamed the Dagger Division, cross the Irrawaddy River. During its 1944–45 campaign in Burma the division fought 18 separate battles in 7 weeks.*

FEBRUARY 20

LAND WAR, *IWO JIMA*
US Marines move forward on Iwo Jima against fanatical resistance. The 277th Regiment of the US Marines defeats a night attack by a battalion-strength Japanese unit around the Motoyama Airstrip No 1 in the south of the island (Iwo Jima has three airstrips). By the morning, the airstrip is in American hands.

TECHNOLOGY, *ATOMIC BOMB*
US scientists and engineers working at the K-25 uranium plant at Oak Ridge, Tennessee, now have enough Uranium-235 to produce an atomic bomb.

POLITICS, *ALLIES*
In the aftermath of the Yalta Conference, US President Roosevelt and British Prime Minister Churchill discuss the Pacific war, pledging a shift in priorities to the East now that the defeat of Germany looks imminent.

▶ *A 17th Indian Division mortar position in Meiktila, Burma. Judging by the relaxed poses, the Japanese are some way off.*

FEBRUARY 21

LAND WAR, *BURMA*
British forces advancing from Shwebo and moving down the Chindwin meet on the Irrawaddy River near Ngazun, only 48km (30 miles) from Mandalay,

▲ *US amphibious assault vehicles knocked out by Japanese mortar and artillery fire lie abandoned on Iwo Jima.*

STRATEGY AND TACTICS

IWO JIMA

Why was the fight for Iwo Jima so costly? By this stage of the war, the Japanese understood that directly contesting a US amphibious landing at the beaches was too risky because of the intensity of US Navy preliminary bombardments. During the US invasion of Peleliu in the Palau Islands in September 1944, the Japanese opted for a defence-in-depth strategy, and avoided wasteful mass counterattacks. Troops were pulled back into the interior where they waited out the coastal bombardments and allowed US forces to land before engaging them heavily from pre-prepared defensive positions. The Japanese utilized this strategy on Iwo Jima. Scattered around the island were more than 800 pillboxes, bunkers, dug-in armoured vehicles and 4.8km (3 miles) of tunnels. The bunkers were well constructed from palm trunks and packed sand, and had an extremely low-profile sloping face resistant to artillery fire. All pillboxes were situated to have over-lapping fields of fire; all beaches, and the slopes leading off them, were zeroed in advance by Japanese machine guns, artillery and mortars.

The Japanese were assisted in the defence of Iwo Jima by the terrain itself. Iwo Jima is a volcanic island, its convoluted rocky landscape full of caves, ravines, ridges and other natural defensive positions. In one 400m x 600m (1312ft x 1968ft) area, US Marines had to neutralize 100 individual defensive caves. The slope of the beaches was extremely steep with crumbly volcanic ash (the Japanese embedded anti-tank mines in the slopes), and US Marines struggled simply to walk across such terrain carrying their 45kg (100lb) packs. Furthermore, US soldiers found in many places that the volcanic landscape was too hot to convert into foxholes. Ultimately, it was only the sheer tenacity of the Marines and the use of overwhelming firepower that took Iwo Jima.

and establish a bridgehead. They immediately launch a major offensive towards Meiktila, directly south of Mandalay, using the 7th and 17th Indian Divisions and the 255th Indian Brigade, cutting into the rear of the Japanese Fifteenth Army.

LAND WAR, *IWO JIMA*
US Marines advance beyond the southern airstrip. Units of the 5th Marine Division make a penetration up the west coast of the island, while 4th Division troops head directly for the Motoyama Airstrip No 2 in the centre of the island. The going is extremely heavy, and the total advance for the day is around 900m (2952ft). On Mount Suribachi, US Marines fighting up the slopes gain only 100m (328ft). US casualties already exceed 3500. The US 3rd Marine division, held in reserve offshore, is now landed to boost the combat effort.

AIR WAR, *IWO JIMA*
Japanese kamikaze air attacks intensify against US shipping around Iwo Jima. Today, the escort carrier USS *Bismarck Sea* is sunk and the carriers USS *Saratoga* and USS *Lunga Point* are badly damaged by kamikaze aircraft.

FEBRUARY 22

LAND WAR, *PHILIPPINES*
Troops of the Japanese Fourteenth Army defending Manila are now pushed back into the old walled city, where they continue to fight tenaciously. Meanwhile, 2000 Japanese defenders on Corregidor kill themselves by detonating a large ammunition dump.

LAND WAR, *BURMA*
British forces make another amphibious landing down the Arakan coastline, this time landing at Kangow in the Bay of Bengal.

FEBRUARY 23

LAND WAR, *IWO JIMA*
Mount Suribachi falls to US forces after a bloody battle on its slopes. Joe Rosenthal, a US combat photographer, immortalizes the moment that Marine soldiers raise the Stars and Stripes on the summit. However, the island will not be secure for another month. Fighting around the central airstrip is extremely heavy, with little progress being made. Today, only 250m (820ft) of ground is won, with Japanese fire contesting every inch of movement.

▼ *US Marine riflemen fire on Japanese positions from cover on Iwo Jima. A burning Sherman tank is on the left.*

▲ *A column of British troops passes a dead Japanese soldier during the advance on Mandalay in Burma.*

FEBRUARY 25

AIR WAR, *TOKYO*
US carrier aircraft attack the Tokyo area, concentrating efforts on shipping and industrial facilities. About three-quarters of the Ota aircraft factory is destroyed, and the Koizuma aircraft plant is badly damaged. In addition, two trains are destroyed in strafing attacks and 158 Japanese aircraft are wiped out, 47 of them in aerial combat. That night, 172 Boeing B-29 bombers devastate the city, dropping nearly 508 tonnes (500 tons) of incendiary bombs.

FEBRUARY 26

LAND WAR, *BURMA*
As British forces close in on Mandalay from the west and south, the 19th Indian Division begins an attack down the Irrawaddy from its bridgeheads around Thabeikkyin and Singu.

LAND WAR, *IWO JIMA*
The central airfield on Iwo Jima is now in US hands. The fighting for the airstrip has been heavy, and US troops have already counted 3568 lost to the Japanese for only 4000m (13,123ft) of ground taken on the island.

FEBRUARY 27–28

LAND WAR, *PHILIPPINES*
Units of XI Corps effectively clear the Bataan Peninsula. Troops from a regiment of XI Corps are landed on the southern coastline of the peninsula on the 28th, meeting up with their comrades advancing down the eastern coastline.

FEBRUARY 28

LAND WAR, *IWO JIMA*
Approximately two-thirds of Iwo Jima is now in American hands, and the centre of the US advance pushes against the southern defences of the Motoyama Airstrip No 3.

▶ *Dead Japanese soldiers on Iwo Jima. Of the island's 27,000 garrison, 20,000 were killed.*

LAND WAR, *PHILIPPINES*
Troops of the US Army 41st Division land at Puerto Princesa on Palawan Island in the southern Philippines against negligible opposition. Palawan offers excellent port facilities for US Navy operations against Japanese shipping passing to and from the Dutch East Indies.

LAND WAR, *BURMA*
Meiktila is surrounded by troops of the 17th Indian Brigade, who begin the assault on the town, which is occupied by 3500 Japanese defenders.

▲ *Bomb damage at Tokyo following a B-29 air raid. Most Japanese dwellings were made of wood, which made them very vulnerable to incendiary bombs.*

MARCH 1–31

LAND WAR, *PHILIPPINES*
Throughout March, US forces invade the many islands of the southern Philippines. By the end of the month, the Philippines are effectively in US hands, and US war leaders start to look towards the Japanese home islands themselves.

MARCH 1

AIR WAR, *RYUKYU ISLANDS*
US aircraft from Vice-Admiral Mitscher's fast carrier task force begin bombarding Okinawa in the Ryukyu chain. It is the beginning of a solid month of aerial and naval bombardment against Okinawa in preparation for the US invasion of the island scheduled for April 1.

LAND WAR, *PHILIPPINES*
US Army troops are landed on Lubang Island, just off the northern coast of Mindoro.

LAND WAR, *IWO JIMA*
US Marines manage to occupy the western end of Iwo Jima's northernmost airstrip, pushing forward after a huge bombardment by US Navy guns and US Marine artillery. Unusually, 17 Japanese prisoners are taken captive.

▼ *A lull in the fighting during the battle for Mandalay. The soldier on the right is pointing a Bren Gun, one of the finest light machine guns of the war.*

LAND WAR, *BURMA*
The British Fourteenth Army begins the assault on Meiktila, attacking through the northern suburbs of the town against a tenacious defence from Major-General Kasuya's garrison. The Japanese have converted the town into a heavy defensive outpost.

MARCH 2

LAND WAR, *IWO JIMA*
US Marines in northern Iwo Jima advance several hundred yards and capture the high ground of Hill 362. In the west, meanwhile, the US 5th Marine Division defeats a large-scale Japanese counterattack.

MARCH 3

LAND WAR, *PHILIPPINES*
Part of the US 40th Division lands on Masbate Island, just north of Leyte.

LAND WAR, *PHILIPPINES*
Having sacrificed 20,000 men in defence of the

▶ *US Marines on Iwo Jima, where over a third of the Leathernecks were either killed, wounded or suffered from battle fatigue.*

▲ *A Royal Air Force B-24 Liberator photographed after droppings its bombs on the railway sidings at Na Nien, Burma.*

▲ *US troops fighting Japanese forces on the island of Panay, which lies between Mindanao and Luzon.*

Philippines capital, Japanese resistance in Manila is finally eradicated. US troops now push out into the north of Luzon and southwards into the Bicol Peninsula.

LAND WAR, *IWO JIMA*
The US advance up Iwo Jima slows to a crawl. Both the 4th

and 5th Marines have moved into rocky terrain, and the Japanese defensive fire is blistering. The 5th Marines engage in hand-to-hand fighting in an attempt to loosen the Japanese grip. A count of enemy casualties reveals that so far in the campaign 12,864 Japanese have been killed. Meanwhile, US evacuation aircraft are starting to use the southern airstrip, though they come under artillery fire when landing and taking off.

LAND WAR, *CENTRAL BURMA*
Chinese troops capture Lashio to the northeast of Mandalay. Lashio includes the northernmost of a series of vital airfields stretching throughout central and southern Burma, and each one captured provides extra logistical capability for the Allied advance.

MARCH 4

LAND WAR, *BURMA*
The 17th Indian Division takes Meiktila. The four-day battle has been ferocious, and more than 2000 Japanese have been killed. Mandalay is the next objective, where the bulk of the Japanese Fifteenth and Thirty-Third Armies are trapped.

MARCH 8

POLITICS, *US*
Vice-Admiral William Ward Smith takes command of the Service Force, US Pacific Fleet. The Service Force has a massive job in providing logistics support to US operations in the Pacific. Smith was formerly chief of staff to Admiral Kimmel, and commanded a

MARCH 8–9

Nearly 2032 tonnes (2000 tons) of incendiary bombs are dropped over the city, resulting in a firestorm that kills between 80,000 and 130,000 of Tokyo's citizens. Around 300,000 buildings, most constructed from wood and plaster, are destroyed. Two nights later, 285 B-29s give Nagoya similar treatment. US aviators now have access to forward air bases captured during the US Pacific campaign. The capture of the Mariana Islands in particular has halved previous operational flying distances.

MARCH 10

POLITICS, *FRENCH INDOCHINA*
The Japanese seize the administration of French Indochina. Although Indochina had essentially been under Japanese occupation, the Japanese allowed the nominal rule of the French colonial government.

▼ *A kamikaze aircraft burns after being hit by anti-aircraft fire from the Essex class carrier USS Wasp, off the Ryukyu Islands in March.*

cruiser task group that saw action in the battles of Coral Sea and Midway.

MARCH 8–9

LAND WAR, *IWO JIMA*
Japanese forces resort to more night-infiltration actions on Iwo Jima. On this night, an infiltration is made in the 4th Marines' sector, resulting in a firefight that leaves 564 Japanese soldiers dead.

MARCH 8–10

LAND WAR, *PHILIPPINES*
US forces gain their first footholds on Mindanao in the southern Philippines.

▲ *The USS Aaron Ward after being hit by kamikaze aircraft off Okinawa. Note the three-bladed aircraft propeller lodged in her superstructure behind the rear guns.*

Two companies of the 24th Division are parachuted around Dipolog.

MARCH 10

LAND WAR, *PHILIPPINES*
With support provided by US Navy gunfire and USAAF ground-attack aircraft, part of the US 41st Division is landed near Zamboanga on the westernmost tip of Mindanao.

MARCH 9–10

AIR WAR, *TOKYO*
The Japanese capital is almost entirely destroyed by a massive night bombing raid by 279 B-29 Superfortress aircraft.

◀ *A light tank and troops of the 19th Indian Division move into their jump-off positions during the advance on Mandalay in Burma.*

MARCH 14

LAND WAR, *IWO JIMA*
The US flag is formally raised over Iwo Jima, despite continuing resistance in pockets in the far north of the island. Iwo Jima – less than 1126km (700 miles) from the Japanese homeland – is now a fully functioning air base for the US Navy, Army and Marine Corps.

MARCH 15

LAND WAR, *BURMA*
The battle for Meiktila rages for two weeks. Around the 15th, General Hoyotaro Kimura, commander of the Japanese Burma Area Army, re-deploys the best part of three divisions from the defence of Mandalay to Meiktila, with its vital rail and communication links. Troops of the 17th Indian Division are now isolated around the town by the Japanese.

MARCH 16

LAND WAR, *IWO JIMA*
Japanese resistance on Iwo Jima breaks down as US Marine forces push their

MARCH 11

KAMIKAZE, *CAROLINE ISLANDS*
The carrier USS *Randolph* is badly damaged by suicide aircraft around Ulithi Atoll in the Carolines.
LAND WAR, *IWO JIMA*
The US 3rd and 4th Marine Divisions make a good advance and capture most of Iwo Jima's east coast. The Japanese are now concentrated in a small section of territory in the north of the island.

MARCH 11–12

LAND WAR, *PHILIPPINES*
Part of the US 24th Division makes an amphibious assault from Mindoro against the island of Romblon.

▼ *The USS* Franklin *ablaze after being hit by two Japanese bombs. The subsequent fire killed 724 crew members. The ship survived after extensive repairs.*

MARCH 12–13

AIR WAR, *JAPAN*
The US strategic bombing campaign against Japan continues. On this night, the city of Osaka is wiped out by a raid of 274 US bombers.

MARCH 13

LAND WAR, *IWO JIMA*
Using explosives and bulldozers, US troops seal up 115 caves with the Japanese defenders still inside.

DECISIVE WEAPONS

YOKOSUKA MXY7 OHKA

The Ohka ("Cherry Blossom") was a rocket-powered piloted bomb designed by naval ensign Mitsuo Ohka in late 1944. Effectively, the aircraft was nothing more than a 1200kg (2646lb) warhead with wings and powered by three solid-fuel Type 4 Mark 1 Model 20 rockets. To deploy the weapon, it was first attached to the modified bomb bay of a Mitsubishi G4M bomber and flown within 40km (25 miles) of the target. Once released, the Ohka's rockets would ignite and the pilot would then fly the bomb into his intended target. To ensure the commitment of the pilot, he was sealed into the cockpit for his one-way trip. Ohkas were a mark of Japanese desperation, and were not a total success. The first attack occurred on March 21, 1945, but all Ohkas missed their targets. Hits were achieved on the battleship USS *West Virginia* on April 1, causing severe damage. The destroyer USS *Mannert L. Abele* was sunk two weeks later, but most Ohkas did not reach launch position before their Mitsubishi transports were shot down by US fighters.

SPECIFICATIONS
CREW: 1
POWERPLANT: three solid-fuel Type 4 Mark 1 Model 20 rockets generating 800kg (1764lb) of thrust
PERFORMANCE: max speed 650kmh (403mph); range 37km (23 miles)
DIMENSIONS: wingspan 5.12m (16.79ft); length 6.07m (19.9ft); height 1.16m (3.75ft)
WARHEAD: 1200kg (2646lb)

▲ *Operation Iceberg, the US invasion of Okinawa, commences. The US fleet assembled off the island prior to the assault numbered 1400 vessels.*

way to Kitano Point, the northernmost tip of the island. A small pocket of disorganized Japanese defenders remains in the northeast, but is easily contained. Today, the central airfield comes into operation.

MARCH 16–17

AIR WAR, *JAPAN*
Kobe is devastated by 307 B-29 bombers in a night raid that kills at least 15,000 people.

MARCH 18

LAND WAR, *PHILIPPINES*
Elements of the US 40th Division land around Loilo on the southern coastline of Panay in the southern Philippines.

MARCH 18–19

AIR WAR, *JAPAN*
On March 18, US carrier aircraft attack naval installations and airfields around Kyushu Island, the southernmost territory of the Japanese homelands. The Japanese stage a major airborne retaliation, and the carriers USS *Enterprise*, USS *Yorktown* and USS *Intrepid* are damaged by bombers and suicide aircraft. Nevertheless, the US attacks continue the next day, the target locations widening to Kobe and Kure. Once again, the Japanese respond with force, and the carriers USS *Franklin*,

USS *Wasp* and USS *Essex* are damaged (the latter, ironically, by misdirected US Navy gunfire).

MARCH 19

AIR WAR, *JAPAN*
US carrier aircraft attacking the Japanese homelands switch their efforts to the Japanese Fleet in the Inland Sea. Two battleships, six aircraft carriers (heavy, light and escort), three cruisers and four destroyers are among the

▼ *Firefighters deal with the aftermath of a kamikaze attack on an aircraft carrier.*

ships badly damaged. In two days of air combat over Japan, 200 Japanese aircraft have been shot down, and 275 destroyed on the ground.

MARCH 20–21

LAND WAR, *BURMA*
Britain's XXXIII Corps takes Mandalay after house-to-house fighting. XXXIII Corps units are now re-deployed to fight around Meiktila. On the 21st, the British 36th Division advancing down from northern Burma with the Chinese New Sixth Army reaches Mandalay, and falls back under the British Fourteenth Army's jurisdiction.

MARCH 21

KAMIKAZE, *PACIFIC*

Japanese Ohka piloted bombs make their first attack against US carriers. They are unsuccessful. However, Japanese air attacks around Iwo Jima today result in the sinking of the carrier USS *Bismarck Sea*. Bombing and kamikaze raids start fires on the ship that rage out of control and force the crew to abandon the carrier.

LAND WAR, *CHINA*

Japan persists in its attempts to capture US air bases in southern China, today launching a fresh offensive towards Laohokow and Ankong.

MARCH 23–24

AIR/SEA WAR, *RYUKYU ISLANDS*

Daily air bombardments against the island of Okinawa begin today. The next day, US battleships, cruisers and destroyers add naval gunfire support to the onslaught.

MARCH 25

KAMIKAZE, *OKINAWA*

Japanese suicide aircraft damage one US destroyer, a destroyer escort, a mine-laying vessel and two high-speed transport ships.

▼ *US forces pour ashore on Okinawa. In the foreground can be seen LVT amphibious vehicles. A total of 1225 LVT-1s were built in the war.*

MARCH 26

LAND WAR, *IWO JIMA*

The final pockets of Japanese resistance on Iwo Jima collapse after a suicide attack by the remaining Japanese troops. Casualties on both sides have been colossal. The US has lost 6821 Marine and navy personnel. Calculating Japanese casualties

▲ *Troops of the US 96th Division climb the sea wall on the western shore of Okinawa on April 1.*

is difficult, for many were killed inside cave complexes that were subsequently sealed. However, the US Navy estimates up to 22,000 Japanese dead.

LAND WAR, *PHILIPPINES*
The Americal Division lands on the eastern coast of Cebu. By this point, almost every island in the southern Philippines is now either under US occupation or in the process of being conquered.

KAMIKAZE, *OKINAWA*
Waves of Japanese suicide aircraft are thrown against US shipping around Okinawa. One battleship (the USS *Nevada*), one cruiser and five destroyers are among the damaged US vessels.

LAND WAR, *RYUKYU ISLANDS*
US Army 77th Division troops land on the islands of the Kerama group west of the southern tip of Okinawa, and occupy them over the next three days. The islands will provide a base for US artillery fire against Okinawa Island itself.

MARCH 27

LAND WAR, *PHILIPPINES*
US Army troops make an amphibious landing on Caballo Island, near the island of Corregidor.

MARCH 28

LAND WAR, *BURMA*
Soldiers of the Burmese National Army (BNA), an independence movement fighting on the side of the Japanese, kill some of their officers. The BNA has, over recent months, been infiltrated by the Allied Special Operations Executive (SOE), which capitalized on the low status afforded to the BNA by the Japanese Army.

MARCH 29

LAND WAR, *BURMA*
With Mandalay taken, and Britain's XXXII Corps now able to support the Indian 17th Division around Meiktila, the Japanese Burma Area Army is ordered to withdraw southwards. General Kimura uses the Mandalay–Thazi rail route to escape with a large number of troops. British forces follow closely, the ultimate objective now being the vital port of Rangoon.

KEY PERSONALITIES

FRANKLIN ROOSEVELT

President Franklin Delano Roosevelt (1882–1945) was coming towards the end of his second term in office when the Japanese attacked the US Pacific Fleet at Pearl Harbor in December 1941. Roosevelt had been tough on the Japanese prior to this incident, imposing oil and metals embargoes in 1940–41 after Japanese attacks against French Indochina. Roosevelt was told that a Japanese attack against US interests would come on December 7, but outdated military intelligence, which underestimated the range of Japanese carrier aircraft, ruled out Pearl Harbor as the target.

Following US entry into the war, Roosevelt sided with the European allies in favour of a Germany First strategy. However, the Pacific theatre still received substantial resources – at least half of US troops and around 30 percent of US aircraft were committed there in 1942. On a strategic level, Roosevelt's early war aims in the Pacific were to maintain the Chinese war effort against Japan through air supply, and ultimately halt the Japanese advance through the South Pacific. Once the war against the Japanese tipped in the US's favour and American forces neared the enemy home islands, Roosevelt decided that the use atomic bombs on Japan would save tens of thousands of US service lives and shorten the war. He never lived to see the defeat of Japan. Roosevelt died of a cerebral haemorrhage on April 12, 1945, during an unprecedented fourth term in office, having struggled with polio most of his life. Although Roosevelt could be pragmatic, especially about the political intentions of the Allies, he brought clarity and momentum to the US war effort.

AIR WAR, *JAPAN*
US aircraft from two carrier task groups attack Japanese shipping and aircraft in the Kagoshima Bay area, Kyushu, Japan.

MARCH 30

KAMIKAZE, *OKINAWA*
A Japanese suicide aircraft damages the US heavy cruiser USS *Indianapolis*.

APRIL 1

LAND WAR, *RYUKYU ISLANDS*
"Operation Iceberg", the invasion of Okinawa, begins with landings by the US Tenth Army along the southeastern

▼ *A Japanese destroyer keels over in the East China Sea following an air attack.*

huge waves of kamikaze aircraft against the 1400-strong Allied fleet. Six vessels are damaged by suicide attack, including the battleship USS *West Virginia*.

HOME FRONT, *JAPAN*

All education for Japanese schoolchildren above the age of six is cancelled, and the young are redirected into war industries to provide a boost to the Japanese labour force.

LAND WAR, *PHILIPPINES*

US Army troops are landed at Legaspi in the south of the Bicol Peninsula, trapping Japanese forces retreating down through the peninsula in the face of a strong southerly advance by US troops.

KAMIKAZE, *EAST CHINA SEA*

The British carrier HMS *Indefatigable* is hit by a kamikaze attack, suffering damage and 14 fatalities.

APRIL 2

LAND WAR, *PHILIPPINES*

US 41st Division troops land on Tawitawi, in the south of the Sulu archipelago near British North Borneo.

LAND WAR, *RYUKYU ISLANDS*

The US XXIV Corps makes good progress across southern Okinawa, reaching the east coast near the village of Tobara. However, US Marines advancing in the centre of the island are beginning to meet increasingly stiff resistance in difficult terrain. Eleven US ships are damaged today, five by suicide aircraft; one by Japanese bombers; and the remainder through collision, grounding and being struck accidentally by US naval gunfire.

▲ *The funeral of President Franklin D. Roosevelt in Washington. Roosevelt died on the verge of victory in Europe, and his loss was keenly felt by the American people.*

coast of the island around Hagushi Bay. The landings are divided into two elements: US III Marine Amphibious Corps (6th Marine Division and 1st Marine Division) takes the left flank, with the objective of advancing to the west and up into the north of the island; while, beneath it, US Army XXIV Corps (7th Infantry Division and 96th Infantry Division) begins operations to clear southern Okinawa. On this first day, re-

sistance is relatively light and the US troops establish a beachhead 5km (3 miles) deep. However, more than 130,000 Japanese soldiers of the Japanese Thirty-Second Army are waiting for them in the interior of the island.

The US invasion is not only protected by US shipping – a large British carrier force under Vice-Admiral Sir Bernard Rawlings operates against enemy positions in the Sakishima group. The Japanese Air Force immediately launches

▶ *A US soldier feeds a young child during the campaign on Okinawa. Fears about the behaviour of US troops prompted many Japanese civilians on the island to commit suicide.*

▲ With combat raging on Okinawa, Japanese aircraft tried to sink US ships offshore. Here, a burning Zero goes down.

APRIL 3

LAND WAR, *RYUKYU ISLANDS*
US Marines cross Okinawa and reach the east coast, cutting off Japanese troops in the Katchin Peninsula. In the south, US Army forces have reached Kuba, with Japanese resistance being light.

APRIL 5

COMMAND STRUCTURE, *PACIFIC*
The US joint chiefs of staff announce changes in the command structure of Pacific operations. General MacArthur is given command of all army forces and related resources for the Pacific theatre. Similarly, Admiral Nimitz takes charge of all US Navy units and resources throughout the Pacific.

LAND WAR, *RYUKYU ISLANDS*
US Marine units reach the Ishikawa isthmus, having advanced around 16km (10 miles) up Okinawa's west coast. Resistance is still light, with only 175 US soldiers killed in the campaign so far. Civilians prove one of the biggest problems. Okinawa has a civilian population of around 450,000, hampering offensive manoeuvres. Today alone, around 9000 civilians surrender to the Americans.

KAMIKAZE, *OKINAWA*
Japanese kamikaze aircraft attack in mass waves around Okinawa. US shipping suffers heavily, with two destroyers sunk and twenty-four other ships damaged.

POLITICS, *TOKYO*
The Japanese prime minister, Koiso Kuniaki, and his cabinet resign as

◀ Following their capture of Pyawbwe, Burma, from the Japanese, Indian troops help to rearm a tank with ammunition.

the war closes in on the Japanese homelands. The 78-year-old Admiral Suzuki Kantaro becomes prime minister, who begins to make ambiguous peace overtures to the Allies.

POLITICS, *MOSCOW*
In an important announcement, the Soviet foreign minister, Vyacheslav Molotov, tells the Japanese ambassador that the USSR will not renew its five-year neutrality pact with Japan. The announcement opens the possibility of Japan fighting against the Russians in Manchuria. Molotov says the change in policy is a consequence of the Japanese alliance with Germany.

APRIL 7

SEA WAR, *EAST CHINA SEA*
The Japanese Navy dispatches a large battle group to attack US shipping around Okinawa. It includes the mighty battleship *Yamato*, an Agano-class cruiser, a light cruiser and a collection of destroyers. The force is spotted by US carrier aircraft south of Kyushu, and is engaged in the East China Sea well before it reaches Okinawa. Japanese aviation losses mean that US aircraft face no aerial opposition, and in the subsequent action the *Yamato*, the Agano-class cruiser, one other cruiser and three destroyers are sunk. This signals the effective end of the Japanese Navy in the Pacific.

▼ On Okinawa, US troops clear a cave with grenades and small-arms fire. Knocking out enemy positions was bloody and time-consuming work.

▲ *US flamethrower tanks of the 7th Infantry Division burn out the enemy defending Hill 178 on Okinawa.*

LAND WAR, *RYUKYU ISLANDS*
Heavy Japanese resistance begins to emerge from the rocky landscape of southern Okinawa, especially around the villages of Uchitomari and Kaniku. Inland areas are laced with networks of defensive positions, and US troops are met by powerful small-arms, artillery and mortar fire. In the north, the Marines are continuing to make good progress, reaching Nago town on the west coast and Ora Bay on the east coast.

APRIL 9

LAND WAR, *RYUKYU ISLANDS*
Around half of the Motobu Peninsula is brought under US control. Enemy resistance in the area is described

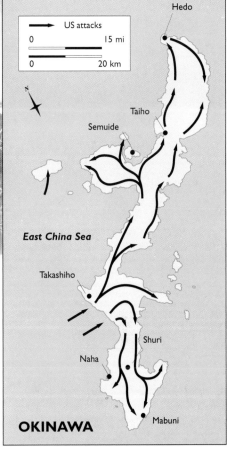

▲ *The US invasion of Okinawa cost the Americans over 12,000 dead (compared to 110,000 Japanese), while at sea 36 US ships were sunk, most by kamikaze attacks. In the air, the Americans lost 763 aircraft to the Japanese 4155.*

APRIL 10

▲ On the road to Rangoon. A column of British tanks and infantry halt after coming under Japanese sniper fire.

in a US report as "scattered and ineffective". Southern-sector operations, by contrast, are extremely slow, as the enemy begins to make repeated counterattacks from a string of heavy defensive positions known as the "Shuri Line". These positions stretch across the island for roughly 7315m (24,000ft) and include interlocking trench and pillbox systems, blockhouses, fortified caves and strongly constructed bunkers. Naval and aerial bombardments are used in an effort to smash enemy emplacements. More than 43,000 Okinawan civilians are now under US protection.

LAND WAR, *PHILIPPINES*
US Army troops of the 41st Division make an amphibious landing on Jolo in the Sulu archipelago, to the west of Mindanao.

APRIL 10

AIR WAR, *OKINAWA*
Heavy Japanese kamikaze and bombing attacks damage the battleship USS *Missouri* and the carriers USS *Enterprise* and USS *Essex*, plus 10 other vessels.

LAND WAR, *PHILIPPINES*
US troops advancing down through Luzon reach Mauban on Lamon Bay, near the entrance to the Bicol Peninsula.

APRIL 11

LAND WAR, *BURMA*
Troops of the 7th Indian Division capture Pyawbwe, about 32km (20 miles) south of Meiktila, on the main rail route between Meiktila and Rangoon. Japanese forces are retreating south at a rapid pace.

APRIL 12

PRESIDENCY, *US*
The US president, Franklin D. Roosevelt, dies at the age of 63. Into his

▼ US Marines engaged against enemy forces on Okinawa. The soldier closest to the camera is armed with an MI Carbine semi-automatic rifle.

place steps the US vice-president, Harry S. Truman.

LAND WAR, *RYUKYU ISLANDS*
While US troops on Okinawa are deadlocked with the Japanese defenders, more kamikaze raids hit the US Navy around the island. Suicide aircraft damage 15 ships, and a piloted bomb sinks the destroyer USS *Mannert L. Abele*.

APRIL 12–15

AIR WAR, *JAPAN*
US Pacific Fleet aircraft carry out three days of attacks over Kyushu, southern Japan. The main targets are air bases at

▲ Allied forces in Burma land at Elephant Point, just south of Rangoon, in the final phase of the campaign to liberate the country from the Japanese.

Kikai, Tanega, Kanoya and Kushira. A total of 246 Japanese aircraft are either destroyed or damaged in the raids.

APRIL 13

LAND WAR, *RYUKYU ISLANDS*
In the south of Okinawa, a battalion-strength Japanese force counterattacks US XXIV Corps troops. The attack is utterly destroyed by US infantry weapons supported by offshore naval gunfire.
AIR WAR, *FORMOSA*
Seafire and Hellcat fighters of the British Pacific Fleet attack Shinchiku and Kiirun airfields on Formosa. Sixteen enemy planes are shot down, one is destroyed on the

THE LIBERATION OF BURMA

- - -▶ Allied advances
──▶ Japanese counterattacks

ground, and five others are badly damaged.

APRIL 14

LAND WAR, *RYUKYU ISLANDS*
Troops of US Marine III Amphibious Corps make good advances in northern Okinawa, reaching Hedo Point, the northernmost tip of the island, as well as securing almost all of the Motobu Penin-

◀ British and Indian paratroopers carry out equipment checks prior to a drop near Rangoon.

▲ Between December 4, 1944, and May 4, 1945, the liberation of Burma was largely complete. However, it took the Allies until August 1945 to wipe out the last pockets of Japanese resistance.

sula and moving to Momubaru town on the west coast, and Arakawa town on the east coast. Through the night of April 14/15, the Japanese in the south make three counterattacks, all of which are defeated with heavy Japanese casualties.
AIR WAR, *TOKYO*
More than 320 US B-29 bombers drop incendiary bombs on Tokyo, obliterating 16 sq km (6.3 sq miles) of the city.

APRIL 16

AIR WAR, *OKINAWA*
In one incident, a single US destroyer is attacked for more than four hours and

is hit by four bombs and two suicide aircraft. However, the destroyer manages to shoot down six enemy aircraft and remain operational. Another destroyer, the USS *Pringle*, is sunk by a suicide attack. The carrier USS *Intrepid* and the battleship USS *Missouri* are also damaged.

LAND WAR, *PHILIPPINES*

US forces land on Carabao to find that the Japanese defenders have gone. Carabao was subjected to two days of bombardment before the landings.

APRIL 16–17

LAND WAR, *RYUKYU ISLANDS*

Troops from XXIV Corps are landed on Ie Shima, a small island off Okinawa's Motobu Peninsula. Ie Shima offers an additional airfield and anchorage for US ships. Japanese resistance intensifies once the US troops advance inland, but by the end of the day the airfield is captured. By the end of the 17th, at least two-thirds of the island is in US hands.

APRIL 17

AIR WAR, *RYUKYU ISLANDS*

A US Navy communiqué reports that, in the period March 18–April 17, 1945, more than 2200 Japanese aircraft have been destroyed in the Ryukyu Islands area, with US carrier aircraft accounting for 1600 of the total. The communiqué also states that British Pacific Fleet aircraft operating off the Sakishimas and Formosa have destroyed more than 80 enemy planes.

LAND WAR, *PHILIPPINES*

The US X Corps puts the 17th Division ashore at Cotabato on Mindanao fol-

lowing heavy bombardments, one of more than 50 amphibious operations conducted around the southern Philippines between February and July 1945. The bulk of the Japanese Thirty-Fifth Army is concentrated on Mindanao, and inland fighting is heavy.

APRIL 18

LAND WAR, *RYUKYU ISLANDS*

While XXIV Corps' positions change little in southern Okinawa, US Marine Corps troops reach the northern tip of the island. On Ie Shima, US troops are struggling to dislodge Japanese defenders from dug-in positions around Iegusugu Peak.

CORRESPONDENTS, *IE SHIMA*

The famous US war correspondent Ernie Pyle is killed by a Japanese sniper

▲ *A US soldier on Okinawa loading a 57mm recoilless rifle with a perforated cartridge, which vented out propellant gases via the breech mechanism.*

at the age of 44. He had followed US soldiers in almost every theatre of their operations, and was deeply loved by the common US soldier.

APRIL 19

LAND WAR, *RYUKYU ISLANDS*

XXIV Corps begins a major offensive to dislodge the Japanese defenders from the Shuri Line in southern Okinawa. The day opens with a huge artillery

▼ *The carrier USS **Bunker Hill** burns after being hit by two kamikaze aircraft off Okinawa. She suffered 346 killed, 43 missing, and 264 wounded, but managed to limp back to port for repairs.*

▲ *A Vought Corsair attacks Japanese positions on Okinawa. The aircraft has just fired its whole complement of eight 5in rockets.*

barrage from US Marine and US Army guns, supported by one of the largest naval support bombardments of the Pacific war. At 06:00 hours, troops of the 7th, 27th and 96th Divisions begin the assault, and against terrible Japanese fire manage to advance about 914m (3000ft) and capture the village of Machinato.

AIR WAR, *TOKYO*
US P-51 Mustang fighters attack Atsugi airfield around Tokyo, shooting down 23 Japanese aircraft and destroying or damaging 51 others.

LAND WAR, *BURMA*
Britain's XXXIII Corps and IV Corps continue to make strong advances towards Rangoon. On the 19th, Pyinmana falls to IV Corps, a position only 64km (40 miles) from the important air base at Toungoo. On the right flank of the advance, troops of XXXIII Corps are closing up against Japanese positions on a 160km (100-mile) stretch of the Irrawaddy River.

▼ *The damage in the hangar deck of USS* Sangamon *following a kamikaze attack. Losses were 11 dead and 21 wounded.*

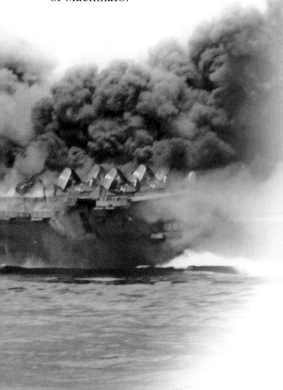

APRIL 21

LAND WAR, *RYUKYU ISLANDS*
The US flag is raised over Iegusugu Peak on Ie Shima, after several days of hard fighting to dislodge Japanese defenders. The island is now under US control, although mopping-up operations continue. Japanese dead number around 100,000.

APRIL 21–25

LAND WAR, *RYUKYU ISLANDS*
XXIV Corps troops make gains on southern Okinawa. US soldiers capture Kakuza town and take key points on Hill 178, a major Japanese stronghold on the left flank of the American advance. By the 25th, the US Navy has recorded a total of 21,269 Japanese troops dead on Okinawa and the surrounding islands.

APRIL 22

LAND WAR, *PHILIPPINES*
The US 31st Division is landed on Mindanao in support of 24th Division operations in the southwest of the island. North of Mindanao, US forces consolidate their hold over Cebu Island.

▼ *A US M1 8in howitzer, nicknamed Comanche, opens fire on the island of Luzon. The M1 fired a 91kg (200lb) shell up to a range of 16,970m (55,676ft).*

▶ *The aftermath of a banzai charge on Mindanao: dead Japanese soldiers litter the ground following their assault against soldiers of the US 124th Regiment.*

APRIL 22–24

LAND WAR, *BURMA*
The Allies capture the air base and town at Toungou, having advanced 80km (50 miles) in three days. The 3000 men of the 1st Division, Indian National Army (INA), surrender to the Allies near Pyu. The INA has been fighting on the Japanese side in Burma since June 1943, and many of those who surrender are subsequently put on trial.

APRIL 25–30

KAMIKAZE, *OKINAWA*
Japanese kamikaze air attacks continue until the end of the month. More than 30 US ships are damaged.

APRIL 29

KAMIKAZE, *RYUKYU ISLANDS*
The US Navy hospital ship USS *Comfort* is hit by a Japanese kamikaze aircraft off Okinawa. Twenty-nine patients and crew are killed, another hundred are missing, and thirty-three are wounded.

LAND WAR, *RYUKYU ISLANDS*
US troops capture Machinato airfield in southern Okinawa.

LAND WAR, *BURMA*
Troops of the 20th Indian Division capture Allanmyo on the Irrawaddy, less than 64km (40 miles) from Prome.

MAY 1

AIR WAR, *RYUKYU ISLANDS*
US carrier aircraft begin strikes throughout the Ryukyu Islands, today hitting Kuro and Kuchino Islands in the north of the chain.

LAND WAR, *BORNEO*
A naval attack force, commanded by Vice-Admiral

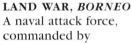

▲ The charred and mangled body of a Japanese soldier following a raid on a US airfield on Okinawa.

MAY 2

LAND WAR, *PHILIPPINES*
US troops of the 158th Regiment advancing northwards through Luzon from Legaspi meet with US soldiers moving south through the Bicol Peninsula. The meeting traps Japanese forces in positions east of Naga.

MAY 3

LAND WAR, *SOUTHERN PHILIPPINES*
US Army troops go ashore at Santa Cruz in the Davao Gulf, establishing a southern flank as part of an offensive against the Japanese Thirty-Fifth

V.E. Barbey, lands a contingent of troops of the Australian 26th Brigade Group and the Royal Australian Air Force on Tarakan Island, Borneo. The 17,000 Australians have the objective of seizing the 24km (15-mile) island, which contains major oil resources and an air base which the Allies wish to use for operations over Borneo. Resistance is fierce from the start, and the campaign to take the island will be one of Australia's bloodiest battles of the war.

MAY 1–2

LAND WAR, *RYUKYU ISLANDS*
On May 1, US troops of the 7th Infantry Division make advances on the eastern flank of operations in the south of the island, reaching the village of Kuhazu. The next day, a heavy offshore bombardment from US Navy vessels destroys a number of enemy emplacements and bunkers, and allows the infantry to make further advances of around 1km (0.6 miles), relying heavily on armour and flame-throwers to make headway.

MAY 1–3

LAND WAR, *BURMA*
The British Fourteenth Army occupies Rangoon after a light-

ning advance down through Burma. On May 1, "Operation Dracula" is launched when soldiers of the Gurkha Parachute Battalion are dropped south of the city, joining the next day with a landing of the 26th Indian Division in the Gulf of Martaban. Rangoon is caught in a pincer movement between the southern advance and the 17th Indian Division advancing down from the north, which reaches Pegu – 64km (40 miles) from Rangoon – on May 2. The Japanese in Rangoon realize their position is untenable, and abandon the city. To the northwest, XXXIII Corps forces take Prome on May 3; Thayetmyo falls two days later.

▶ A US Marine makes a dash for cover on Okinawa, at a site nicknamed "Death Valley". At this particular place the Marines suffered 125 casualties in 8 hours.

MAY 3-4

▶ A Corsair of Marine Air Group 33 at Okinawa, one of 700 US Marine aircraft that took part in the campaign.

Army, which occupies strong positions in central Mindanao.

MAY 3-4

LAND WAR, *RYUKYU ISLANDS*
Japanese forces attempt two ambitious amphibious counterattacks in southern Okinawa. Approximately 600 Japanese soldiers try to land on the east and west coasts of Okinawa behind US lines. Predictably, the attacks are defeated, the east coast assault being repulsed at sea, while the west coast group lands but is contained and destroyed. One of the attacks is coordinated with an air strike on Yontan airfield, but Japanese aviators suffer heavy losses.

MAY 3-4

SEA/AIR WAR, *OKINAWA*
Japanese kamikaze and conventional aircraft make a major attack on US shipping around Okinawa. On May 3, three US destroyers – USS *Luce*, USS *Morrison* and USS *Little* – are sunk by suicide aircraft, and eight other vessels are severely damaged. The next day, a further 10 vessels are damaged, including the escort carrier USS Sangamon, but 168 Japanese aircraft are shot down.

MAY 4

AIR WAR, *PACIFIC*
The US Navy establishes a major air operating base on Guam known as Fleet Air Wing 18. The aircraft stationed there will be capable of major air operations over the central and western Pacific.

LAND WAR, *RYUKYU ISLANDS*
The Japanese carry out a general counterattack in southern Okinawa,

firing a heavy preliminary artillery bombardment and supporting the attack with tanks and other armoured vehicles. The attack is beaten off by massive US artillery supremacy and destructive strafing by US carrier aircraft. US forces respond to the Japanese defeat by resuming the advance, beginning an assault against the key high ground of Hill 187. US estimates place the Japanese death toll in the Okinawa campaign to date at around 33,000.

MAY 4-5

SEA WAR, *SAKISHIMA GROUP*
Warships of the British Pacific Fleet bombard Miyako Island in the Sakishima Group, southeast of Okinawa. The firepower is directed against the Hirara and Nobara airfields, and is coordinated with a strike by British carrier aircraft that destroys at least 22 Japanese aircraft.

MAY 5

AIR WAR, *KOREA STRAITS*
US aircraft of Fleet Air Wing One flying from Okinawa attack Japanese vessels sailing along the coastline of western Korea. Two large oilers and five cargo ships are sunk, and fourteen other ships are left badly damaged.

▼ American M4 Sherman tanks on Okinawa. The spare tracks attached to the front of the hulls gave additional protection to the crew.

KAMIKAZE, *OKINAWA*
Seventeen US ships are sunk by a mass kamikaze attack off Okinawa. Yesterday, the British carriers HMS *Indomitable* and HMS *Formidable* were hit by kamikaze strikes off Japan, but suffered little damage owing to heavily armoured flight decks.

AIR WAR, *USA*
The US suffers its first civilian fatalities of the Pacific war. A Japanese bomb balloon, one of the hundreds released in the Pacific weeks earlier, kills six US civilians – a teacher and five children – in Oregon.

MAY 9

LAND WAR, *RYUKYU ISLANDS*
In celebration of the final unconditional surrender of Germany, which was signed two days ago, every US naval gun and artillery piece on and around Okinawa fires a single shell at Japanese positions. Bad weather over the last couple of days has led to reduced

▲ *Major-General Lemuel C. Shepherd, who commanded the US 6th Marine Division during the campaign on Okinawa.*

Japanese air activity over the island, although today two US destroyers are damaged by kamikaze aircraft.

MAY 10

LAND WAR, *PHILIPPINES*
Part of the US 40th Division is landed on the northern coast of Mindanao around Cagayan. The landing now means that the Japanese on Mindanao are effectively trapped between the northern, western and southern points of the US advance.

AIR WAR, *OKINAWA*
In a courageous attack, a US fighter of the 2nd Marine Aircraft Wing whose guns have jammed destroys a Japanese bomber by cutting off its tail assembly using the fighter's propeller. He attacks the Japanese bomber three times in this way before downing the aircraft.

LAND WAR, *RYUKYU ISLANDS*
The 6th Marine Division bridges the Asa River in southern Okinawa. The bridging effort is delayed for some hours by two Japanese human bomb attacks, but eventually the crossing is secured. Elsewhere in the south, particularly around the Shuri Line, US progress is slow, with hand-to-hand fighting in some sectors. The Japanese are attempting constant night attacks and night infiltration into the Tenth Army's lines.

MAY 11–12

KAMIKAZE, *OKINAWA*
Japanese suicide aircraft damage the carriers USS *Bunker Hill* and USS *Enterprise* and the destroyer USS *Evans*. The destroyer USS *Hugh W. Hadley* is also hit and damaged by an Ohka piloted bomb. The Americans, however, shoot down 93 enemy aircraft in reply – one destroyer alone shoots down 19

Japanese aircraft with sustained and intense anti-aircraft fire.

LAND WAR, *RYUKYU ISLANDS*
US forces launch a major offensive against the Okinawan capital, Naha, with elements of the 6th Marine Division penetrating the outer suburbs.

LAND WAR, *NEW GUINEA*
The 6th Australian Division attacks and occupies Wewak on the New Guinea coast. Wewak was the headquarters of the Japanese Eighteenth Army, and the remaining Japanese troops in the country are now widely dispersed and unable to mount organized resistance.

▼ *Japanese soldiers taken prisoner on Okinawa await interrogation. Only 7400 Japanese troops gave themselves up during the fighting.*

MAY 12

MAY 12

LAND WAR, *RYUKYU ISLANDS*
US Army forces are landed on Tori Shima, another island in the Ryukyu chain. The island, approximately 88km (55 miles) west of Okinawa, is captured without resistance.

MAY 13

AIR WAR, *JAPAN*
US carrier aircraft begin two days of air attacks over Kyushu, crippling its rail network, damaging its aviation production plans and destroying or damaging 272 Japanese aircraft. The aircraft carrier USS *Enterprise* is damaged by a suicide attack off the Japanese coast. All of Kyushu's airfields are now knocked out.

MAY 14

LAND WAR, *RYUKYU ISLANDS*
After a bloody five-day battle, US troops capture "Chocolate Drop Hill" east of Ishimmi and the Yonabaru airfield.

AIR WAR, *JAPAN*
The Japanese mainland is further devastated after 472 B-29 Superfortress bombers drop 2540 tonnes (2500 tons) of incendiary bombs on Nagoya. Nearly 15 sq km (6 sq miles) of the city are incinerated, and the Aichi and Mitsubishi aircraft works practically destroyed. In the air, 20 Japanese fighters are shot down by the bombers' fighter escorts.

MAY 15

POLITICS, *BURMA*
With the defeat of the Japanese Army in Burma essentially complete, the Burmese nationalist leader, Aung Sun, gives full cooperation to the Allied war effort.

▶ A column of US M4 Sherman tanks ford a river on Luzon while infantry use a makeshift bridge.

MAY 15–16

SEA WAR, *INDIAN OCEAN*
The Japanese heavy cruiser *Haguro* is sunk by a force of five British destroyers in the Malacca Strait as it attempts to evacuate Japanese Army troops from Andaman Island in the eastern Bay of Benghal.

MAY 16–18

LAND WAR, *RYUKYU ISLANDS*
US troops of the 96th Infantry Division engage in a ferocious evening battle to take "Conical Hill", southern Okinawa, against Japanese counterattacks. One company fights a one-hour grenade battle before ousting the Japanese from the summit. Another hill, known as "Sugar Loaf Hill", is taken by the 6th Marine Division on the 18th, the fifth time the summit has changed hands (it will change hands a total of 11 times during the course of the Okinawa battle). US troops have, over the last few days, advanced from the Asa to the Asato River, crushing two battalions of Japanese soldiers in the process.

◀ The wreckage of a Japanese fighter lies abandoned on a disused airstrip in Burma. By May 1945, the Japanese Fifteenth Army in Burma had largely disintegrated.

MAY 17

AIR WAR, *JAPAN*
USAAF P-51 Mustang fighters make a low-level attack on Atsugi airfield, Tokyo, and destroy or damage 42 Japanese aircraft with the loss of 1 of their number to anti-aircraft fire.

MAY 19

SEA WAR, *CHINA*
Japanese forces abandon the port of Foochow on the Chinese coast. Japanese-occupied Chinese ports have become untenable since the US capture of the Philippines, putting US air bases within striking range of Chinese coastal towns such as Amoy and Swatow, which have also been deserted by the enemy.

AIR WAR, *JAPAN*
The city of Hamamatsu is bombed by 279 Boeing B-29s.

MAY 20

LAND WAR, *RYUKYU ISLANDS*
The US Tenth Army surrounds the Japan-

◀ *After a hard-fought campaign in the Philippines, Douglas MacArthur reads the country's proclamation of liberation.*

▲ *Soldiers of the 6th Australian Division take cover from enemy fire during the capture of Wewak, off New Guinea.*

ese-held citadel of Shuri. Japanese troops make counterattacks across the southern sector, but all are repulsed. In a new variation on Japanese tactics, numbers of Japanese soldiers are found to be wearing US Marine uniforms and carrying US weapons. The US advance leads to the withdrawal of Japanese troops from the Shuri Line, although US troops still face hundreds of enemy emplacements in the far south of the island.

MAY 23

LAND WAR, *PHILIPPINES*
US X Corps and elements of the US 40th Division meet in central Mindanao in positions around Impalutao. Japanese forces are increasingly compressed into a small pocket of resistance in the east of the island, around 160km (100 miles) long by 80km (50 miles) wide.

MAY 26

LAND WAR, *BURMA*
Britain's XXXIII Corps occupies Bassein, an important railway town 128km (80 miles) to the west of Rangoon.

AIR WAR, *JAPAN*
A large B-29 raid (464 aircraft) on Tokyo nearly claims the lives of Emperor Hirohito and his family after the Imperial Palace is surrounded by fires.

MAY 27

AIR WAR, *OKINAWA*
Combined bombing and suicide attacks on US Navy vessels around Okinawa

sink the destroyer USS *Drexler* and damage eight other ships.

LAND WAR, *RYUKYU ISLANDS*
US infantry and Marines secure most of Naha, the Okinawan capital. Appalling rains slow the US advance even more, however. On average, US troops in the south of Okinawa have advanced only around 274m (900ft) a day.

LAND WAR, *CHINA*
Chinese Nationalist troops win an important victory in southern China by capturing the city of Nanning, the capital of Kwangsi Province. Nanning is only 128km (80 miles) from the border of Indochina, and its loss means that the Japanese Army in China is cut off from its forces in Burma, Thailand, Indochina and Malaya.

May 29

AIR WAR, *JAPAN*
Tokyo is devastated once again by B-29 raids, which this time burn up nearly 44 sq km (17 sq miles) of the battered city.

June 1

AIR WAR, *PACIFIC*
A US naval air facility is established on Peleliu in the Palau Group.

AIR WAR, *JAPAN*
The Japanese city of Osaka is devastated by a huge B-29 raid in which 3048 tonnes (3000 tons) of incendiary munitions are dropped. Osaka becomes a non-functioning city, as most of its workforce has been dispersed.

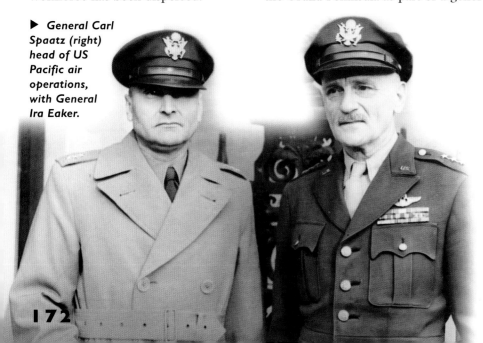

▶ **General Carl Spaatz (right) head of US Pacific air operations, with General Ira Eaker.**

▲ *Japanese civil defence measures: an officer instructs women civilians on the proper use of gas masks.*

June 3

LAND WAR, *RYUKYU ISLANDS*
US Marines are landed on Iheya Shima in the Ryukyu Islands.

June 4

LAND WAR, *RYUKYU ISLANDS*
The US 6th Marine Division makes an amphibious landing on the coastline of the Oruku Peninsula as part of a gener-

al US offensive to take Naha and its airfield in southern Okinawa. Fighting is extremely heavy.

JUNE 5

TYPHOON, *RYUKYU ISLANDS*

A huge typhoon hits the US fleet off Okinawa, causing massive destruction. Thirty-five ships are damaged, including four battleships and eight carriers.

AIR WAR, *JAPAN*

More than 3048 tonnes (3000 tons) of incendiaries are dropped over Kobe in a raid by 473 B-29 bombers.

JUNE 6

LAND WAR, *CHINA*

Japanese forces in southern China retreat back to Kweilin, the whole Ichi-Go offensive having collapsed with the Japanese being pushed back nearly 320km (200 miles) in two weeks.

JUNE 8

AIR WAR, *JAPAN*

US carrier aircraft attack Kanoya airfield on Kyushu, inflicting further damage on Japanese homeland air resources.

SEA WAR, *JAVA SEA*

The Japanese cruiser Ashigara is torpedoed and sunk by the British submarine HMS *Trenchant*.

JUNE 8–9

SEA WAR, *BORNEO*

Allied cruisers and destroyers lay down a heavy two-day bombardment on Japanese facilities around Brunei Bay, on North Borneo's northwest coast.

JUNE 9

LAND WAR, *RYUKYU ISLANDS*

US Marines go ashore on Aguni Shima in the Ryukyu chain.

LAND WAR, *PHILIPPINES*

The Japanese forces on Mindanao lose their defensive positions at Mandong, critically weakening any attempt to mount organized resistance.

JUNE 10–13

LAND WAR, *RYUKYU ISLANDS*

US forces in the Oruku Peninsula make slow progress against the Japanese, compressing them into an area of little more than 1000 sq m (10,800 sq ft). Many Japanese troops begin committing suicide as they realize their defeat is near. By the 13th, all resistance in the peninsula has been crushed, and a US victory on Okinawa is at last in sight.

▼ *A Japanese mother and son eat a meal in a shack amidst the rubble of a Japanese city devastated by US airpower.*

KEY PERSONALITIES

EMPEROR HIROHITO

Michinomiya Hirohito (1901–89) was the longest-reigning monarch in Japanese history, taking the throne in 1926 and keeping it until his death in 1989. Although the figurehead of Japanese power, with a quasi-divine status among his people, Hirohito's control over the events that led to war was limited, de facto power residing in the control of the Japanese state by the military establishment. Recent research has shown that Hirohito was actually opposed both to an alliance with Germany and Italy in the Tripartite Pact, and to the Japanese war with the US. Hideki Tojo was the true instigator of the Pacific War, and it was he who rejected a note from President Roosevelt on December 6, 1941, that attempted to avert a conflict.

Hirohito did not believe that Japan could sustain a war against the US, and even in 1942 was urging Tojo to end the conflict. By 1945, Tojo was gone from office and a large number of senior politicians had joined the peace movement. Following the devastation of Hiroshima and Nagasaki by atomic bombs, Hirohito broke with imperial precedent (traditionally, the Emperor is publicly silent) and announced on radio on August 15, 1945 that Japan would accept the US demand for unconditional surrender. In a further step, on January 1, 1946, he announced to the Japanese people that there was no divine status in his office or person. By so doing, and for his role in closing the Japanese resistance, Hirohito managed to escape Allied war crime trials.

JUNE 10

JUNE 10

LAND WAR, *BORNEO*
Following a two-day bombardment, Australian troops are landed at Brunei Bay (a proposed advanced base for the British Pacific Fleet) and on Labuan and Muara Islands. More than 30,000 Japanese troops are located in Borneo's interior, and at this late stage in the war the Australians do not want to waste lives with unnecessary campaigning. Consequently, the Australian troops consolidate only the coastal strip around the landing area, while Allied Special Operations Australia (SOA) units control Japanese forces inland.

JUNE 14–16

AIR WAR, *CAROLINE ISLANDS*
British carrier aircraft mount a two-day attack against remaining Japanese bases in the Caroline Islands. Such is the weakened state of the Japanese Air Force by this stage that they meet no aerial resistance.

JUNE 15

AIR WAR, *JAPAN*
The blighted city of Osaka is revisited by US B-29s, and is bombarded with a further 3048 tonnes (3000 tons) of bombs and incendiaries.

JUNE 17–18

LAND WAR, *RYUKYU ISLANDS*
Both sides on Okinawa suffer the loss of senior commanders. On the 17th, the commander of the Japanese naval base on Okinawa, Admiral Minoru Ota, commits suicide. The next day, the C-in-C of the US Tenth Army, Lieutenant-General Simon B. Buckner, is killed by shrapnel from an exploding shell, only three days before the final US victory.

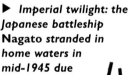

▶ *Imperial twilight: the Japanese battleship* **Nagato** *stranded in home waters in mid-1945 due to severe fuel shortages.*

JUNE 20–25

LAND WAR, *BORNEO*
Australian soldiers capture major oil fields at Seria on the 20th; two days later, the island of Tarakan is finally secured. On the 25th, the Miri oil fields on Sarawak also fall into Allied hands.

JUNE 21

LAND WAR, *RYUKYU ISLANDS*
The hard-fought battle to capture Okinawa comes to an end as US forces finally overwhelm Japanese defenders in the south of the island. The Japanese commander, Lieutenant-General Ushijima Mitsuru, commits suicide. Although Japanese casualties are not confirmed, the figure is around 100,000 dead – unusually, nearly 7500 Japanese soldiers surrender. The US also

◀ *The Japanese city of Hamamatsu after the B-29 raid on June 18, which destroyed 15,160 houses and killed 1157 civilians. Air force bases and munitions factories were positioned in and around the city.*

suffers badly in the campaign, with 7613 US Marines and US Army infantry being killed, and 31,807 wounded. In addition, the US Navy loses 4900 seamen with 36 vessels sunk and 368 damaged. The air war over Okinawa has been equally bitter. Japanese aviation losses number around 8000; 4000 of these shot down during combat missions. US aviation has lost 763 aircraft. The capture of Okinawa gives the Americans an invaluable operating base only 550km (340 miles) from Japan.

POLITICS, *JAPAN*

Emperor Hirohito pleads with the Japanese cabinet to find a diplomatic way to negotiate peace with the US. US forces are now less than 643km (400 miles) away, and Japanese cities are being devastated by B-29 strikes almost every night.

JUNE 23

LAND WAR, *PHILIPPINES*

Part of the 511th Parachute Infantry Regiment is dropped on the far north coast of Luzon around Aparri. It joins with other US Army forces and advances southwards to meet US Sixth Army units moving northwards towards Tuguegarao.

JUNE 24

THAILAND, RIVER KWAI

The bridge over the River Kwai, symbol of the horrifying use of slave and POW labour by the Japanese, is destroyed in a British bombing raid. The Japanese rail link to Thailand is being cut to pieces by Allied bombing, with US forces even using new radar-guided bombs to make accurate hits on bridges and depots.

◀ *The heavy American raids on Japanese cities in 1945 made tens of thousand of people homeless, such as these two factory workers.*

JUNE 25

LAND WAR, *PHILIPPINES*
Tuguegarao and its air base fall into US hands. The next day, US troops advancing from Aparri meet up with US troops coming up from the south, thus completing the encirclement of Japanese forces in northern Luzon.

▼ *At the Potsdam Conference, Stalin (right) met the new leaders of the US and Britain: Truman (centre) and Attlee (left).*

JUNE 26

LAND WAR, *RYUKYU ISLANDS*
US Marine units are landed on Kume Shima in the Ryukyu Islands.
LAND WAR, *CHINA*
The Chinese begin to claw back southern air bases lost to the Japanese. Today, the airfield at Liuchow is recaptured.

JUNE 28

LAND WAR, *PHILIPPINES*
General MacArthur announces the

▲ *A Japanese Kaiten "human torpedo" is launched from a cruiser near Kure, Japan. Over 300 were built in 1944–45.*

effective recapture of Luzon from the Japanese. Although organized Japanese resistance has collapsed, there is much mopping-up work to do. US forces have lost 7933 men killed and 32,732 wounded retaking Luzon, as opposed to 192,000 Japanese dead.

JUNE 29

STRATEGY, *PACIFIC*
Capitalizing on the release of troops from the European theatre, US President Truman approves a joint chiefs of

▶ *USS Indianapolis, seen here shelling Saipan, delivered bomb components for "Little Boy" to Tinian. She was sunk on July 30.*

staff plan for an invasion of mainland Japan. Two operations are outlined, involving a total of 36 US divisions. The first, "Operation Olympic", proposes landing 13 divisions on Kyushu on November 1, 1945. The second, "Operation Coronet", looks to land the remaining 23 divisions on Honshu on March 1, 1946.

JULY 1

SEA WAR, *PACIFIC*

The American submarine USS *Barb* attacks enemy coastal installations at Kaihyo Island off the east coast of Karafuto. It is the first time a submarine has used rockets to attack an enemy shore position.

LAND WAR, *CHINA*

Chinese troops advancing through southern China capture Liuchow, a key town astride the main north–south rail line and featuring a large air base formerly used by US air units. USAAF forces are now working to reopen captured air bases for the strategic bombing campaign against mainland Japan.

JULY 2

HOME WAR, *JAPAN*

The Japanese Government states that the US air raids have caused five million casualties among the Japanese civilian population.

JULY 3–5

LAND WAR, *BORNEO*

Australian forces capture the airfield at Sepinggang. Two days later, further troops are landed at Balikpapen Bay, and

the Australian 7th Division is now making good advances into Borneo's interior and along its coastline.

JULY 5

LAND WAR, *PHILIPPINES*

General MacArthur announces that the Philippines are now liberated from Japanese control. The Philippines campaign has been the largest operation for US forces in the Pacific, and the Japanese have lost well over 200,000 men. However, many other Japanese troops remain on the island – around 50,000 will surrender at the end of the war.

POLITICS, *AUSTRALIA*

The Australian prime minister, John Curtin, dies at the age of 60. Curtin had held the post since October 1941, and although his political power was tenuous at times he had fully mobilized Australia for war, often against internal government opposition. More than 30,000 people attend his funeral in Perth on July 9.

POLITICS, *US*

General Carl A. "Tooey" Spaatz is appointed head of US Strategic Air Forces in the Pacific. Spaatz had formerly commanded the US bombing effort against Germany, and now he will oversee the air campaign against Japan and the deployment of the atomic bombs.

▲ *A victim of US airpower. The battleship* Ise *lies wrecked in Kure harbour after being hit 23 times by bombs dropped from aircraft belonging to Task Force 38.*

▲ *Under mortar and small-arms fire, British Lee tanks near a Japanese position during mopping-up operations in Burma.*

JULY 7–10

AIR WAR, *JAPAN*

US carrier aircraft attack Japanese airfields on the Tokyo plain. A total of 173 Japanese machines are destroyed, utterly overwhelmed by more than 1000 US fighter-bombers. Japan still has huge numbers of aircraft on the mainland, although many are committed to suicide missions. Japan also has an appalling deficit of trained pilots, and veteran US aviators easily pick off young crews with only a few hours' flying experience.

JULY 13

POLITICS, *ITALY*

In a largely symbolic gesture, Italy declares war on Japan.

POLITICS, *JAPAN*

The Japanese ambassador in Moscow, Naotake Sato, meets with the Soviet foreign minister, Molotov, and discusses possible peace initiatives with the Allies that do not involve Japan's unconditional surrender.

JULY 14–15

AIR WAR, *JAPAN*

US carrier-based aircraft bomb rail facilities, industrial targets and shipping around northern Honshu and Hokkaido, causing substantial infrastructure damage and sinking the destroyer *Tachibana*. Supporting the attacks is a naval group of battleships, cruisers and destroyers under Rear-Admiral J.F. Shafroth, which attacks coastal targets around Kamaishi, Honshu, on the 14th; and steel and iron works around Muroran, Hokkaido, on the 15th. This is the first time US warships have fired directly at Japan, and such attacks now become daily events.

JULY 16

TECHNOLOGY, *ATOMIC BOMB*

The first atomic bomb is successfully exploded in the

◀ *A member of the Japanese Fifteenth Army in Burma (right) who chose to give himself up to the British.*

desert at Alamogordo, New Mexico. The bomb is a 20-kiloton device (explosive force equivalent to 20,320 tonnes/20,000 tons of TNT) and raises a mushroom cloud that towers to 12,200m (40,000ft).

POLITICS, *POTSDAM*

Churchill, Stalin and Roosevelt meet in Potsdam to discuss the strategy of completing World War II, and the politics of dividing up conquered Europe. They are told of the successful detonation of the first atomic bomb.

JULY 18

AIR WAR, *JAPAN*

US carrier aircraft from the Third Fleet attack Yokosuka naval base and airfields around Tokyo. Japan's last big warship, the battleship *Nagato*, is sunk.

SEA WAR, *JAPAN*

The coastal city of Hitachi is pounded by a fierce one-hour bombardment

◄ *A B-29 Superfortress accompanied by a swarm of North American P-51 Mustang fighters. With drop tanks the P-51 had an operational range of 2080km (1300 miles).*

(an island located between Japan and mainland Asia). Once ashore, they blow up a Japanese train before escaping.

JULY 24

SEA WAR, *PHILIPPINES*
The US destroyer USS *Underhill* is critically damaged by a Japanese piloted torpedo, and is later scuttled. The Japanese piloted torpedoes (Kaiten) were essentially Long Lance torpedoes fitted with an operating compartment and a conning tower for use by a single crewman.

JULY 24–25

AIR WAR, *JAPAN*
The remaining strength of the Japanese Navy is further devastated by a two-day

from US Navy warships, which fire 2032 tonnes (2000 tons) of shells.

JULY 19

KAMIKAZE, *OKINAWA*
The US destroyer USS *Thatcher* is hit and badly damaged in a suicide attack.

JULY 21–25

POLITICS, ATOMIC BOMB
At the Potsdam Conference, Roosevelt and Churchill agree to the use of the atomic bomb; and, after Tokyo issues a rebuttal of Allied surrender demands, President Truman gives the order that the A-bomb can be used operationally after August 3.

JULY 23

RAID, *KARAFUTO*
The submarine USS *Barb* lands US raiding forces on the east coast of Karafuto

STRATEGY AND TACTICS

THE INVASION OF JAPAN

Although the atomic bombs removed the need for a conventional invasion of Japan, the campaign was planned in detail and forces gathered for its execution. The invasion had two proposed stages. First, Operation Olympic would land the US Sixth Army, 13 divisions strong, on Kyushu in the far south of Japan on November 1, 1945, securing key naval and aviation bases and pulling enemy forces down into the south of Japan. Then, on March 1, 1946, Operation Coronet would be launched against Tokyo. Here, the US Eighth Army and US First Army, totalling 14 divisions, would land in a pincer movement around Tokyo itself, driving with heavy armoured forces to Kumagaya and Koga and isolating the capital for capture.

Despite undeniable US superiority in the Pacific at this stage of the war, there were deep fears about levels of US casualties. The experience of island clearance in places such as Iwo Jima and Okinawa led US Army and Marine Corps chiefs to predict some 500,000 US casualties to take Japan. This level of human loss was unacceptable to the US president and his staff, and the preference was for the deployment of atomic bombs.

DECISIVE WEAPONS

THE MANHATTAN PROJECT

The "Manhattan Project" was the codename for the US atomic weapons programme. The origins of the project go back to 1939, when top US scientists, including the influential Albert Einstein, persuaded President Roosevelt of the military possibilities for fission chain reactions of atomic elements. Official work began in February 1940 with a grant of $6000, but on December 6, 1941 – with war raging in Europe and threatening in the Far East – the programme was substantially upgraded and placed under the jurisdiction of the Office of Scientific Research and Development. The War Department took joint management following the Japanese attack on Pearl Harbor.

The programme assumed the name Manhattan Project in 1942 after the US Army engineers of the Manhattan district, who were given the task of constructing the initial plants for the work.

Scientists such as Ernest Orlando Lawrence and Philip Hauge Alberson spent the next three years working on methods of producing usable amounts of uranium-235 and plutonium-239 suitable for the fission process. Most of this work was conducted at the Oak Ridge reactor plant near Knoxville, Tennessee; the metallurgical department of the University of Chicago; and the Hanford Engineer Works near Pasco, Washington.

The job of turning fissionable material into a nuclear weapon fell to Robert Oppenheimer and the staff of his laboratory established in 1943 in the desert at Los Alamos, New Mexico. Oppenheimer had to devise a weapon that could create a supercritical mass of fissionable material to produce an explosion, and in the summer of 1945 the Hanford Works gave him enough plutonium-239 to conduct his first test. On July 16, 1945, the first atomic bomb was exploded at Alamogordo, New Mexico, producing a blast the equivalent of 20,320 tonnes (20,000 tons) of TNT, sending a mushroom cloud 12,200m (40,000ft) into the air and fusing the desert sand into glass. The US, having ultimately invested two billion dollars in the Manhattan Project, now had its atomic bomb.

▲ *Enola Gay, the B-29 Superfortress commanded by Colonel Paul W. Tibbets that dropped the first atomic bomb on August 6, 1945.*

attack by carrier aircraft over the Inland Sea, hitting Kure Naval Base and airfields at Nagoya, Osaka and Miho. Three battleships, one escort carrier and two heavy cruisers are sunk. Kure is hit again three days later, and one aircraft carrier and five other vessels are sunk.

JULY 26

POLITICS, *PACIFIC*
The Potsdam Declaration is delivered to the Japanese Government. It calls for

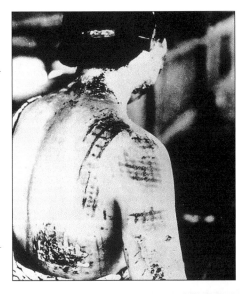

JULY 28

KAMIKAZE, *OKINAWA*

The US destroyer USS *Callaghan* is hit and sunk by Japanese kamikaze aircraft around Okinawa. USS *Callaghan* will be the last Allied warship in the Pacific campaign to be sunk by a kamikaze attack, although the next day a suicide plane damages the destroyer USS *Cassin Young*.

POLITICS, JAPAN

The Japanese Government rejects the Potsdam Declaration: the peacemakers in the cabinet are overridden by belligerent military leaders such as Korechika Anami, the war minister; and army chief of staff Yoshijiro Umezu.

JULY 30

SEA WAR, *PHILIPPINE SEA*

The US heavy cruiser USS *Indianapolis* is sunk by a Japanese submarine in the Philippine Sea, having first delivered to Tinian the uranium for the atomic bomb. Only 316 of the 1196 crew survive, many dying slowly over three days in the remote Philippine Sea, suffering dehydration, shark attacks and drowning.

AUGUST 1

AIR/SEA WAR, *WAKE ISLAND*

US carrier aircraft and battleships bombard Japanese forces on Wake Island. The Japanese reply with coastal guns, damaging the battleship USS *Pennsylvania*.

AUGUST 2

POLITICS, *POTSDAM*

The Potsdam Conference comes to an end with a clear Allied commitment to deploy the atomic bomb to bring about the defeat of Japan.

AIR WAR, *JAPAN*

B-29 raids devastate Nagasaki and Toyama. The next day, B-29s drop huge volumes of sea mines around the Japanese coast, blockading harbours. In recent months, air-dropped sea mines have been sinking more Japanese ships than US submarines.

▲ *The atomic blast produced heat rays that caused terrible injuries. Here, a kimono pattern was branded onto skin.*

the unconditional surrender of Japan, the alternative being Japan's "prompt and utter destruction".

ATOMIC BOMB, *MARIANA ISLANDS*

The cruiser USS *Indianapolis* delivers a lethal consignment – enough uranium-235 to make the first atomic bomb – to Tinian air base in the Mariana Islands. A USAAF bomber unit, the 509th Composite Group, has been specially created and trained for the deployment of the atomic bomb against Japan.

▼ *Hiroshima after the atomic blast. By the end of December 1945, 140,000 of its 350,000 inhabitants had died either during the blast or from radiation poisoning.*

AUGUST 4

AUGUST 4

LAND WAR, *BURMA*
The final organized elements of the Japanese Twenty-Eighth Army are destroyed in heavy battle around the Pegu Yoma range, nearly 8500 of the 10,000 Japanese troops being killed. Although Burma is in Allied hands, isolated concentrations of Japanese troops remain throughout southern Burma, pushed up against the Irrawaddy and Sittang rivers.

AUGUST 4–6

AIR WAR, *JAPAN*
US B-29 bombers drop leaflets over Japan warning that, without a surrender, strategic bombing will destroy 12 more cities. On the night of August 5/6, six cities are totally devastated during incendiary attacks.

▼ *The ruins of Nagasaki following the dropping of the second atomic bomb on Japan by the Americans. After the bomb was dropped "black rain" fell in some areas, carrying radioactive materials from within the rising cloud of fission products.*

AUGUST 6

ATOMIC BOMB, *HIROSHIMA*
A 20-kiloton atomic bomb is dropped over the city of Hiroshima from the B-29 Enola Gay, piloted by Colonel Paul Tibbets. The initial blast kills around 100,000 people, leaving most of the survivors wounded and irradiated.

AUGUST 7

TECHNOLOGY, *JAPAN*
Japan flies its first and only turbojet aircraft, the Nakajima Kikka ("Orange Blossom"). The Kikka is essentially a smaller version of Germany's Me 262, and only 19 prototypes are built before the war comes to an end.

AUGUST 8

POLITICS, *SOVIET UNION*
The USSR declares war on Japan.

AUGUST 9

ATOMIC BOMB, *NAGASAKI*
Nagasaki is devastated by a second atomic bomb, this time dropped from the B-29 Bockscar. Around 35,000 people are killed and 60,000 wounded.

▲ *The B-29 nicknamed Bockscar dropped the atomic bomb on Nagasaki. Today, about a million visitors each year view Bockscar in the US Air Force Museum.*

SEA WAR, *JAPAN*
US battleships and cruisers attack Japanese industrial targets along the coast of Honshu, Japan.

LAND WAR, *MANCHURIA*
A huge Soviet offensive deploying more than 1.5 million troops is launched against the Japanese Army in Manchuria. The Japanese defence by the Kwantung Army crumbles, and the Soviet forces drive at speed towards the southern Manchurian coast.

▲ *President Truman announces Japan's surrender to members of the press at the White House in Washington.*

AUGUST 10

POLITICS, *JAPAN*
Emperor Hirohito tells the Japanese Government that he wishes to accept the terms of the Potsdam Declaration, and to announce Japan's unconditional surrender to the Allies.

AUGUST 11

POLITICS, *PACIFIC*
General MacArthur is declared the Allied Supreme Commander, giving him the authority to accept

the Japanese surrender on behalf of all the Allied nations.

AUGUST 13–14

AIR WAR, *TOKYO*
As a further incentive to get the Japanese to surrender, around 1600 US aircraft bomb Tokyo.

◄ *In accordance with their emperor's wishes, the military leaders of Japan's forces surrendered to the Allies. Here, General Takazo Numata (left) and Admiral Kaigye Chudo (centre) arrive at Rangoon to surrender their units.*

▲ *For the invasion of Manchuria the Soviets massed 1.6 million troops and 5550 tanks. The Japanese had 1 million troops and 1200 obsolete tanks.*

AUGUST 15

POLITICS, *JAPAN*
Emperor Hirohito breaks imperial silence and makes a radio broadcast to the Japanese people. He tells of his move to surrender Japan's forces, and asks the Japanese people not to resist the Allies. The next day, Hirohito orders Japanese troops at home and throughout the Pacific to lay down their arms.

AUGUST 17

AIR WAR, *JAPAN*
Carrier aircraft from the Third Fleet attack Japanese air bases around Tokyo, encountering surprisingly heavy opposition from Japanese aircraft.

POLITICS, *CHINA*
The Chinese Communist leadership tells the US Government that it wants territorial gains from any postwar settlement with Japan. The Soviet Union pledges to return Manchuria to China within three months of the end of hostilities with Japan.

AUGUST 17

POLITICS, *JAPAN*
General Prince Higashikuni becomes Japan's new prime minister, and forms a new cabinet to oversee the Japanese surrender to the Allies.

POLITICS, *DUTCH EAST INDIES*
Nationalist leaders in the Dutch East Indies declare independence from the Netherlands, renaming the country the Independent Republic of Indonesia.

AUGUST 18

INDIAN NATIONAL ARMY, *FORMOSA*
The Indian National Army's leader, Subhas Chandra Bose is killed in an air crash.

AUGUST 18–20

LAND WAR, *MANCHURIA*

In a massive offensive from the west, north and east, Soviet forces overwhelm the Kwantung Army in central Manchuria, capturing the cities of Harbin, Tsitsihar and Changchun in three successive days of campaigning.

AUGUST 21

SURRENDER, *MARSHALL ISLANDS*

The Japanese garrison at Mili Atoll in the Marshall Islands becomes the first to surrender in the Pacific theatre.

AUGUST 23

LAND WAR, *MANCHURIA*

Soviet forces reach the coastline of southern Manchuria, concluding a 12-day defeat of the Kwantung Army. It is the quickest campaign in Soviet history, killing 80,000 Japanese soldiers for Soviet losses of 8000 dead and 22,000 wounded.

AUGUST 25

ALLIES, *JAPAN*

US carrier aircraft begin uncontested flights over Japan, monitoring the surrender of Japanese military facilities and also locating and supplying Allied prisoners of war formerly held in Japanese camps.

AUGUST 27

SEA WAR, *TOKYO*

Vessels of the US Third Fleet anchor

◀ *Foreign Minister Mamoru Shigemitsu (in top hat and tails) and representatives of the Japanese armed forces on the USS Missouri during the surrender ceremony.*

▲ *US aircraft fly in formation during the surrender ceremonies in Tokyo Bay, a photograph that amply illustrates US military might.*

themselves in Sagami Bay in the approaches to Tokyo harbour.

AUGUST 28

OCCUPATION, *JAPAN*

The first US troops land in Japan. They are US Air Force technicians who go to inspect Atsugi airfield near Tokyo.

SURRENDER, *BURMA*

Japanese officers sign surrender documents in Rangoon, finalizing the defeat of Japan in Burma.

AUGUST 29–31

SURRENDER, *PACIFIC*

Japanese forces throughout the Pacific theatre begin to surrender en masse, with troops on Singapore, Marcus Island and the Philippines capitulating to the US and British.

AUGUST 30

OCCUPATION, *JAPAN*

US occupation forces begin major landings in Tokyo Bay with the US Third Fleet and its aircraft providing security. Yokosuka Naval Base is officially handed over to the Allies. General MacArthur makes it his Supreme Allied Command headquarters.

SEPTEMBER 2

SURRENDER, *USS MISSOURI*

The Japanese foreign minister, Mamoru Shigemitsu, and General Yoshijiro

Umezo sign the final Instrument of Surrender aboard the US battleship USS *Missouri* anchored in Tokyo Bay. General MacArthur's signature concludes Japanese hostilities with all Allied nations, and it is MacArthur who will oversee the occupation of Japan. The Japanese surrender brings the Pacific war, and World War II, to an end.

▼ *Having just landed, US Marines smash Japanese field artillery pieces and small arms at Yokosuka Naval Base in Japan on August 29, 1945.*

AFTERMATH

In attempting to create an empire in East Asia and the Pacific, Japan had lost 1,506,000 soldiers. In addition, 900,000 of its civilians were killed, most in one year of US fire bombing and two atomic explosions. The aftermath of the atomic blasts – which killed around 135,000 people – was to be a further 200,000 deaths caused by radiation. Even cities such as Tokyo, which had escaped an atomic strike, were utter wastelands. Following its unconditional surrender, Japan was placed under military administration headed by General Douglas MacArthur, and did not become self-governing again until 1952.

China

The Chinese death toll of World War II is often given scant regard in the history books, but in addition to 1,324,000 military deaths, around 10 million civilians were killed in one of the most apocalyptic civil disasters in history. The death toll was compounded by the internecine warfare between the Communists and Nationalists, and the defeat of the Japanese once again raised the spectre of civil war.

The flashpoint was Manchuria. Although the Soviets, who had taken Manchuria from the Japanese in a lightning 10-day campaign, were committed to withdrawal by February 1, 1946, the Nationalist leader Chiang Kai-shek rightly feared that Mao Tse Tung's Communists would attempt to occupy the country in the Soviets' wake. To pre-empt a possible Communist takeover, Chiang began deploying troops in southern Manchuria. Escalation was inevitable, and by 1946 the Nationalists and Communists were once again locked in a bitter civil war. The US gave some aid to the Nationalist cause but was reluctant to commit itself to a land

VENGEANCE

Over 5000 Japanese soldiers and officials were brought to trial for war crimes between May 1946 and November 19, 1948. The Allies held a major trial equivalent to the Nuremberg trial in Germany, hosted symbolically in the Japanese Army Ministry building in Tokyo. Trial judgments led to the execution of 900 high-ranking Japanese for atrocities committed against Allied POWs – of whom 27 percent had died in Japanese camps – and the indigenous populations of the Far East. Those put to trial included two former Japanese prime ministers – Hideki Tojo, the man had effectively took Japan into the war, and Koiso Juniaki, Tojo's successor. Tojo was hanged and Juniaki died while serving a sentence of life imprisonment.

war on the Asian mainland. The Nationalist forces outnumbered those of the communists by three to one, but gradually drained away after defeat in Manchuria where Nationalist garrisons became isolated and were picked off by Communist forces. By the end of 1949, China was a Communist nation.

Decolonization

China was not the only country to experience political upheaval and conflict following the collapse of Japan. Throughout the Far East, many European colonies were now no longer willing to see their former masters return, and began the push for independence. Over the next three decades, the indigenous peoples of almost all European colonies in East Asia would shake off colonial rule, often through guerrilla warfare.

In Vietnam, part of pre-war French Indochina, the disarming of Japanese occupiers in the north by Chinese troops and in the south by the British, led to the effective partition of the

▼ *Former colonial masters humbled by the indigenous population: French officers captured by the Viet Minh in Indochina.*

country at the 16th Parallel, with Communist strength concentrated in the north. As the French returned to take office, the Communist Viet Minh organization led by Ho Chi Minh – whose forces had originally fought against the Japanese occupiers with full sponsorship from the US – began a nine-year guerrilla war with backing from Communist China and the Soviet Union. Ho's insistent guerrilla tactics wore the French down. Following defeat at Dien Bien Phu in 1954, the French gave up all of Indochina. Independent nations were established in Laos and Cambodia. Vietnam was effectively split at the 17th Parallel into a Communist North and a US-backed, independent South, with the promise of future reunificatory elections. But the South avoided the elections and the North Vietnamese Army (NVA) and Viet Cong Communist guerrillas in South Vietnam began a military campaign to take the South by force. By 1965 this campaign had sucked the US into the 10-year Vietnam War, a huge action which cost the US 58,000 dead combatants and North Vietnam, whose forces eventually took Saigon in 1975, over one million dead soldiers and civilians.

▲ *The Vietnamese nationalist leader Ho Chi Minh, who was one of the prime movers of the post-World War II anti-colonial movement in Asia. He organized a crushing defeat of French forces at Dien Bien Phu in 1954.*

Aftermath

The United Kingdom's once mighty empire also contracted. India – a country which had lost 36,000 troops fighting for the British during World War II – was partitioned into the independent states of India and Pakistan, the British having pledged in the last years of the war to relinquish its most mighty colony. Ceylon and Burma gained their independence over the next year. The British did re-colonize Malaya, and fought a largely successful counter-insurgency campaign against the Malayan Races Liberation Army, a force under the direction of the Malayan Communist Party, from 1948. However, the sun was setting over imperial politics, and in 1957 the British granted Malaya full independence, the hostilities ending with the effective defeat of the MRLA in July 1960.

Holland was the other European power to shed colonies in the Far East. At the end of war, the leader of the In-

▲ Cold War warrior: General Douglas MacArthur (right), the hero of the Pacific War, shown here during the Korean War.

donesian Nationalist Party, Achmed Sukarno, declared Indonesia's independence from the Netherlands. Dutch attempts to take back its colony were vigorously resisted, and they were forced to withdraw in 1949, leaving Sukarno as president, and Indonesia became fully independent on August 15, 1950. The Netherlands retained control of West New Guinea, but in 1963 they were compelled to give this up also.

The US gave their colony the Philippines formal independence after the war, but there was fighting there too as the new government had to defeat a guerrilla army of so-called Hukbalahap insurgents in the 1940s.

New World Order

Many of the wars of independence became associated with the Cold War, with the Soviet Union and China tending to support groups that aimed to throw off Western control. In addition, some of the independence movements throughout the Far East started with Communist credentials. The stand-off between the Soviets and the West may not have led to outright war, but it did produce a whole series of proxy wars throughout Africa and the Far East. War in Korea ran from 1950–53, and fighting in

Indochina/Vietnam lasted effectively from 1945 until 1975, and was sponsored by the US, China and the Soviet Union.

Ironically, it would be Japan who would emerge as the success story of post-war Asia. By the 1980s it had become one of the world's largest economies, basing its success around the manufacture of vehicles and hi-tech electrical goods. It has considerable influence and close relations with its great source of raw materials, Indonesia, once the Dutch East Indies, over which so much blood had been spilt in the 1940s.

▼ President Sukarno, the leader of the Indonesian independence movement and the country's first president.

▼ A British Army truck blown up by Communist rebels in Malaya. British military efforts in the country were aimed at a peaceful handover to an elected government.

INDEX

INDEX